ONE THOUSAND YEARS

A Concise History of Hungary

ONE THOUSAND YEARS

A Concise History of Hungary

Written by
Kálmán Benda
Péter Hanák
Zsuzsa L. Nagy
László Makkai
Emil Niederhauser
György Spira
Károly Vörös

Edited by
Péter Hanák

Corvina

Written by

László Makkai pp. 9–65   Emil Niederhauser pp. 110–113
Kálmán Benda pp. 66–97   György Spira pp. 114–121
Károly Vörös pp. 97–109 | Péter Hanák pp. 122–176
Zsuzsa L. Nagy pp. 177–249

Edited by Péter Hanák

Translated by Zsuzsa Béres
Translation revised by Christopher Sullivan
Cover design by Anikó Környei

CONTENTS

I. HUNGARY IN THE MIDDLE AGES

Migration and the Founding of the Hungarian State

The History of the Carpathian Basin up to the End of Roman Rule

The Carpathian Basin has been a populated area for thousands of years. In the course of its history it has witnessed the settlement, migrations and struggles of sucessive peoples. Relics of these historic times are still found today. Some of the buildings which were erected in pre-Magyar days, and later by people living alongside the Magyars, still stand, over many thousand years the collective efforts of the peoples living in this area transformed its forests and the steppes into a land fit for human habitation.

One of the oldest human finds in Europe was unearthed at Vértesszőlős, in Hungary, about a quarter of a century ago. Beetween 400,000 and 500,000 years previously, hunters settled close to the hot-water springs and the animal and human footprints made on the alkaline mud became covered and subsequently preserved. After a long interval, about 100,000 years ago a new type of human being, the so-called Neanderthal man, hunted for mammoths and bears in the area which now makes up Hungary. The first human beings of today's species arrived in this region from the southeast at some time around 50,000 B.C. Their knapped flint tools are perfect, and a whistle with three holes which was discovered suggests that they played music. The fact that they buried their dead with some ceremony (they decorated the corpses with red paint symbolizing blood, and therefore life) would indicate their belief in an afterworld. At Lovas, near Lake Balaton, the source of the pigments they used was also excavated. They hunted for large animals, especially reindeer. However, the gradual increase in temperature and the development of greater humidity forced those animal species who liked dry cold weather to move northwards. Of the animals formerly hunted, the aurochs, bison, deer, the wild boars and brown bears remained in the area.

About 10,000 years ago, the climate of the Carpathian Basin was much the same as it is today. Deciduous forests and lowland steppes alternated with each other and in the south was brushwood together with chestnut trees, vines and figtrees. Changes in the natural environment compelled the inhabitants of the Carpathian Basin to switch to animal husbandry and the cultivation of crops at around 5000 B.C. Wheat, barley, sheep and goats had been brought to the area by peoples migrating from the Balkans, while cattle and pigs were domesticated from indigenous wild species. It was through the Danube Basin that, by 4000 B.C., Neolithic culture spread to the more northerly and westerly parts of Europe. This involved livestock breeding, land cultivation, weaving and spinning, as well as the production of pots and the building of houses.

The newcomers from the southeast who brought these innovations with them partly assimilated to the existing local population and partly moved on. From time to time their descendants were forced back, while further waves of people repeatedly arrived from the southeast. The Carpathian Basin was in this way the great melting-pot of peoples, into which there came a succession of newcomers from the west, east and south. These peoples either brought new cultural assets with them or destroyed the ones they found. They also created flourishing cultures there which lasted for various periods of time.

The Neolithic era lasted three thousand years and was followed, at around 2000 B.C., by the Copper Age. This lasted just a few centuries. The new technology was introduced by people arriving on four-wheel carts and originating from the Balkans. The carts were drawn by oxen and these settlers made good use of the abundant copper supplies which they found locally. They made not only tools but also weapons from the metal they extracted. It was also from the southeast that another wave of people arrived. They brought with them the technique of casting bronze and a flourishing local bronze culture in the area also attracted various additional settlers from the East. These ethnic groups in turn introduced the domesticated horse to the Carpathian Basin.

During the Bronze Age, a military aristocracy, living in earthwork forts, well-armed and sporting gold ornamentation, ruled the masses. At around 1000 B.C., the Illyrians and Thracians from the West, and the Scythians from the East introduced the use of iron. The local bronze culture, which thrived on abundant raw material and perfection of craftsmanship, was not entirely superseded though. It was only in the middle of the first century B.C. that iron became a commonly used metal in the Carpathian Basin. The peoples responsible for this were, in the west, the Celts and, in the east, the Dacians.

In the years after Christ, the Carpathian Basin became linked with the culture of Greece and Rome, and this connection lasted some 400 years. This occurred as a result of the Roman conquest of Transdanubia and Transylvania, which became the provinces of Pannonia and Dacia respectively. The arrival of Roman power marked the beginning of the use of written records at local level, as well as monumental stone architecture and urban life-style, the appearance of vineyards on the hillsides of Pannonia and the beginnings of Christianity. Traces of this Roman presence are found in the remains of amphitheatres, water mains, temples, basilicas, chapels and sarcophagi, as well as in the objects found among them. Roman settlements were Aquincum (now Óbuda), Sopianae (now Pécs), Scarabantia (now Sopron), Sabaria (now Szombathely) and Gorsium (now Tác). Further indications are the ancient form of the pruning knives used in Transdanubian viticulture and the cult, which eventually spread through Europe, of the early Christian martyrs in Pannonia. One should also not forget St. Martin who was born in Sabaria, later lived in Gaul and eventually became the patron saint of France. For a few centuries therefore the Carpathian Basin became a civilized region. Only later did it sink back into barbarity in the wake of the Great Migrations.

Huns, Teutons, Avars and Slavs in the Carpathian Basin

The Hungarian chroniclers of the Middle Ages regarded the Huns and the Hungarians (Magyars) as one and the same people. According to these chroniclers, Árpád based his claim to the Carpathian Basin and its inhabitants on the fact that the region had formerly belonged to his ancestor, Attila. Also according to the chronicles, the Szeklers were the last group of Huns remaining in the area and joined with the conquering Magyars. Although the question is rather more complex, the idea of Hun–Magyar kinship cannot be entirely discarded, as it was at one time by Hungarian historians.

The Huns were a Turkish-speaking people of North-Central Asia who were famous in world history not only for their wide-ranging military campaigns, but also for their invention of the stirrup. This device made horse riding safe and later became the technical basis of medieval European chivalry. The Huns crossed the Volga in 375 and the Magyars, who lived in the valley of the Lower Volga, became their subjects. The Huns conquered the Ostrogoths, who lived on the northern shore of the Black Sea and, in the course of the fifth century (A.D.) the Romans evacuated Pannonia. The great Hun king, Attila then moved to the region of River Tisza, which had formerly been inhabited by the Sarmats. The Romans had abandoned Dacia long before and the Germanic Visigoths settled there after 271. The Visigoths, who had fled to the Balkans in the face of a Hunnish attack, were replaced by the Gepids, another Germanic people.

The three major geographical regions of the Carpathian Basin, Transdanubia, the Great Plain and Transylvania, first became a single political unit under Hunnish sway. At the same time the Carpathian Basin also became the base for the large-scale military operations led by Attila. These

11

took the Hunnish king (often called "The Scourge of God") right into the Western Roman Empire, first to Rome and later to Gaul where, at Catalaunum a dozen peoples fought a great battle. After Attila's sudden death in 453, the conquered Germanic peoples rose in arms against their Hunnish masters. Those Huns remaining withdrew to the area between the Don and the Volga rivers. From them emerged the Khazars who, together with other peoples, ruled over the Onogur (i.e. "Ten Peoples") tribal alliance. This alliance incorporated the Magyars. The rulers of both the Magyars and Danubian Bulgars then left the Onogur grouping. Since they regarded Attila to be their ancestor, it may be presupposed that both peoples received their rulers from the Hunnish royal family at the time when the Magyars and Danubian Bulgars still lived together.

For over a century the Carpathian Basin was taken over by Germanic peoples. For the time being, Transdanubia was occupied by the Ostrogoths, while the Gepids continued to inhabit the eastern area. The Lombards pushed into the territory now occupied by the Ostrogoths, who migrated to Italy. The Lombards then became entangled in a bloody war with the Gepids and were only able to defeat them with the assistance of another conquering people from Central Asia, the Avars. After this, the Lombards themselves set out for Italy. In 568, the bellicose Avar king, Bayan, became ruler of the Carpathian Basin. He settled the Slavic tribes he had brought with him in the surrounding mountain areas and the Gepids, now divested of their leaders, assimilated to these Slavic settlers.

In addition to archeological finds, the memory of the Slav settlers is preserved only by the ethnic name *tót*. This derives from the word *teut*, meaning "people", the name they themselves used. Incidentally, *tót* was used by the Magyars to describe every native speaker of Slavic languages in the Carpathian Basin.

For two and a half centuries the Avars maintained Transdanubia, the Great Plain and Transylvania as a single political entity. Although their predominance was seriously jeopardized by an insurrection among the Slavs, they drove new strength from a group of Bulgaro-Turks who came to the area around 670. A growing number of Hungarian archaeologists now think that these new settlers may have been Magyars, or, rather, Szeklers. Although archaeological finds support this theory, there is as yet no evidence to suggest that these people spoke a Finno-Ugric language —that is, that they were indeed Magyars.

Where then did the Magyars, a people speaking such a language, come from?

From the Urals to the Danube: Hungarian Prehistory

Linguists agreed long ago that the ancestors of the Magyar people belonged to the most easterly, Ugric branch of the Finno-Ugric peoples. However, the precise geographical location of the Finno-Ugric homeland continues to be the subject of debate. For many years it was considered to have been situated between the middle Volga and the Ural Mountains, north of the River Kama. This was where the common ancestors of the Finno-Ugric language speakers were supposed to have lived until 2000 B.C. More recently, however, both linguistic and archaeological arguments have given rise to the view that the Finno-Ugrians hunted and fished on both sides of the Central Urals. The Finno-Ugrian hunters followed the reindeer and moose from the western regions—wet and rich in grass during summer but covered with thick snow in winter—to the drier eastern slopes. They used sledges drawn by dogs, as well as skis. In the wake of these animals, they returned for summer hunting. The Finno-Ugrians travelled across the Ural Mountains, rocks of which were covered during the third millennium B.C. with drawings which depicted scenes from the chase. They travelled in boats on the estuaries of the Tobol and Kama rivers. Around 4000 B.C. they still used knapped flint implements but by this time also had earthenware dishes decorated with drawings of water birds. The Finno-Ugrians regarded the wild duck as a sacred animal. This was because, according to an ancient myth preserved from the *Kalevala,* the world came into being from the egg of such a creature.

> From the cracked egg's upper fragment,
> Rose the lofty arch of heaven,
> From the yolk, the upper portion,
> Now became the sun's bright lustre;
> From the white, the upper portion,
> Rose the moon that shines so brightly;
> Whatso in the egg was mottled,
> Now became the stars in heaven,
> Whatso in the egg was blackish,
> In the air as cloudlets floated.

Kalevala; translated by W. F. Kirby,
The Athlone Press, London, 1985, p. 7.

Around 2000 B.C. population growth forced the western Finnish branch of the ancient Finno-Ugric people to move to the Volga and later to the Baltic Sea. On the other hand, the Ugric branch, which, in addition to the ancestors of the Magyars, also included the ancestors of the Ostyaks and Voguls, spread from the southeastern slopes of the Ural Mountains to the valleys of the big rivers in the area. Here they switched from hunting and fishing to farming and above all, to livestock raising. The words for "horse", "saddle", "halter", and "whip" are the same in all Ugric languages. In Hungarian, the Persian words *tehén* (cow), *tej* (milk), *nemez* (felt) and *szekér* (cart) originate from the Persian peoples living in the Aral region. These peoples acquainted the ancestors of the Magyars with Copper Age and Bronze Age civilization. Shortly afterwards, the Ugrian peoples created their own Bronze-Age culture which generated works of art depicting their new way of life and subsequently enriched the world of their beliefs. An important symbol in this was that of the horse. Indeed, the horse is often depicted as a sacred animal, but nevertheless one which was sacrificed as well.

Having become equestrian nomads, the Ugrians left the mountain regions and moved to the steppes. As a result of an increase in temperature between 1500 and 1000 B.C., these expanded northwards by as much as 200–300 kilometres and thinned the forests. To escape the drought which was caused, the Voguls and the Ostyaks followed the forests northwards. When, after 800 B.C., the climate turned cold and wet, they were encircled by the returning taiga and the reindeer replaced the horse in their homeland along the River Ob. The Magyars remained on the steppes which, after a period of increasing dryness, became green again after 800. These people became nomadic herdsmen and at this time Persian and Scythian influence among them was at its greatest. Indicative of the latter is that in addition to the Hungarian word *kard* (sword), other things came from the Scythians. These included the famous bow, as well as a religious cult based on the stag, and the frequent delineation of that animal. While the symbol of the horse did not disappear, that of the tame wild-duck did. The latter was replaced as a symbol by that of the *turul*, a predatory eagle. During this time, iron became regularly used and at this time also the people who called themselves "Magyars" broke away from the other Ugrian peoples. This last event probably took place when the Magyars moved across the Urals to the area of present-day Bashkiria some time after 500 B.C. Here they became the neighbours of other alien peoples, the Persians, Alans and the Turkic Bulgars. According to more recent linguistic suppositions, it was to distinguish the Magyars from these peoples that the actual word "Magyar" was created. This was done by putting together the Finno-Ugrian *mon* (speak) and *er* (man). Other peoples also called themselves "speakers" and referred to foreigners as *néma* (mute). A case in point is the Hungarian word *német* (German), which is of Slavic origin.

Although the "speakers", that is, the Magyars, seemed conscious of some kind of ethnic identity, neighbouring peoples did not remain "mute" for long. Words which the Hungarians took from their languages reveal that under the influence of the neighbouring tribes, the Magyars underwent a decisive socio-economic transformation. Some of the Bulgars, and especially the Onogur group which settled near the Magyars after 700, learned

14

the use of the plough from the Alans of the Caucasus. This knowledge they handed on the Magyars. This is shown by the Hungarian words *eke* (plough), *sarló* (sickle), *búza* (wheat), *árpa* (barley), as well as *ökör* (ox), *tinó* (steer), *borjú* (calf), and so on which the Magyars acquired from them. Although the Magyars probably did not entirely give up hoeing as an aid to cultivation, the use of the ox-drawn plough paved the way for a far more advanced agriculture as well as for the opportunity of more lasting settlement. Although the Magyars continued to drink *kumis* (fermented horse's milk), they now, as a result of Bulgarian influence, also drank wine which they made from their own grapes. In addition to mutton, they also ate the meat of the settlers' favourite animals—both *disznó* (pig) and *tyúk* (hen) are taken from Bulgarian. In summer the Magyars lived in tents, but in winter they lived in cottages in their permanent settlements along the big rivers. From the Alans the Magyars adopted the curved sabre and from the Bulgars, armour and the stirrup. In this way, there came into being a constantly armed group of warriors which rallied around a chieftain and which fought with arrows and sabres. These warriors no longer lived from the work of their own two hands, but from war booty and the work of slaves captured in foreign lands. In keeping with the Bulgarian model, the clans rallied into military organizations, known as tribes. As their name *Ungarn, hongrois, vengier*, etc. suggests, the Magyar tribes probably belonged temporarily to the Onogur tribal alliance which lived in the Don area after 500 and which was subordinated to the Khazar Khanate. After throwing off Khazar rule, some of the Magyar tribes moved, at around 800, to Levedia, in the Don region. A couple of generations later, and under pressure from the Pechenegs, they moved on to the Etelköz, the area between the Dnepr and the Lower Danube. Before the Mongol invasion of Hungary in 1241, the Hungarian Dominican friar, Julian, visited Bashkiria. There he found Magyars who had stayed behind. These Magyars eventually assimilated with the neighbouring peoples.

The Conquest and the Raids

Both the chronicles and historiography have regarded Árpád as the leader who led the conquest of the Carpathian Basin single-handed in 895–6. This is despite the fact that contemporary Byzantine and German authors speak of the involvement of two Magyar princes in this, Árpád and Kurszán. Furthermore, from Muslim and Byzantine sources we know that—as in the case of the Avars and Khazars—power over the Magyars was shared between three persons. These were the *kende*, the commander of the warriors, the *gyula* and the *harka*. According to the Magyar chronicles, Kurszán was the *kende* and Tétény the *harka*. (The chronicler Anonymus says the *harka* was Tuhutum.) Accordingly, Árpád must have been the *gyula*, the chief

15

military commander. This also explains why tradition has regarded him as the principal figure in the Conquest.

In 895, when the Pechenegs crossed the River Don and took the Magyars by surprise, most of the Magyar army was away fighting the Bulgars. With the bulk of the Magyar forces along the Lower Danube and the River Tisza, the Magyars at home were without adequate protection. Árpád and his son Levente were abroad with the army, and a Pecheneg attack forced the remaining Magyars to take refuge in the Transylvanian mountains. Árpád's father, Álmos, died a voluntary death because he was unable to protect successfully the homeland of the Magyar people. The Etelköz (land between rivers), as this was called, was the Magyar's last homeland prior to the conquest of Hungary. In the course of the next few years the Magyars allied themselves with the three Kabar (perhaps Szekler) tribes which had joined them. Re-inforced by the fighters who had returned from the Bulgarian campaign, the Magyars prepared to strike. They drove the Bulgars out of the Great Plain and Transylvania, evicted the Franks from Transdanubia and freed the western part of Upper Hungary from Moravian control. In 904, Kurszán, the chief ruler, fell victim to Bavarian intrigue. He was invited to a peace feast where he and his retinue were murdered. Magyar pagan tradition regarded such deaths as divine punishment. Accordingly, Kurszán's family was stripped of its hold on the chief rulership and Kurszán's place was taken by Árpád. To avenge Kurszán's death, the Magyar army defeated the Bavarians, whose prince also fell in the battle. The Conquest was now practically completed; the Carpathian Basin was under Magyar domination.

Shortly after the Conquest, the Magyars launched a series of plundering raids to the West. The Italian and German princes often called in the Magyars as allies in their wars against each other, and paid them for their services. Torn apart by internal strife, the Carolingian Empire was initially unable to defend itself when confronted with the special Hungarian cavalry tactics. Like other equestrian nomads, the Magyars carried out lightning attacks followed by a feigned withdrawal. These deceived the enemy and reduced his alertness. The Magyars would then turn and shower the foe with arrows. In the hand-to-hand combat which followed, the Magyar horsemen would finish off the enemy. "From the arrows of the Magyars, Lord, save us", prayed the inhabitants of Italian, German and French monasteries. This was all to no avail, however, until the German king, Henry the Fowler, took charge of the situation. In 933, the German cavalry, strengthened and reorganized, defeated the Magyars for the first time at Merseburg.

The Magyar tribal chiefs, just like contemporary Bohemian, Polish and Russian princes, maintained their military forces from foreign money and from war booty captured. Their land was cultivated by foreign slaves, and these they refused to relinquish. As a final great effort, Bulcsú, the *harka* of the tribal alliance, led a series of campaigns against the Western countries. To ensure that there would be not threat to him from the south, Bulcsú went to Byzantium in 948 and was converted to Christianity there. In 955, however, he suffered grave defeat at Augsburg. The German king, Otto I, the subsequent founder of the Holy Roman Empire, annihilated most of the Magyar army and Bulcsú himself, together with Prince Lél (Lehel), was captured and executed. This catastrophe put an end to the raids in the West. Soon the South also became closed to the Magyars. In 970, the Pechenegs murdered the Russian prince, Svyatoslav. Svyatoslav, accompanied by his army, had been on his way home after failing to occupy Byzantium. The Magyars had been his allies and now, like the neighbouring Slav peoples, they had to accommodate themselves to one of their two powerful neighbours. These were the Holy Roman Empire and the Byzantine Empire and either way the Magyars would have to join the community of Christian peoples.

This process was, however, hindered by the socio-political composition of the Magyar people and, to a lesser extent, by their pagan beliefs. Magyar society was based on blood kinship and the clan. Each clan was under the leadership of a clan chief *(fő)*. The latter owed his authority not only to wealth accumulated during the raids, but also to his vast number of slaves. These slaves were called in and worked on the chief's own land—arbitrarily expropriated from the common land of the clan. Also important were the warriors or *jobbágy* who rallied around him and the fact that he officiated in the cult of the clan's ancestors. The clan chief's martial glory was sung by the bards, who in turn were closely associated with the sorcerer, or *táltos* who evoked the spirit of the ancestors to help the clan. Comprising five to six clans, a military organization, the tribe, supported the rule of the haves over the have-nots. Each tribe was headed by a chieftain, who led the plundering raids. Major campaigns and delegations abroad were led jointly by the chief ruler, or a member of his family and the *gyula* or the *harka*.

In time, however, the tribal chieftains, especially the *gyula*s and the *harka*s attempted to act independently of the chief ruler. The *gyula*s were the most successful in this and in Transylvania they formed an almost independent province for themselves. Bulcsú emphasized his wish to secede by receiving baptism at Byzantium in 948. This contrasted with the House of Árpád, who were looking to Western Christianity. Although Bulcsú himself would probably have aligned himself with the West by creating an independent Transdanubia, the defeat at Augsburg frustrated this. The disaster not only prevented him from founding a dynasty but cost him his position as *harka* as well. Only the strengthening of the chief ruler's power could save the Magyar tribal alliance from disintegration and the Magyar people from assimilation to the neighbouring peoples. The positive consequences of the Augsburg catastrophe ultimately brought about the opportunity for this.

EASTERN EUROPE IN THE 9th CENTURY AND THE MAGYARS' ROAD TO PRESENT-DAY HUNGARY

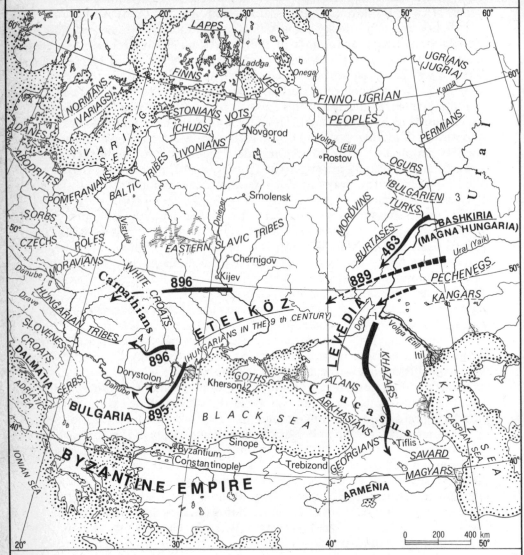

FINNO-UGRIAN PEOPLES

TURKIC PEOPLES

SLAVIC PEOPLES

GERMANIC PEOPLES

OTHER PEOPLES

1 SARKEL

2 BYZANTINES

3 ANCIENT HOME OF THE HUNGARIANS

4 TRANSYLVANIA

⟵ The direction of Hungarian migrations

⟵--- The direction of the Pecheneg attack in 889

K. V. Bp. 1987. 668086

The Founding of the State

The Magyar conquest of the Carpathian Basin, and the subsequent emergence of the Bohemian, Polish and Russian states, closed Eastern Europe as a source of slaves for the warriors of the Carolingian Empire. In Western Europe serfdom emerged by allowing slaves to own land and by subjugating the freemen. The same factors also made the transformation of Magyar society important. Árpád's descendants, following Western models, organized their slave settlements and the indigenous Slav population into manors *(udvarhely)*. Freemen were also forced to serve. To guard the manors' *jobbágy* from the upper, warrior castes of the seven Magyar tribes were settled. The memory of these tribes has been preserved in place-names found in various parts of the country (Nyék, Megyer, Kürt-Gyarmat, Tarján, Jenő, Kér and Keszi).

Taksony (955–972), the grandson of Árpád, learned the lessons of the Augsburg defeat and sought contact with Western Christianity. In 961, he asked the Pope in Rome to send a bishop. He ordained Bishop Zacheus who was, however, prevented from reaching Hungary by the German king, later emperor of the Holy Roman Empire, Otto I. Otto wished to thwart the establishment of a Magyar bishopric owing direct allegiance to the Holy See.

Prince Géza (972–997) continued the domestic policy of his predecessors and also pursued a far-sighted foreign policy. Shortly after he came to power, in 973, Géza was invited by Emperor Otto to Quedlinburg. Otto also invited the Danish, Bohemian and Polish princes and it was his intention to extract oaths of allegiance from all four rulers. Prince Géza, however, sent only envoys who were not authorized to take such an oath. These representantives did, on the other hand, express Géza's friendly intentions by asking the Emperor to send missionaries to Hungary. These missionaries did in fact reach the country and were headed by Bruno, the monk of Sankt Gallen, who was ordained Bishop of the Magyars. Géza also admitted a few German knights into his princely escort. It was their task to prepare the prince's armed forces for battle against both possible Western enemies and against any resistance in Hungary. The prince himself received baptism and encouraged his entourage to follow suit. What he regarded as even more important, however, was to break tribal opposition. This he did by speeding up the resettlement of the warriors leaving the tribal framework and entering his service in his fortresses and manors. The tribal chieftains and clan chiefs thereby lost the military basis of their power. Even Géza, however, did not feel strong enough to break the power of the *gyula*s in Transylvania, the principal centre of resistance to him. He therefore sought compromise with them for the time being.

Vajk, the son of Prince Géza and his wife Sarolt (herself the daughter of the Transylvanian *gyula*), was christened Stephen. After a Christian up-

19

bringing, Stephen took over from his father in 997. He established the institutional framework for social and political transformation and organized the Hungarian state. Stephen confiscated the fortresses belonging to the clan chiefs, together with two-thirds of the clan territory and people. From these lands emerged the counties. Their inhabitants became the "castle-people" and "castle-serfs", who were responsible for the economic and military upkeep of the castles. Some proprietors of the remaining clan land joined the retinue of the prince. From these there emerged an élite, the *ispán*s, appointed royal officials who headed the counties, and the soldiers who served in the prince's regular army. The former estates of the princes were enlarged by means of new acquisitions and became independent economic units. Blood kinship thereby ceased to be the fundamental relationship in society. Everyone became the subject of the ruler, who organized his country on a purely regional basis.

Social and political transformation had to be accompanied by ideological change. With the help of missionaries, but by force if necessary, Stephen led the entire population of the country into the Christian fold. Christianity did not recognize differences of social origin and was a universal religion organized on a territorial basis. The Church filled the vacuum left by disintegrating tribal and clan relations. Stephen issued orders that every ten villages build a church and support its priest. The counties roughly coincided with the decanal districts. The latter formed ten bishoprics, two of which (those of Esztergom and Kalocsa) were made archbishoprics. Christian culture was spread by Italian, German and Czech monks. Monasteries were founded and subsequently supervised by the Benedictine house at Szentmártonhegy (Pannonhalma). Bishop Gellért of Csanád, who died a martyr, was the first ecclesiastical writer in Hungary. Stephen himself was the first Hungarian to write a literary work, in the form of admonitions to his son. The keeping of Latin records started at local level in the monasteries.

Stephen carried out his great work with the assistance of both Hungarians and foreigners. Naturally, he encountered powerful internal opposition. In bloody battles he defeated his relations, Koppány of Somogy and the *gyula* of Transylvania. Yet there remained pockets of resistance even after this. Such continuing opposition did not, however, alter the fact that the feudal Hungarian state had come into existence. This state was formally recognized when the Pope sent a crown to its creator. At the coronation, in AD 1000, Stephen became King of Hungary. However Stephen I's whole work became endangered when his only son, the legendary Prince Imre (Emeric) fell victim to a hunting accident. Vászoly, the last male descendent of the House of Árpád, was a pagan and a supporter of the old order. To prevent him from asserting his rights, Vászoly was blinded and molten lead poured into his ears. Vászoly's sons fled the country and Stephen named Peter Orseolo as his heir. Orseolo was the son of Stephen's sister and his father was the Doge of Venice.

Medieval Hungary

Struggles for the Survival of the Hungarian State

A critical period for Hungary ensued after the death of King (Saint) Stephen I in 1038. The independence, indeed the very existence, of the young Hungarian state became seriously jeopardized.

There were several reasons for the crises which occurred during the period of early feudalism. Discontent among the subjugated freemen and the rivalry between temporal and ecclesiastical lords gave rise to rebellion and conspiracy. The new order placed great burdens on the poor and tedious restrictions on the rich. From without, two neighbouring powers threatened the young Hungarian state. These were the Holy Roman Empire, which had already made the Czechs and the Poles its vassals, and the Byzantine Empire which had by this time swallowed up the Bulgarian state. Both powers had designs on Hungary.

Although the descendants of King Stephen, the talented Árpád dynasty, had great determination, they often channeled vast energies into family feuds. The princes of the House of Árpád fought primarily over the principle of succession. One fraction held that the oldest male member of the dynasty should succeed to the throne when the reigning king died. The other considered that the king's eldest son should be heir. When they were forced to compromise, they divided the country among each other. Consequently, large parts of the country were under the rule of the princes, almost independently of the king. Yet, the will to preserve state and the people conquered selfishness and dissension. The eleventh and twelfth-century kings from the House of Árpád consistently strove to ensure firm royal authority and the country's independence. To this end, they utilized both external and internal forces, the same forces that exploited the personal ambitions of these rulers for their own benefit.

The rule of St Stephen's successor, Peter Orseolo (1038–41 and 1044–6) was threatened by rebellion among Hungarian feudal lords who were jealous of the foreigner. Peter Orseolo turned for assistance to the German emperor, then at the height of his power. The price of this support was the recognition of German suzerainty. Feeling concern for the country's independence, the feudal lords turned to Princes Andrew and Levente, the exiled sons of the executed Vászoly, and asked them to re-establish order. The princes encountered a pagan rebellion of elemental force, which even claimed the life of Bishop Gellért. After Peter Orseolo was overthrown, Andrew was crowned King of Hungary in 1046. Andrew I (1046–60) did

21

not want to put the clock back. He suppressed the pagan rebels and restored St Stephen's state. In his efforts he could count on support from Byzantium, ever-jealous of German expansionism. Andrew's younger brother, Béla, repelled German attack by scoring a victory over the invaders.

Andrew I wanted to establish family links with his powerful German neighbour. Prince Béla used this connection to procure the throne (1060–3). After Béla I's sudden death, Solomon became king. Solomon, the son of Andrew I and the brother-in-law of the German emperor Henry IV, reigned from 1063 until 1074. Béla's sons, Géza and Ladislas, were granted dukedoms. As a result of German and Byzantine intrigues, the king and the princes came into conflict with each other. Géza (1074–7) emerged victorious from this family feud and at his coronation wore a crown presented to him by the Byzantine Emperor. The first great period of crises in Christian Hungary ended with the succession to the throne of King (Saint) Ladislas I (1077–95). The international situation favoured Ladislas. It was at this time that the Investiture Controversy broke out between the papacy and the Holy Roman Empire. Ladislas sided with the Pope in order to free himself from German pressure, but rejected the Pope's ambition to make Hungary his vassal, as had already happened with neighbouring Croatia. Byzantium was preoccupied at this time with attacks from the Seljuk Turks and she was therefore unable to prevent Ladislas from beginning the occupation of Croatia and Dalmatia. Threatened by Venice, an ally of Byzantium, the Dalmatian towns welcomed the protection of the Hungarian king.

The Hungarian conquests in the south certainly conflicted with the interests of the Byzantine Empire. Byzantium therefore sent her allies, the Pechenegs, against Hungary. Solomon and his commander, László, sucessfully repelled their onslaught. By means of Draconian laws, Ladislas restored domestic calm, which had been shaky for a long time. He supported the Church, the guardian of ideological order, not only with lavish gifts, but by canonizing, in 1083, Stephen, Imre and Gellért. Ladislas was succeeded on the throne by his nephew, Coloman I (1095–1116), called "Könyves" ("the Book-Lover"). Coloman completed the occupation of Croatia and Dalmatia and defeated the Pope's attempts to make Hungary his vassal. He himself was an educated man. Coloman opened his court to those Hungarians who encouraged literature written in Latin, as well as to the numerous drafters of laws and writers of legends and chronicles. It was at this time that Romanesque art in Hungary achieved European standard, primarily in the works of the Pécs architectural school.

By the early twelfth century the German threat to Hungary had been averted and the Pope reconciled to the existence of the Hungarian state. Byzantium also considered it advisable to improve relations with her Hungarian neighbour. As a sign of rapprochement, Piroska, Ladislas's daughter, married the Byzantine emperor. (She was henceforth called Eiréné to signify peace between the two countries.) After Piroska's death, the Byzantine Church canonized her, thereby paying tribute to her life of self-restraint and charity. Piroska was the first of many Árpád dynasty princesses to lead saintly lives. However, Piroska's son, Emperor Manuel, attempted to use his Magyar origins as a pretext to occupy Hungary. First he supported pretenders to the throne. He then took the younger son of Géza II (1141–62) hostage with the promise that he would make him his successor. This younger son, Béla, possessed ducal provinces, Syrmia, Croatia and Dalmatia, and Manuel's real reason for this promise was to acquire them immediately. However, Manuel encountered stiff resistance in Hungary and finally had to relinquish his grand design, the union of Byzantium and Hungary. In 1172 Prince Béla returned to his native land to occupy the vacant throne and was crowned Béla III. After Manuel's death in 1180, he retrieved the southern province that had been taken away from Hungary.

Hungary thus survived her second major political crisis and, after nearly one and a half centuries of struggle, both her western and eastern neighbours had learned to fear and respect her. One typical foreign opinion of the Hungarians at this time is found in the work of a Byzantine historiographer. He speaks of the "Magyar people, who have good horses, good weapons and wear iron and armour". They constitute "an uncountable mass, are as numerous as the sands of the seashore, their audacity is insuperable, and their boldness invincible. They are irresistible in battle, independent, free, walk with their heads held high, love liberty and are their own masters..."

The Consolidation of the Feudal State

With the accession of Béla III (1172–96), Hungary acquired a very talented ruler. Béla was an outstanding politician and could operate under favourable international conditions. The Holy Roman Empire was very much distracted by its conflict with the Pope, as well as with internal opposition. Accordingly, the Empire had relinquished its claims of suzerainty over Hungary. Byzantium, too, was paralysed by dynastic struggles and her Serbian and Bulgarian subjects had also risen in arms. For a while Béla III acted as the protector of the Byzantine Empire, but eventually accepted the independence of the Serbs and the Bulgars. This meant an end to direct links between Byzantium and Hungary for good. During the two centuries after this time, Venice became Hungary's great rival, and attempted to acquire Dalmatia from the Hungarian king. Venice, the "Queen of the Seas", was now at the height of her influence but nevertheless repeated Venetian attacks on Dalmatia were frustrated by Hungarian arms and the loyalty of the Dalmatian towns themselves. These towns were concerned for their commercial independence. A turning-point occurred in 1202 when crusaders, bribed by Venice, occupied Zara and, two years later, Constantinople.

Dynamic economic and social progress along with closer bonds with a generally developing Europe strengthened Hungary. Later, however, a number of serious problems were to arise as a result of this. Waves of French and German settlers flocked to Hungary from the West and the immigrants from France spread viticulture north and east of the Danube. Western settlers *(hospes)* also brought with them the idea of crop rotation system. More efficient agriculture led to the emergence of towns. The "Latin" (that is, the French and Italian) merchants of the two earliest such settlements, Esztergom and Székesfehérvár, carried on a profitable trade. They exchanged precious metals from Hungarian mines, wax and animal skins for Western luxury goods. These included cloth from Flanders, French enamelled bronze items, German weapons and Italian silk. Esztergom and Székesfehérvár also served as the locations of royal residences. During the reign of Béla III, the requirements of the royal court increased significantly. Béla himself had been accustomed to a life of luxury in Byzantium. Through his two French wives he had also become familiar with Western fashion. Previously, the king and his entourage had been content with the primitive articles made by the rural craftsmen on the royal estates. The services of rural cooks, dog-catchers and minstrels who were ordered to the palace once a week had in the past satisfied the requirements of the royal party. At this time Hungary did not have a permanent capital. The king travelled from one royal estate to another, using up the revenue of each on the spot, as well as the two-thirds of the county revenues that were his due. Now, however, the court purchased better quality goods. These were either imported from abroad or made by craftsmen who had settled in Hungarian towns. A class of professional officials also emerged. Béla III had a permanent residence built at Esztergom. This was a splendid palace where he could even receive the Holy Roman Emperor Frederick I Barbarossa as befitted the latter's rank.

Changes in economic conditions and demands were accompanied by changes in the structure of the economy. The use of money began. Only a quarter of Béla III's annual revenues came from the counties. This income was 166,000 marks yearly (1 mark equalled approximately 200 grams of silver) and was substantial even by European standards. Béla now demanded only one-third of the counties' revenue. The rest of his income derived from foreign settlers, minting money and from the mines which produced salt and precious metals. With the growth of these sources of revenue, the financial importance of the royal estates and the counties declined. The king could afford to cede these to the ambitious feudal lords and the latter gradually adopted the expensive life-style of the knights in Western Europe. The feudal lords were not satisfied with the income received as *ispán*, namely, one-third, and later two-thirds of the county revenues. They wished to acquire estates of their own, in the same way as the feudal aristocracy in the West had done. These aspirations were lavishly satisfied by Béla III's younger son, Andrew II (1205–35). The new king was himself full of ambition and much attached to pomp. Having entangled himself in a hopeless war with Russia, Andrew even ceded Zara to Venice in exchange for the latter's assistance in his crusade adventure (1217). Andrew bestowed royal and county estates on the feudal lords and attempted to offset the resulting loss of revenue by levying taxes and customs duties.

The money economy received forceful encouragement in this way. However, the process produced too great a burden for society and engendered general discontent. Already worried by the territorial acquisitions of the secular magnates, leading churchmen felt that their old trading privileges in salt and wine were being jeopardized. Discontent ran high among the king's professional court soldiers, the so-called *servientes*. These men were oppressed by the aristocracy and the same held true for the commoners who had lost all their assets. The *servientes* organized themselves into a nationwide movement in defence of their interests. A group of barons led this movement and, in 1222, compelled the king to sign the *Golden Bull*. Deriving its name from the gold seal appended to it, this document guaranteed protection for the *servientes* against harassment from the magnates, promised to put an end to financial abuses and recognized the barons' right of armed rebellion should the monarch fail to honour its provisions.

The greatest opponent of Andrew II's policy was his own son, who later ruled as Béla IV (1235–70). Prince Béla was quite different from his father, who was a light-hearted person and who often lapsed into frivolity. Béla was also a devout Christian who took inspiration from St Francis, St Dominic and from his (Béla's) sister, St Elizabeth. It was as though Béla had a premonition of the danger which was to threaten Hungary in the wake of Mongol expansionism. Even before he succeeded to the throne, Béla tried to fortify the Transylvanian frontiers and after he became king he made every effort to reconstitute the disintegrating crown lands and counties. However, this was not a viable path of social development. Béla also sought help from abroad. He sent Julian, a Dominican friar, to Bashkiria where he was to invite the remaining Magyars there to move to Hungary. Afterwards, he invited the Cuman people, who had already been attacked by the Mongols, to settle in the country also. However, Béla's measures gave rise to internal tensions which contributed to the devastating defeat of 1241. In that year Béla's army was routed by Batu Khan at Muhi on River Sajó. The Mongols ravaged the country for more than twelve months and, after they eventually left, the Hungarian state had to be refounded.

Hungarian Culture in the Early Middle Ages

The Magyar conquest of the Carpathian Basin marked the end of the Great Migrations in this area. After the consolidation of the Hungarian state, culture began to flourish. The royal household, the *ispáns*'s castles, the episcopal sees and the Benedictine monasteries all served as the early centres of Christian civilization.

The material and intellectual achievements of European culture generally soon found their way to Hungary. As a result, the cultural heritage of the pagan period disappeared almost entirely. The memories of this age survived only in the songs of minstrels and, from these, the legends of the mythical stag, the *turul,* the white horse, Lehel's horn, Botond's war-axe and others were incorporated into the Magyar chronicles. The minstrels' tunes were preserved for a thousand years in pentatonic folk music and were rediscovered in the twentieth century by Béla Bartók and Zoltán Kodály. From the ancient shamanism the Hungarian folktale saved, among other things, the myth of the tree of life and that of the shamans, who fought in the guise of animals.

The Hungarian fine arts of the early Middle Ages still contained something of the Magyars' pre-Conquest times. The palmette, a popular ornamental motif during the period of the Conquest and used then in wood carving, gold work and textiles, was now applied to stone work. With Lombard inspiration also, the palmette continued to develop in the foliated scroll carvings of the Pécs school of architecture. St Ladislas's frescoes in the churches of the Szekler Land (in eastern Transylvania) depict the tree of life and the animal fights. A good example of such work is to be found at Erdőfüle.

As time passed, however, the heritage of the pagan era gradually disappeared from Hungarian art and gave way to European inspiration. Initially, Christian culture found its way to the country through Czechs and Germans. Priests, friars and knights coming from these ethnic groups would introduce this but, nevertheless, Hungarian literature and art followed Italian and French models. The earliest Hungarian school of architecture was inspired by Lombard art and the late eleventh century Pécs and late twelfth century Esztergom schools were influenced by French architectural achievement. All three had a nationwide impact and raised imitation to the level of national practice. Although the Romanesque style at this time was international, its details mirrored Hungarian reality. A case in point is the Hungarian sandal, which had straps going up to the knee, satchel and stick. These were standard equipment for Hungarian herdsmen during the twelfth century and are depicted on the commoners' altar in Pécs Cathedral. (In the early Middle Ages a separate altar was erected in front of the chair and was for the commoners.)

Literature was predominantly ecclesiastic. Rites, monastery annuals, the legends of saints and secular works were all in the hands of the sole experts in writing at the time, the Benedictine friars. Among other tasks, they recorded the early chronicles, tabulated the laws of St Stephen, St Ladislas and Coloman the Book Lover and, for the most part, drew up legal documents. The larger monasteries and the collective chapters founded by St Ladislas were authorized to draft official documents and eventually acquired the functions of notaries.

In spite of all this though, culture did not remain of an exclusively ecclesiastical character. As the lay aristocracy strenghtened its position and became increasingly prosperous, so the secular element in culture increased. During the twelfth century the ecclesiastical intelligentsia, who had visited the universities of Oxford and Paris, introduced to Hungary the courtly culture of England and France. By this time the material trappings of this culture were already established in the country. Stockings and tunics sewn from Flemish cloth, body armour helmets, the straight sword and war-horses had already found their way, through foreign merchants and Western enemies, to the Hungarian élite. Béla III's notary, "Magister P." (commonly referred to as Anonymus) worked during the early years of the thirteenth century. Anonymus did not consider introduction of Christianity as the most important result of the Conquest. He regarded the legacy of the pagan Attila and the family histories of the Hungarian feudal lords to be the main objective of his work, the *Gesta Ungarorum* (The Exploits of the Hungarians).

However, not all of courtly culture spread in the Latin language. It was probably Anonymus himself who wrote an account in Hungarian of the Trojan War, the favourite reading of the knights at the time. In any event, it was during Anonymus's time that it became fashionable in aristocratic circles to name offspring after the figures in the Trojan legend. Ecsellő, Perjámos and Iktár—the equivalents in Hungarian of Achilles, Priam and Hector—survive in place-names to this day. Famous representatives of Western courtly culture visited Hungary. The Provençal troubadour Peire Vidal and the eminent German singer Tannhäuser visited King Andrew's court, as did Villard d'Honnecourt, the most distinguished French architect of the age.

The early thirteenth century was, however, also a period of fundamental change. A secular era was again followed by a religious revival, chief representatives of which were the Dominican friars. They converted the Cumans to Christianity and searched for those Magyars who remained in the East. Also important were St Elizabeth, the House of Árpád princess, who corresponded with St Francis, and, above all, Béla IV and his whole family. The mendicant orders now determined the whole character of Hungarian culture and their influence was to last for the next two centuries.

27

The Kings' Struggles with the Barons (1242–1308)

The catastrophe represented by the Mongol Invasion accelerated the changes already begun by economic and social development. The population of the crown lands had either fled or been killed and the same was true of the former inhabitants of the disintegrating counties. Béla IV had no choice but to donate the devastated land to the feudal lords. The king's reasoning was that the magnates would resettle the countryside, partly with liberated serfs attracted by special benefits and partly with immigrants from abroad.

Previously, too, settlers had come to Hungary. These had primarily been Germans (the so-called Saxons) who had moved across to Transylvania. The numbers of these Saxons in the country had been small until after the Mongol Invasion, when many more arrived. Moravian, Ruthenian and Roumanian peasants came with them and from this time onwards Hungary became a truly multinational country. The economy began to flourish as hitherto uncultivated areas, primarily the forested mountain regions, were drawn into the mainstream of production. The resettlement of the country also improved the lot of the Hungarian peasantry. Hungarian bondsmen won the liberty enjoyed by the foreign settlers. By 1300 there emerged a homogenous peasantry that farmed independently, was free to move and owed dues to the landlords in kind. It inherited the appellation *jobbágy* from the freemen who had acted as officials during the early feudal period and who had served in the royal castles.

The magnates who re-populated their estates with settlers new to the country profited most. The king was compelled by circumstances to give them a free hand to increase their power. These landlords were allowed to recruit private armies from among the ranks of the lesser nobility (the former *servientes*). They built castles for themselves, and these were initially designed on the multi-storey keep pattern. By doing this the feudal lords contributed, albeit indirectly, to the defence of the country and allayed fears of a possible new Mongol attack. Isolated from the rest of the nobility, the feudal lords, or barons as they came to be called, increasingly broke with royal power. To stop this process, Béla IV encouraged a new type of county formed from the royal knights, the *jobbágy* and the *servientes*. After 1267, this new kind of county institutionalized the autonomy of the lesser nobility—an autonomy which received military backing from the head, the *ispán*.

The king settled foreign, primarily German "guests" in some of the former royal castles, for example, Sopron, Győr and Kolozsvár. These new arrivals became assimilated with the existing castle inhabitants and this mixture gave rise to Hungary's urban, burgher population. The *cívis* (citizen) of the previous era now became a burgher, a word of identical meaning but of German, not Latin, origin. Mining towns began to flourish and acquired special importance. Through them Hungary became one of the major precious metalproducing areas in medieval Europe.

In addition to the lesser nobility and the town population, Béla IV also regarded the Cumans as a support for royal power. Béla had offered this people asylum in Hungary. The Cumans lived as nomads and were organized along tribal lines but, because their men were all soldiers, constituted a significant force. In order to strengthen its bond with the Cumans, the royal house allied itself in marriage to the Cumans. Stephen, heir to the Hungarian throne, married the daughter of the Cumans' prince. This girl was christened Elizabeth.

However, Béla IV's efforts to offset the power of the barons proved to be futile. The wealth and power of these magnates were constantly increasing. Not only did the latter split into warring factions, but they also tried to subject large parts of the country to their own rule. Exploitation of tensions within the royal family had for long been an effective policy. As a result of the barons' machinations, Béla IV and his son, Stephen, became entangled in bloody conflicts with each other and the country was plunged into civil war. It was in vain that Béla's saintly and charitable daughter, Margaret, tried to mediate between them. Matters were made worse by the international situation. In 1254, the Austrian Babenberg dynasty, which had constantly been at war with the House of Árpád kings, died out. Béla was determined to thwart the expansionist ambitions of the Bohemian kings, who were aspiring to hegemony in East-Central Europe. Béla IV occupied Styria and placed his son, Stephen, in power. A few years later, however, Ottokar II, the King of Bohemia, occupied not only Styria, but the other provinces of Austria as well. Ottokar enlisted the help of the Kőszegi family, who were barons and owned land along the western frontier of the country. The Bohemian king then mobilized traitors inside Hungary against Béla IV, who by this time had again fallen out with Stephen.

After his father's death, Stephen V (1270–72) himself fell victim to the anarchy which his own rebellion had done so much to precipitate. The ten-year old heir to the throne, Ladislas IV, entitled "the Cuman", was brought up by his mother, herself of Cuman origin. Ladislas was initially the plaything of the warring baronial factions. In 1278 they forcefully took him to the battlefield at Dürnkrut, where Hungarian arms helped lay the foundations of the power and imperial authority of the House of Habsburg.

When Ladislas IV (1272–90) grew up, he turned against the baronial factions and sought support from the Cumans, from whom his mother descended. Since, however, the Cumans still observed pagan ritual, the Church also opposed Ladislas. The king consequently became isolated and was eventually assassinated. Since Ladislas had no heir, he was succeeded by Andrew III, the grandson of Andrew II, who had lived in Venice. He too, however, was unable to overcome the anarchy which paralysed Hungary. The most powerful barons, the Kőszegis, Máté Csák, László Kán and

29

others tore the country into independent provinces and ruled them as kings. They maintained their own courts, entered into alliances with foreign powers and ignored the legitimate monarch.

Andrew III tried to use the lesser nobility against the barons and established one of the first feudal diets in Europe. Although this body enacted legislation and excluded the barons from its proceedings, at this time it did not wield sufficient power to be effective. In fact, for a long time it ceased to function at all.

With the death of Andrew III in 1301, the male line of the House of Árpád died out. A struggle for the throne immediately began between descendants of the House of Árpád through the female line. First Wenceslas II, king of Bohemia, and later Otto, Prince of Bavaria, organized factions for themselves but failed to win over the majority of the barons. Finally, the barons crowned the Pope's candidate, Charles Robert of Anjou, King of Hungary in 1308. He too, however, needed a long time to stamp out anarchy in the country.

The Loss of Hungarian Possessions in the Adriatic

The century which followed the extinction of the House of Árpád also witnessed an end to Hungarian expansionism towards the Adriatic. At first it seemed that the succession of Charles Robert, who belonged to the Neapolitan Anjou dynasty and who was a descendant of the House of Árpád through his grandmother, would strengthen links between Hungary and Italy. Charles Robert consolidated his rule with moral backing from the Pope and financial support from the Italian bankers. Moreover, he tried to guarantee his authority in Italy by betrothing his younger son, Andrew, to Johanna, heir to the throne of Naples. However, Hungary's grave internal problems did not make it possible for Charles Robert to pursue an active foreign policy. It was only in 1321, after defeating the last rebellious barons, that he succeeded in establishing his control over the whole of Hungary. In 1323, Charles Robert transferred his seat from Temesvár to Visegrád, which by now was the site of a magnificent Gothic castle.

It was around this time that Charles Robert also put the royal finances in order. It did not even occur to him to re-constitute the decayed royal counties. He entrusted the governing of the new county system to chief *ispán*s appointed by him and to justices elected by the nobility. From the barons and the nobility generally, Charles Robert required only military service. The county and baronial armies fighting under their own flags were called *banderia*. The barons marched off to war with their *familiares* (vassals), while those nobles who did not enlist in the army of one of the barons, fought under the command of the county *ispán*. The remaining royal estates were organized around castles and made independent of the county administration. Charles Robert based his incomes on directly and indirectly raised royal revenues. These were known as *regalia* and derived from customs dues, taxes and, above all, the royal monopoly of precious metals. The mining of silver had been carried on for a long time in Hungary and during Charles Robert's reign the mining of gold also greatly increased (at Körmöcbánya, Nagybánya). As a result minting of the gold florin was started in 1325.

Military and economic reforms guaranteed internal order for the country, as well as favourable conditions for foreign trade. Trade with the West suffered considerably from Vienna's ability to stop the passage of goods. In 1335 Charles Robert convened a highly important meeting at Visegrád of the kings of Hungary, Bohemia and Poland. There the monarchs concluded a trade agreement and established alternative international routes for merchants. This success indicates that it was primarily with his northern neighbours that Charles Robert was able to achieve good political relations. As for the south, however, he was unable to retrieve anything from the legacy of the Árpád kings. Dalmatia, Croatia and Slavonia accepted Charles Robert as their king in name only and were in fact under the control of local rulers. In former Cumania, the Roumanian voivodes, who had been appointed as chief officials under the Árpád kings, governed independently of the Hungarian monarch. Wallachia was the first to secede and Moldavia then followed suit. After this, only a loose and often abrogated oath of allegiance bound them to the kingdom of Hungary.

Charles Robert's son became King Louis I in 1342. Louis was to occupy the throne for forty years and came to be called "the Great" on account of his grandiose plans and ambitious military campaigns. The new king wished to get back not only the southern provinces which had broken away, but also wished to extend Hungarian power into the Balkans. In addition, Louis coveted territory even further afield. On the basis of dynastic right, he attempted to acquire the throne of Naples and in 1370 he succeeded in acquiring the kingdom of Poland, a legacy from his uncle. However, Louis's excessive ambition in Italy was unacceptable both to Venice and to the Pope. The Hungarian king fought two campaigns against Naples and, with the help of Genoa, also made war on Venice. His Italian victories, however, could not bring the result Louis aimed at. In the south, he succeeded in procuring only Dalmatia and Croatia, and his Bulgarian, Serbian, Bosnian and Roumanian vassals were shortly afterwards conquered by the Turks. Louis himself launched one campaign against these invaders from Asia who, later on, would advance still further.

Louis I died in 1382 and without a male issue. He was succeeded on the throne by his daughter Mary, and, from 1387 on, by her husband, Sigismund of Luxembourg. The latter had to defend his throne against the Anjous of Naples. Their candidate, Charles of Durazzo, was actually crowned king of Hungary in 1385 but was murdered a few weeks later. His son, Ladislas allied with Venice against Sigismund, who was helped to retain Dalmatia by Florence, herself jealous of Venetian power. From Florence Sigismund acquired the services of the excellent military commander and financial expert, Filippo Scolari. When, however, the Medicis came to power, Florence entered into alliance with Venice. The result of this was that Sigismund lost his Italian possessions.

The situation was aggravated by Ottoman expansionism in the Balkans which was now threatening the frontiers of Hungary. Sigismund of Luxembourg (1387–437) tried to ensure Hungarian hegemony in the Balkans, but his multinational campaign against the Turks there met with resounding defeat at Nicopolis in 1396. After 1420 Sigismund (now also king of Bohemia and, from 1433, Holy Roman Emperor too) was preoccupied with the suppression of the Hussite uprising and ending the struggles of the anti-popes. However, he was unable to solve permanently either these problems or to counter the Ottoman threat, to which he had paid very little attention. Sigismund did, however, score one significant success for Hungary. In 1404 he issued an edict, the *placetum regium,* in which he laid down that no papal bull or encyclical could be published or read in the country without his prior approval. In 1428 Sigismund suffered another defeat at the hands of the Turks at Galambóc. Even earlier than this he was compelled to give up Dalmatia. Thenceforth Hungary was no longer in a position to pursue an expansionist policy along her southern borders. Indeed, she now had to make desperate efforts to defend herself.

Early Struggles with the Turks

In 1418 the Turks broke into Croatia and, in the following year, entered Transylvania. Wherever the Turks went they burnt, looted and took prisoners. Their attacks became frequent and, although King Sigismund's military commanders were more or less successful in organizing Hungary's defence, the people who lived in the southern frontier regions suffered increasingly from the war. It was no coincidence that it was precisely in these areas that Hussitism, the embodiment of anti-feudal discontent, became widespread. Ruthlessly persecuted by the Inquisition, some Hussites fled to Moldavia where the Bible was being translated into Hungarian. Others joined the peasants of Transylvania who were rebelling against demands for excessive tithes.

In 1437 Hungarian and Roumanian peasants, headed by Antal Budai Nagy, rose in arms against their oppressors and sought justice from King Sigismund. At the time, the latter lay seriously ill in Moravia and died shortly afterwards. The peasants scored two victories over the forces of the bishop and the nobility. Indeed, they won the town of Kolozsvár to their cause. In spite of this, they were finally defeated by the forces of the Kápolna League, an alliance between the Hungarian nobility, the Saxon patricians and the Szekler leaders.

This internal dissension did nothing to avert the growing Ottoman threat to the country. Only King Albert of Habsburg (1437–39) was able to take effective action with regard to this. Albert entrusted the defence of the southern frontiers to János Hunyadi, the son of a Transylvanian landowning family. As a child, Hunyadi was taken to King Sigismund's court. (Contemporaries regarded him as Sigismund's illegitimate son.) There he was instructed in modern warfare by Italian professional mercenary commanders, but he also learned a great deal from the fighting tactics of the Hussites. In addition to making use of the Hungarian lesser nobility and the ennobled Roumanian mayors, he often instigated popular uprisings as an aid to his military campaigns. Hunyadi's achievements were amply rewarded by the king who bestowed on him offices and estates. At the time of his death Hunyadi had acquired some two million hectares of land, and had become the greatest Hungarian landowner of all time. However, Hunyadi did not spend his vast revenues merely on furthering his own political career; his income primarily went on defence needs.

In his capacity as Voivode of Transylvania, Hunyadi had already fought a successful battle against Mezid Bey, a Turkish commander who was killed in that encounter. In 1443, Hunyadi launched an offensive and, after a string of victories, was forced only by a harsh winter to return from the Balkan Mountains. King Wladislas I (1440–44) denounced his treaty with the Turks, but died in the Battle of Varna, from which Hunyadi himself barely escaped. Wladislas I was succeeded by the child Ladislas V (Albert's son) and Hunyadi was elected Regent. He was to occupy this position from 1446 until 1453, when Ladislas came of age.

As Regent, Hunyadi concentrated all his energies on realizing his great plan—to expel the Turks from Europe. In this he counted on the help of the Balkan peoples, the Serbs, Bulgars and Roumanians. They, however, were so intimidated by the Ottoman invaders that they dared not, indeed could not, hold out as the Hungarians were doing. Accordingly, in 1448 Hunyadi's last major undertaking at Kosovo polje, in Serbia, failed.

The struggle against the Turks was not, however, handicapped merely by the enemy's superior numbers and weakness on the part of the allies. Internecine strife also played its part. The early fifteenth century witnessed the intensification of the rivalry between the barons and the rest of the nobility. The lesser nobles also demanded representation in the running of the country. This gave rise to the re-establishment of the feudal diet. In 1440, the lower house, which was made up of lesser nobles, won the concession that any future laws would require the approval of the Diet before they could be enforced. The various baronial factions, the so-called leagues, now quarrelled among themselves and the resulting disharmony in these leading circles undermined the country's unity still further. What usually happened at this time was that one of the baronial factions sided with the king, and the other with the rest of the nobility. The lesser nobility tried to counter-balance the wealth of the barons with the power it derived from its numerical strength.

The lesser nobility supported the Hunyadi faction and, because of this, the Cillei–Garai–Brankovics clique had to bide its time. When Ladislas came of age in 1453, Hunyadi's own pre-eminent position dramatically changed. He had to step down as Regent and be satisfied with the office of captain-general of Hungary. The new king, Ladislas V, was just thirteen years old and had been entirely under the influence of his relative, Ulric Cillei. Through Cillei other enemies of the Hunyadi faction also had access to the young king. This made matters potentially difficult for Hunyadi himself.

In this tense situation news arrived that Sultan Mohammed II, having occupied Constantinople in 1453, had now launched a campaign against Hungary. In 1456 he laid siege to Nándorfehérvár (now Belgrade). At the head of an army composed of mercenaries, lesser nobles and crusaders recruited from among the people, Hunyadi raised the siege of this important border fortress. Hunyadi's victory halted the Ottoman advance for nearly a century. In honour of this great victory and to encourage further resistance, Pope Calixtus III ordered Christian churches to toll their bells at noon each day—a practice followed ever since. However, immediately after Hunyadi's victory, plague broke out in the Hungarian camp and the great military commander fell victim to it. After Hunyadi's death the Cillei and the Hunyadi factions launched a life-and-death struggle against each other. Hunyadi's supporters murdered Ulric Cillei. The king arrested both Hunyadi's sons, had the elder one, Ladislas, beheaded, and imprisoned the younger one, Matthias, in Prague. In 1457, Ladislas V died unexpectedly and the country was faced with the problem of having to elect a new monarch.

The Attempt to Create a Danubian Empire

The Hunyadis were the most powerful baronial family in Hungary at this time and, in alliance with the lesser nobility, they forced the other magnates to elect Matthias, the only surviving son of the former Regent, king of Hungary. Matthias Hunyadi was, however, still a prisoner of George Podiebrad in Prague, and his mother, Erzsébet Szilágyi, had to pay a large ransom for his release. Matthias's uncle, Mihály Szilágyi, now demanded the price for his assistance—the title of Regent and the power that went with it. Matthias, however, rejected his family's patronizing attitude and relied for advice on János Vitéz, his excellent humanist tutor, whom he made Archbishop of Esztergom as well as Chancellor. Following Vitéz's advice, Matthias strengthened royal power against the barons. The new king curtailed the power of the magnates and chose his officials from the rank of the lesser nobility, town burghers and indeed sometimes from among the peasantry.

Matthias did not wish to rely on the private armies of the barons. He therefore hired mercenary forces, which later became the famous "Black Army" and which were under his personal command. Matthias was obliged to put finances on an entirely new footing. By introducing a new system of taxation and, above all, by stringently monitoring the collection of taxes, Matthias created a sound financial foundation for his reign. As a result, he could follow the example of his illustrious father and launch a military campaign against the Turks. In 1464, Matthias took the fortress of Jajce in Bosnia. However, owing to the sudden death of Pope Pius II, the promised help of a crusader army did not materialize. Matthias could not, therefore, continue the fighting.

From this episode Matthias learned the very important lesson that Hungary's military strength was, in itself, insufficient to halt the Ottoman advance. In addition, he realized that, even casual alliances were useless, as they tended to collapse at the critical moment. A united empire must be organized from the peoples of the Danube area which would alone be strong enough to resist the Turks. Matthias therefore made peace with the Sultan, a peace which, during the reign, was disrupted only by sporadic Turkish incursions and Hungarian reprisals. In 1479, one such Turkish onslaught was defeated by Matthias's military commanders, Pál Kinizsi and István Báthori. This engagement took place between Alkenyér and Szászváros.

Matthias devoted the last twenty years of his life to attempts to establish the Danubian empire he considered so important. The idea of such an empire was nothing new however. As early as the thirteenth century, king Ottokar II of Bohemia, strove to establish a kingdom out of the Bohemian, Hungarian and Polish lands. Sigismund was Holy Roman Emperor as well as the King of Hungary and Bohemia, while the Austrian duke, Albert, procured the Hungarian and Bohemian thrones. Among Matthias's contemporaries the Emperor Frederick III and members of the Polish Jagiellon dynasty pursued policies that strove to bring countries together. Matthias aimed to conquer Bohemia, but Frederick III and the Jagiellons joined forces against him.

In Hungary many felt that Matthias's designs on Bohemia were motivated by personal ambition and that he was neglecting the Turkish threat to the country. Another criticism was that his expansionist schemes in the West would make new enemies for Hungary at a time when the Ottoman danger was already great. Archbishop János Vitéz headed those who were dissatisfied with Matthias's policies, but his conspiracy against the king was discovered. Vitéz was imprisoned and died not long afterwards. Matthias, however, went on to confound his critics. In 1474 the united Polish and Bohemian armies broke into Silesia and besieged Breslau, with Matthias himself inside the town. The siege was soon given up and peace was established by the Treaty of Olmütz, signed in 1478. Under this, both Matthias and Wladislaw recognized each other as Kings of Bohemia and that country was divided between the two rulers. Matthias retained Moravia and Silesia, while Bohemia went to Wladislas.

Silesia was a flourishing province during this period. Its capital, Breslau, was a centre of trade in East-Central Europe, with Vienna being the other important commercial town in the Danube region. Matthias knew that these two cities supplied foreign commodities to the Hungarian market and that much Hungarian gold went to them in payment. This was one reason why Matthias wanted to bring these towns under his control. Matthias entered into conflict with Frederick III, from whom he captured Vienna in 1485. Matthias moved his seat of government to this city.

By this time Matthias was not only known as a great king, but also as a generous patron of the arts and sciences. In 1476 he married Beatrice of Aragon, the daughter of the king of Naples. Matthias's queen introduced Renaissance culture into the Royal Castle at Buda. To the existing Gothic palace were added doors, windows and statues in the Renaissance style. Gardens and wells were also created which bore the same stamp. A splendid library, the "Bibliotheca Corviniana", was set up and contained beautifully illustrated codices. The castle's own pottery workshop made colourful utensils and tiles. Buda developed into a densely populated and affluent town—the worthy seat of a great king.

The memory of Matthias, the greatest of Hungarian kings, survived not only because of his grandiose political designs, his victorious wars and his generous patronage of the arts. The common people referred to him as the "just king" long after his death. It was not as though Matthias had shown much financial consideration for his subjects. On the contrary, he made them pay heavy taxes. In return for their sacrifices though, Matthias created order and security for them. "In this country no one can rely absolutely on his power and cannot be completely certain of it. Everyone is entitled to maintain, if need be even against Us, his right... Here officials and powerful men do not dare to oppress the people with any form of servitude because they know that they themselves serve only for a time. And the source and supervisor of this just legal system is not law, but the king who is not slave to or tool of the law, but who stands above the law and rules over it." This was how Matthias described his own conception of royal power to the Italian humanist Brandolini. Matthias's early attempt to centralize power was made in the spirit of righteousness. Legends about that remarkable king, who travelled the country in disguise and brought powerful wrongdoers to book, lived on in folklore.

The Hungarian Economy in the Middle Ages

Contemporary Hungarian and foreign sources praised the natural resources of Hungary during this period. Historic Hungary offered numerous economic opportunities. The country was the meeting-place of three major climatic regions of Europe. These were the Atlantic region, which was characterized by forestry and grain production, the Mediterranean, which ripened grape and figs, and the Continental, which produced grasslands for grazing. The Magyars, as well as the other peoples living in the Carpathian Basin, made good use of this diversity.

The twelfth century memoirs of Abu Hamid, a Moslem trader, described Hungary as belonging "to those countries in which prosperity and abundance are the greatest". The German bishop, Otto of Freising, was understandably angry with the Hungarians for defeating his fellow countrymen. During the same period he wrote that "Fate may justifiably be blamed, or rather the divine error wondered at that gave these human beasts (for they cannot be called human beings), such a beautiful country."

But whatever others thought about the Magyars, the fruits of their labour had to be acknowledged. As early as 1300, a French Dominican travelling in Hungary recalled the fertility of the Hungarian soil. "Formerly the Kingdom of Hungary was not called Hungary, but Moesia and Pannonia. Moesia received her name as a result of her rich harvests and Pannonia received hers because of her abundance of bread. And this is only natural as from a good harvest there follows an abundance of bread." (In Latin, *messio* means "harvest" and *panis* "bread". It was mere coincidence that the pronunciation of these words resembled the "Moesia" and "Pannonia" of Roman times.) The Magyars had cultivated the soil even in their ancient homeland. In Hungary they learned how to grow oats and rye, in addition to wheat and barley, although for a long time arable farming was subordinated to livestock breeding. Ploughed land appeared as small islands in the vast sea of pasture. On the grassy expanses of the Great Plain, the Magyars raised horses and cattle, while the Slavs and Roumanians who lived in the mountains bred sheep and goats.

At the beginning of the fifteenth century a Burgundian knight, Bertrandon de Brocquière, made interesting observations on the Hungarian horses of the time. "There are quite a few horse dealers in Pest", he wrote, "should anyone want to buy two thousand good horses, he could probably do so here. Horses are sold in lots of ten and the price of each lot is two hundred forints. I have seen two or three horses of which are worth this price. Most are from the Transylvanian mountains which surround Hungary's frontiers. I myself bought an excellent running horse, but generally those available are saddle horses. Abundant fine pasture facilitates horse breeding in this country. It is, however, a fault of Hungarian horses that they are slightly unruly and difficult to shoe."

HUNGARY
IN THE 15th CENTURY

0   50   100 km

HOLY ROMAN EMPIRE

Danube

TRENCSÉN

Zsolna
Beszterce   Rózsahegy   Németlipcse
Turóc   Szt. Miklós
Szakolca   Trencsén   Lipcse
Hollós   Bolondóc   Breznóbánya
Csejte   Besztercebánya
Sasvár   Körmöcbánya
NYITRA   Zólyom
Nagyszombat   Modor   Galgóc   Nyitra   Újbánya   Korpona
Szt. György   Léva   Szt. Benedek   Losonc   Fülek
Dévény   Oroszvár   BARS   Surány   Ság   Gyarmat   Szécsény
Pozsony   ESZTERGOM   Pásztó
Kismarton   Óvár   Szerdahely   Komárom   Vác   Gyöngyös
Nagymarton   Moson   Hédervár   Esztergom   Visegrád   Hatvan
Frakno   Sopron   Győr   Gönyű   Tata   Óbuda   Tura   Berényszállás
Kőszeg   Csorna   PANNON   Zsámbék   Buda   Pest
Szalónak   Pápóc   Pápa   Martonvásár   Tököl   PEST   Szászberek
Szombathely   Vép   Sárvár   Palota   Fehérvár   Keve   Cegléd
Újvár   Vasvár   Veszprém   Hontsegyháza   Kőrös   Kecskemét
Körmend   Sümeg   Keszthely   Simontornya   Paks   Csongrád
Dobra   Zalavár   Tamási   Kalocsa   Szer
Muraszombat   Marcali   Somogyvár   TOLNA   Halas   Hódmező
Alsó-Lendva   Kanizsa   Kaposújvár   Szekszárd   Szabadka
Csáktornya   Hedrehely   Pécsvárad   Baja   Györgye
Varasd   Csurgó   Babócsa   Szigetvár   Pécs   Bátmonostora   Coborszentmihály
Krapina   Kőrös   Siklós   Baranyavár
Klava   Sztréza   Veröce   Váska   Szaplonca   Tarda   Erdőd   BÁCS
Zagreb   Izdenc   Peker-Szerdahely   Nekcse   Eszél   Bács
Szamobor   Csázma   Pozsegavár   Gara   Valkóvár   Péterváradja
Nova Csicsa   Monoszló   Orbova   Nevna   Diako   Újlak   SZERÉM
Petrinya   ZÁGRÁB   Szincse   Nempti   Szávaszentdemeter
Lippa   Dubica   ORBÁSZ   Orbászvásárhely   Szabács
Modrus   Pesnye   Kozora   Banjaluka   Szerebernik   BANATE OF MACSÓ
Atak   SZANA   Só
Bihig   Korbávia   BANATE OF JAJCA
(Bihács)   Jajca
Busán   Tenen (Knin)   BANATE OF SZREBERNIK
Vrana (Aurania)   Senj

ADRIATIC SEA

Clissa

OTTOMAN

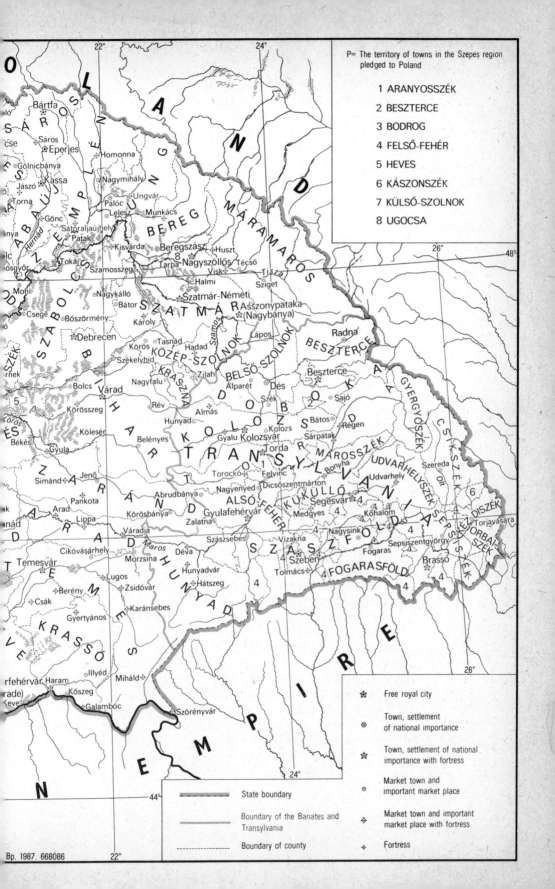

P= The territory of towns in the Szepes region pledged to Poland

1 ARANYOSSZÉK
2 BESZTERCE
3 BODROG
4 FELSŐ-FEHÉR
5 HEVES
6 KÁSZONSZÉK
7 KÜLSŐ-SZOLNOK
8 UGOCSA

Free royal city

Town, settlement of national importance

Town, settlement of national importance with fortress

Market town and important market place

Market town and important market place with fortress

Fortress

State boundary

Boundary of the Banates and Transylvania

Boundary of county

Bp. 1987. 668086

For a long time it was generally believed that the large, long-horned, greyish-white cattle in Hungary had been introduced to the country during the Conquest. Bone finds have since revealed, though, that, up to the end of the fourteenth century, only the small Central European reddish-brown cattle were bred by the Magyars. The long-horned, grey breed appeared almost without antecedent. From this (and from the subsequent breeding areas of this grey variety), it is reasonable to conclude that these animals were brought in by the Cumans. Following the settlement in Hungary of these people during the thirteenth century, the breed spread. The new cattle were bred by the burghers who lived in the market-towns of the Great Plain. During the fourteenth century, the Italian chronicler Villani wrote that in Hungary "many oxen and cows are raised which are not used as draught animals. They therefore grow fast and become fat on the lush pastures. They are slaughtered and their skins and fat traded on a large scale. The meat is boiled in big cauldrons and, when it is cooked, it is salted and removed from the bone. The meat is dried in ovens or elsewhere, ground into a fine powder. This is how it is preserved." At first ox skin and fat were sold abroad but, from the second half of the fourteenth century onwards, a growing number of fattened Hungarian oxen were driven on foot to Germany and to Venice. During the course of the fifteenth century, the number of cattle involved in this trade was more than 100,000 annually. Cattle constituted Hungary's most important export commodity at this time.

The wines of Tokaj were just as famous. The Romans were the first to produce wine in the Tokaj area and French settlers helped to expand its boundaries northwards. Large quantities of Tokaj wine were exported to Poland. Sheep breeding was one of the important branches of agriculture. The Hungarian *racka* variety of sheep provided the wool needed for broad-cloth. At the same time the *purzsa,* the type raised by the Roumanian mountain herdsmen, supplied the whole population with ewe cheese. This was an important part of their diet.

Hungary was also rich in natural resources. As early as in the twelfth century written records mention silver and gold mines, as well as the salt of Transylvania. Germans were the chief mining experts in Hungary and, prior to the appearance on the market of precious metals from Africa and the Americas, Hungary supplied most of Europe with gold and silver. Even more important than this was Hungarian copper, which had a high silver content. As early as the fifteenth century, copper mining was mechanized when the Hungarian Thurzó family introduced the water-wheel into the industry. Later, the Thurzós joined forces with the Fuggers, a banking family, and concluded deals worth millions on the world market.

Up to the end of the sixteenth century, Hungary was a major raw material supplier in Europe. Precisely because of this, however, she remained an industrially backward country. This had serious economic consequences afterwards.

The Peasant War of 1514 and the Battle of Mohács

The successful realization of king Matthias's far-reaching plans would have required both an obedient civil service and a mercenary army. However, the weakness of urban development in Hungary meant that the king was unable to reward good service with grants of money. Accordingly therefore military commanders were given estates in payment for their achievements and officials received leading posts in the Church. Despite his intentions, Matthias in this way contributed to the strengthening of the large landed estate and, at the same time, the Palatine István Szapolyai, the head of what was now the wealthiest baronial family, and Tamás Bakócz, Matthias's secretary and Bishop of Győr, agreed that a king must be elected who would not curtail the power of the magnates. Therefore, in 1490, the weak Wladislas II succeeded to the throne. Wladislas was to be king of Bohemia too until 1516 but to prevent him exercising power even Matthias's Black Army was disbanded. The barons' private forces once again monopolized military power in the country. These they maintained from public taxation and forced even the royal court to economize dramatically.

Wladislas II turned to the leading churchmen for assistance against the barons. He made Tamás Bakócz his confidant, and appointed him Archbishop of Esztergom and Chancellor. In effect Wladislas entrusted the entire government of the country to this man. Bakócz was an intelligent, albeit ruthless, prelate who was quite prepared to augment his wealth by any means possible. The pomp of Bakócz's surroundings rivalled the splendour of the royal court. The nobility rallied behind the Szapolyais in their struggle against Bakócz. In 1505, the Diet declared that, should Wladislaw die without an heir, a "national" king should be elected to rule over Hungary. The nobility was thinking of János Szapolyai, and the growing popularity of this particular magnate led the king and Bakócz to seek an alliance with the Habsburgs.

While the "national" and "Court" parties were locked in conflict with each other, popular discontent grew. The ordinary people were defenceless against the powerful and special mention must be made of burghers of the market-towns. This stratum bred cattle and produced wine for export. Growing prosperity for these people had brought greater consciousness and they were hard by the Diet's resolution that, instead of the former lump-sum payment they would now have to pay a ninth of their cereal and wine production to the landowner. In this way the bitterness of the poor peasants was now compounded by the despair of the more affluent. In 1513 Bakócz was defeated in the papal election and Leo X (of Medici) ascended the Throne of Saint Peter. By way of compensation, the Pope commissioned Bakócz to lead a crusade against the Turks. The resentments of the people were soon to receive dramatic expression.

41

In spring 1514 the Franciscan friars entrusted with the recruitment of crusaders had collected such a vast army of peasants outside Buda that it was endangering not only spring agricultural work, but also the security of the landowners. The Franciscans, who lived in the market-towns and sympathized with the people, advocated the idea of a peasant kingdom based on equality of assets. The barons together with the nobles, therefore forced the king and Bakócz to order the army of crusaders to disperse on May 15.

By this time, however, the first troops had set off across the Great Plain on their way to engage the Turks. Their response to the disbandment order was to turn against the landowners. They elected György Székely (Dózsa), a soldier of Szekler origin, to be their leader. Dózsa had earned a reputation for bravery in his skirmishes with the Turks and wanted to lead the peasant army to Transylvania. There, they would unite with the dissatisfied Szeklers and would establish popular power. However, János Szapolyai, already Voivode of Transylvania by this time, used his troops to block the road leading to Transylvania. Dózsa's army therefore marched south against Temesvár, a town defended by István Báthori, the *ispán* of Temes. Szapolyai hastened to the relief of Temesvár and by 15 July had dispersed the peasant army. Dózsa was burnt alive on a red-hot iron throne and his associates were tortured to death. The Diet passed a law which declared that the peasants were to be perpetually and without exception bound to the land and deprived of their right to own it. Peasants were from this time on to become socagers tied to their landowner. For centuries to come the peasants were outcasts in their own country, for the development of which their work had been largely responsible.

After the defeat of the peasant insurrection, the conflicts between the barons and the nobles continued. Bakócz and his clique tried to offset the growth of Szapolyai's authority by concluding a succession settlement between the Hungarian Jagiellons and the Austrian Habsburgs. After the death of Wladislas II, his son, Louis II was crowned King of Hungary in 1516. Louis married Mary of Habsburg, whose brother Ferdinand in turn married Anna Jagiello. This constituted a violation of the 1505 law which had stipulated the election of a "national" king. The struggle between the baronial faction and the lesser nobility became more acute than ever.

After the death of Bakócz in 1521, Palatine István Báthori, the second wealthiest person in Hungary after the Szapolyais, became the leader of the "Court" faction. In 1525, however, Báthori was ousted by István Werbőczy, the influential mouthpiece of the Szapolyai faction and the compiler of the famous *Tripartitum,* a work on Hungarian common law. (The *Tripartitum* recognized the equality of barons and nobles and listed their rights, but also included were the punitive laws against the peasantry.) The voting power of the lesser nobility overthrew Báthori and made Werbőczy Palatine. The first thing the new Palatine did was to deprive the Fuggers of their lucrative mining leases. The miners, now without pay, rebelled

—only to be suppressed and punished by Werbőczy. This antagonism of the Fuggers served to deny the country of credit from that family at the time when the Turkish threat was growing.

In 1521 Sultan Suleiman the Great occupied Nándorfehérvár (Belgrade) and in 1526 launched a new campaign against Hungary. Louis II could rally only 25,000 troops against almost 100,000 Turks. Unable to wait for Szapolyai's 10,000 men who were already on their way to unite with his forces, Louis II was forced to accept a battle with the Ottomans at Mohács (29 August 1526). Under the command of Pál Tomori, Archbishop of Kalocsa, the Hungarian army attacked the enemy—only to be dispersed by the Turkish artillery. In his flight from the battleground, Louis was drowned in the Csele stream. Half of the Hungarian troops present, including numerous barons and prelates, also died. The prosperous days of medieval Hungary were over.

Gothic Culture in Hungary

In Hungary, the Gothic style of architecture became established in the middle of the thirteenth century. The first major Gothic buildings were commissioned by the royal court and, the earliest Gothic edifices still surviving are the Mary (now Matthias) Church and the tower of Mary Magdalene Church in Buda. The former was built for the German burghers and the latter for the Hungarian ones and both were founded by Béla IV—although their present form is not the original. King Béla IV also had a convent built for his daughter Margaret on what is now the Margaret Island. Of this only a few fragments now remain. Béla IV started the construction in the thirteenth century of one section of Buda Castle but today only the foundation walls of this have survived. The most impressive examples of Hungarian Gothic architecture were to be found in that central part of the country which was later devastated during the Ottoman invasion. Castles and churches in this region were indiscriminately destroyed.

In the second half of the thirteenth century, the castles of the secular lords still took the form of keeps. The fourteenth century witnessed the emergence of the fortified castle with towers encompassed by an outer wall. The royal residences were the finest examples of these and were to be found at Visegrád, Buda and Diósgyőr. Secular lords also built in the same way —as, for instance, the Laczfis did at Tata and János Hunyadi did at Vajdahunyad, in the more complex style of late Gothic architecture.

The evolution of Gothic architecture was accompanied by the emergence of a new type of residential building for the burghers and the peasantry. The burghers' houses in fourteenth and fifteenth-century Hungarian towns faced the street with their sloping roofs. Under the "palace" of the first storey, which rested on supports, there opened an enormous gateway. This

43

gateway opened into a wide passage with Gothic sediles to the right and to the left. These awaited the paying guests of the winegrower host. During the same period, the single-room shack of the early Middle Ages was replaced by the tripartite peasant house. The windows of this type of building faced the street and its entrance was from a yard. One went into this yard through a gateway. Opposite the entrance to the house itself was the kitchen with an open fire. On one side there opened a door to the guest room which was heated by a stove. This stove would burn coal and would be staked from outside the room. On the other side was an unheated pantry. This type of peasant dwelling became widespread even amongst the nobility and the burghers of the market-towns. However, the houses of these people were of better quality, built of stone and with domed ceilings.

The mendicant orders of monks produced the finest examples of Gothic ecclesiastical architecture in Hungary. The examples provided by the monasteries were soon followed, in the second half of the fourteenth century, by the towns. The most important Gothic town parish churches that have survived are located in Kassa, Kolozsvár and Brassó. In the fifteenth century the hall-type church became common, especially in the market-towns of eastern Hungary. The most beautiful examples are Szeged's Lower City Church and the church in Farkas Street, Kolozsvár.

Whilst Hungarian architecture was dominated by French and German influences, painting and sculpture were powerfully inspired by Italian art. This was only to be expected during the reign of the Anjou kings. In addition to fresco painting (e.g. the St Ladislas series in the Szekler Land) which flourished during the fifteenth century, Hungarian miniature painting also revealed Italian influence, especially in the *Nekcsei Bible* and the *Illustrated Chronicle (Képes Krónika)*, the latter a masterpiece by Miklós Meggyesi. At the beginning of the fourteenth century, panel painting also became widespread and examples of it were often found in churches. Tamás Kolozsvári, whose work was also influenced by Italian art, was the greatest master of this type of painting. Among other things, he painted the winged altar-screen at Garamszentbenedek. This can be seen today in Esztergom.

Italian influence is even more obvious in the sculpture of the period, primarily in the works of the Kolozsvári brothers, Márton and György. It was they who sculpted the statues of Hungary's canonized kings which once stood outside Nagyvárad Cathedral. (They were destroyed by the Turks in 1660.) However, their St George statue, made for Prague in 1372, has survived. This statue is a very early example of one which stands apart from a building, and its style combines realism with a touch of Renaissance influence. The statues of knights and prophets which were made in the Buda Castle around 1440, showed signs of the "Northern Renaissance" represented in the Dutch and Burgundian art of the time. The same was true of the carvings of Pál Lőcsei, who lived at the beginning of the sixteenth century.

The two centuries of Hungarian Gothic art were dominated by the influence of the mendicant orders, the Dominicans and the Franciscans. These orders were based in the towns and their preachings, in the vernacular, were primarily addressed to the burghers and well-to-do peasants who lived there. To draw attention to what they had to say, they introduced motives from old fables and this was how numerous eastern stories became known by the Hungarian people. They were also the first educators of Hungarian women: the so-called "beginas" who were affiliated to their orders. It was probably for these that the first known poem in the Hungarian language, (The Lament of the Holy Virgin) was written. In the fourteenth century, these orders wrote and performed most of the legends, hymns, passion plays and meditations, and in doing so served all sections of Hungarian society. Towards the end of the period, the "beginas" themselves cultivated literature in the vernacular, or at least translated religious texts into Hungarian. (Lea Ráskai, and Márta Sövényházi are examples.)

The predominance of ecclesiastical art did not entirely eclipse the activities of the secular intelligentsia. A large number of people pursued university studies without intending to embark on a career in the Church. In 1367, Louis the Great founded a university at Pécs. This, however, did not measure up to foreign standards and accordingly the Hungarian clergy continued to attend universities abroad—primarily Vienna, Prague, Cracow, Bologna and Padua. It was from the clergy that the officials of the royal chancery were picked. Master Simon Kézai, who lived in the court of Ladislas the Cuman, was the first to expound the idea of Hun–Magyar kinship in the chronicle that he wrote. He thereby gave support to his monarch's policy of looking to the pagan Cumans for backing and of turning against the Church. In the middle of the fourteenth century, János Küküllei wrote an account of the reign of Louis the Great. Although this has not survived in its original version, the Toldi and Tar legends prove that the secular epic also flourished during this period. A well-known, albeit late, example of this kind of writing is *Szabács viadala* (Szabács's Fight).

Early Renaissance Culture in Hungary

Up to the early sixteenth century Renaissance culture was largely confined to Italy and seldom penetrated northwards across the Alps. Hungary was therefore especially fortunate in being an early centre of Renaissance art, in spite of her geographical position. While in the Western European countries Gothic art still predominated, in Hungary Renaissance achievement appeared alongside a flourishing Gothic culture. Naturally the royal court was the first centre of this. From 1476 onwards, Beatrice of Aragon —Matthias Hunyadi's second wife—strove to transform Hungarian practices and to bring them into line with Italian ideas. Beatrice regarded the existing Hungarian culture as barbaric, and King Matthias, receptive to anything that was new and beautiful, supported her. Matthias himself soon took the initiative in this transformation and set very high standards.

The stone carvings and furniture at Buda and Visegrád Castles soon changed their style. It was probably at this time that the splendid Gothic well built by the Anjou at Visegrád was demolished, being replaced by the new Renaissance basin made of red marble from Piszke and decorated with representations of Hercules as a child. The Gothic statues at Buda, which had been made just a few decades earlier, were also removed and buried during this period. They were replaced by the works of Italian masters. Not only foreign experts worked at Buda, however. Hungarians also became proficient in the skills of these. For instance, Italian faience ceramic art was first introduced into Hungary through imported pottery, floor and mosaic tiles. Soon, however, King Matthias set up his own ceramic works in Buda. Indeed, as the latest finds have revealed, this type of ceramic art also became established in Pécs.

Hungarian goldsmiths had less to learn from the Renaissance. Abounding in gold and silver, Hungary had never lacked fine jewellers. Silver fittings from belts and headdresses have been found even in medieval peasant graves. The application of *cloisonné* enamel made the Hungarian goldsmith's art, which otherwise used international Gothic motifs, especially appealing.

Local traditions also persisted in panel and mural painting. The great painter who used the initials M. S. and who worked during the early sixteenth century, was familiar with the works of Albrecht Dürer—his contemporary and a Hungarian by origin. It was not, however, Renaissance inspiration that he took from Dürer, but rather his Gothic forms. The window frames, door frames and statues at Buda and Visegrád are splendid relics of Renaissance stone carving and sculpture. The same is true of the Bakócz Chapel in Esztergom and the Báthory Madonna. In addition, numerous Gothic churches and burghers' houses, carved altars and items of furniture have survived from this period. Not only did the Gothic and Renaissance styles exist alongside each other, but there was a certain amount of intermingling between them as well. This took place in the fine arts and also in literature.

King Matthias invited foreign humanists to his court and these were mainly Italians. Among the latter were Antonio Bonfini, the historian, Galeotto Marzio, who recorded the king's witty sayings, and Naldo Naldi, who preserved and described the magnificently illustrated codices of the famous Corvina Library. There were many others also, for example the most famous German astronomers of the age, Regiomontanus and Peuerbach. A number of Hungarians also represented the new, secular spirit in literature and science. They included János Vitéz, a writer of fine letters, and his nephew Janus Pannonius, Bishop of Pécs and one of the most talented of Europe's medieval Latin poets. Janus wrote odes on the Hunyadi's exploits, elegies lamenting Hungary's backwardness, satirical epigrams and lyrical poems. These last were imbued with gentle emotion and a sensitive love of nature, and were admired even in Italy.

At the same time, however, at the Franciscans' monastery in Buda, Pelbárt Temesvári and his disciple Osvát Laskai castigated humanist thinking which they considered to be faithless and immoral. Not even King Matthias himself was spared criticism. They demanded of him the devout religiosity of the "Holy Kings", albeit in a new form—that of the pre-Reformation "New Piety". This represented the spiritual side to Renaissance thinking and was advocated by no lesser figures than Thomas Kempis and Erasmus. The words of the Franciscan friars did not reach the King but nevertheless did elicit a considerable response among the burghers of the towns and in the ranks of the lesser nobility. Indeed, because their preachings were published also in Latin, the Franciscans were able to spread their views even beyond Hungary's borders.

The printing of books in Hungary also began during Matthias's reign. In 1473 András Hess set up a printing press in Buda and brought out the *Chronica Hungarorum*. Another printing press also existed in Hungary at this time but both were short-lived, new ones being started only after 1536. The chronicle of János Thuróczy, Matthias's Hungarian historian, was published in Brno in 1488. Thuróczi's work, imbued with national pride and identifying the Magyars with the Huns, compares Matthias to Attila. This work greatly influenced the outlook of the Hungarian nobility and for many decades determined national consciousness. Although a large number of works from the reign of King Matthias perished later on, this historical idea was passed on to subsequent generations. It was to provide emotional strength during the grave misfortunes that were in store.

II. HUNGARY AT THE BEGINNING OF MODERN TIMES

The Division of Hungary into Three Parts

Contemporaries regarded the Ottoman invasion of Hungary as divine punishment for internal anarchy, party strife, social injustice and moral and intellectual profligacy. Although each of these had in fact weakened Hungary in her struggle againts the Turks, it was also true that the Ottoman Empire was a very formidable adversary. The Turks were incomparably stronger economically and possessed an army which far outnumbered that of the Hungarians. Only assistance from outside could have enabled Hungary to resist the Ottoman onslaught with success.

When the childless Louis II died at the Battle of Mohács in 1526, it was of paramount importance that the new king be able to mobilize adequate foreign help against the Turks. The lesser nobility wished to see János Szapolyai, Voivode of Transylvania, son-in-law of Sigismund I, King of Poland, a state then at the zenith of her power, and could therefore offer support. The Diet elected Szapolyai king, with the title John I. However, led by Palatine István Báthori, a small group of barons proclaimed a rival king, the Austrian Archduke Ferdinand of Habsburg. As the Bohemians had also elected Ferdinand king, the tradition of a common king for Hungary and Bohemia would be upheld. Indeed, there was even hope that, through Ferdinand's brother, the powerful Emperor Charles V, the Holy Roman Empire would also aid Hungary against the Turks.

Szapolyai offered to marry Mary, the widow of Louis II and the sister of Ferdinand of Habsburg, but was rejected. Charles V helped Ferdinand against Szapolyai but did nothing against the Turks. Ferdinand drove Szapolyai out of the country and the latter fled to Poland. With Polish and French assistance, Szapolyai now won the support of Sultan Suleiman II, the Ottoman leader. In 1529, the Sultan used force to restore Szapolyai's rule and, what is more, even tried to occupy Vienna, Ferdinand's seat. In 1532, the Sultan's second advance was halted by the heroic efforts of Miklós Jurisics, the defender of the fortress at Kőszeg.

Szapolyai died in 1540 and Ferdinand took the opportunity to besiege Buda. However, Bishop György Martinuzzi, governor of the country, wanted to ensure the succession to the throne of Szapolyai's infant son. The child was John Sigismund, who was also the Bishop's ward. Martinuzzi therefore turned to Suleiman II for assistance. In 1541 the Sultan drove off the Germans besieging Buda, but then occupied the city for himself. John Sigismund—the Sultan's adopted son by now—was sent to Transylvania, along with his mother, the Polish princess, Isabella Jagiello. The Turkish-occupied part of Hungary—the Pécs-Esztergom-Szeged triangle—was wedged in between Habsburg Western Hungary and the eastern, Szapolyai kingdom.

The country was now divided into three parts. Martinuzzi, who governed the kingdom in the east, regarded Habsburg assistance as vital to Hungary's reunification. However, a powerful army would be required to overcome the inevitable Ottoman resistance to this. In 1551, nevertheless, Ferdinand of Habsburg sent an army to Transylvania which, according to contemporaries, "was too big to conduct a diplomatic mission, but too small for fighting a battle". Martinuzzi asked for reinforcements and, to gain time, entered into negotiations with the Turks as well. Afraid of treason, the commander, Castaldo, had Martinuzzi assassinated but was unable to prevent Ottoman revenge. In 1552, the important border fortresses fell to the Turks one after the other: the towns of Temesvár, Szolnok and Drégely all came under Ottoman control. However, the Turkish advance was checked at Eger, where the garrison, under István Dobó's leadership, put up a heroic defence.

In 1556, the kingdom in Eastern Hungary was re-established under the rule of John Sigismund and became an Ottoman protectorate. For a whole decade there followed a struggle to fix the frontiers of the two Hungarian states. István Báthori, the commander of Várad, would have liked to end internecine strife by arriving at a compromise agreement. This would have acknowledged the duality of the kingdom, but would, at the same time, have given war-torn Hungary a chance to recover. However, while Báthori was negotiating in Vienna, Suleiman II launched an offensive against that city in 1566. The Sultan promised John Sigismund that he would enlarge the latter's kingdom three-fold but in fact occupied additional Hungarian territories for himself. These included the castle of Gyula in the east, formerly in Habsburg possession.

However, Suleiman's campaign against Vienna soon encountered difficulties. At Szigetvár the Turks encountered stiff resistance. The Ottomans' siege of that castle dragged on and, by the time victory was theirs, the elderly Sultan was already dead. At the very last moment, Miklós Zrínyi, the commander of Szigetvár, broke out of his devastated and burning castle at the head of his Hungarian and Croatian soldiers. All of them died in the battle which followed. In the meantime, King Maximilian I (1564–76), Ferdinand's successor, had been waiting at Győr together with a large mercenary force. However, Maximilian refused to heed Zrínyi's desperate calls for assistance and to risk his army, which had been assigned to the defence of Vienna. It was at this time that the Habsburgs' policy towards the Hungarian territories became absolutely clear. The Habsburgs regarded Western Hungary as a buffer zone to protect their hereditary provinces. For the time being at least, they were not contemplating the expulsion of the Turks from Hungary's central regions.

The heroic feat of Zrínyi and his soldiers was, however, sufficient in itself to stem Ottoman advance temporarily. Owing to time lost during the lengthy siege and because of the Sultan's death, the Ottoman army withdrew. The new Sultan was unable to match his father's efforts and in 1568 concluded the Peace of Adrianople with Maximilian. Under this treaty, the conquests of Suleiman II remained in Ottoman possession. The front line between the two great powers now stabilized and both sides established an extensive network of border fortresses. Hostilities were reduced to the level of regular skirmishes between the Habsburg and Ottoman forces and this state of affairs persisted for a very long time.

The Rise of Transylvania and the Long War

The era of the Ottoman conquest in Hungary was not only characterized by defeats. It also abounded in victories. As early as the late sixteenth century it seemed that the Turks might well be driven out if the two Hungarian states joined forces against their common foe. Such a bold undertaking held out hope of success for two reasons. Firstly, the Habsburgs were able to mobilize foreign assistance and, secondly, Hungarian state in the east had also become stronger.

In 1570, John Sigismund (Szapolyai) concluded the Treaty of Speyer. By this he relinquished the Hungarian crown to the Habsburgs and became Prince of Transylvania. (Transylvania had now annexed the territories east of the River Tisza.) His successor, István Báthori (1571–86) defended Transylvania against the Habsburgs and, in competition with Maximilian, also became king of Poland in 1576. However, through his brother, Kristóf, who had been appointed voivode, Báthori retained control over Transylvania which was now united with Poland for all practical purposes. For the time being, the Poles enjoyed the advantages of this union. Báthori (as King Stephen of Poland) fought his successful battles against Russia's Ivan the Terrible largely with Transylvanian mercenaries. Of these the majority were Szeklers.

In 1562 John Sigismund I made serfs of the Szekler commoners and for some thirty years their only opportunity to rise socially was through military service. Generally speaking, the sixteenth century witnessed the deterioration of the peasantry's lot in Hungary. It was then that "perpetual

51

serfdom" was instituted in both east and west. István Báthori's military policy not only alleviated the misery of the serfs, but also laid the foundations of a Transylvanian army which could later challenge the Turks with some chance of success.

In 1591, and after a long period of peace, Hassan, the pasha of Bosnia, laid siege to Sziszek castle. This move marked the beginning of renewed hostilities between the Habsburgs and the Turks. The army of Habsburg Emperor Rudolph was largely made up of German and Hungarian mercenaries. This scored a victory against the Ottomans at Sziszek in 1593, and later one at Pákozd. Although Rudolph's troops surrendered the fortress of Győr, they had every chance of successfully continuing the struggle. Zsigmond Báthori, the new Prince of Transylvania, headed the advice of his uncle István Bocskai, the commander at Várad. Bocskai realized that Transylvania could not appear to be pro-Turkish at a time when Ottoman fortunes might begin to wane. With the Ottomans expelled from Hungary a principality aligned with the Sultan would be in great danger from victorious Habsburg forces. Accordingly, Zsigmond Báthori eradicated the pro-Ottoman faction in Transylvania, restored the liberties of the Szekler commoners and extracted oaths of allegiance from the voivodes of Wallachia and Moldavia. In this way, he was able to enter into an alliance with Rudolph on equal terms.

In 1595, Bocskai's Szekler forces, who were fighting in defence of their liberty, together with the Roumanian and Serbian troops of Mihai, the Voivode of Wallachia, conducted an impressive campaign against the Turks. An Ottoman attack through Wallachia was beaten off and the enemy driven back as far as the Danube. Most of the Turkish troops who tried to escape across the bridge at Giurgiu were massacred. At the same time Báthori, the captains György Borbély and Mózes Székely, occupied Lippa, Jenő and numerous other castles along River Maros. The nobility was not, however, prepared to accept the loss of its Szekler serfs. With Zsigmond Báthori's tacit approval, the nobles therefore once again made serfs of the Szekler commoners at the so-called "Bloody Carnival" of 1596. Deprived of his finest soldiers, Báthori could not render much assistance to the Habsburg army, which was then seriously defeated by the Turks at Mezőkeresztes. Eger also fell.

After this, the war ground to a halt. The Turks ruthlessly devastated the Great Plain. The free Heyducks in turn revenged themselves on the Ottomans capturing their supplies and burning their principal crossing point, the bridge over River Drava at Eszék. Although Győr was recaptured from the Turks in 1598, Kanizsa was lost in 1600. Gradually both sides became exhausted, while the country itself was devastated and depopulated.

Having lost all hope, Zsigmond Báthori relinquished his title of Prince and decided to cede Transylvania to the Habsburgs. Later, however, he changed his mind and handed over the throne to his cousin, Cardinal András Báthori. In 1599, Mihai, Voivode of Wallachia, occupied Transylvania with the help of vengeful Szeklers. Although claiming to act on behalf of the Habsburgs, Mihai was in reality pursuing his own objectives. Fleeing from the scene of the lost battle, András Báthori was killed by the Szeklers in the mountains. However, Voivode Mihai's ascendancy was short-lived. The Transylvanian nobility enlisted the support of George Basta, the Habsburgs' famous general. Basta defeated Mihai and, in 1601 had him murdered.

The Transylvanian nobility was not enamoured with the prospect of Habsburg rule though, and wished to make peace with the Turks. Mózes Székely, the former hero of the struggles against the Ottomans wanted to organize the principality with their assistance. In 1603, however, Székely's army was defeated by Habsburg troops at Brassó and Székely himself was killed. His followers, among them the young Gábor Bethlen, fled to Turkish territory. Basta took bloody revenge on Transylvania. His mercenaries looted and set fire to the villages. The people fled to the mountains to escape death, and famine and plague swept the land. When Basta left Transylvania in the spring of 1604, the country lay in ruins. It seemed that the two Hungarian states had again been reunited, albeit at great cost.

Humanistic Culture and the Reformation in Hungary

Although Hungarian culture entered a period of decline after 1526, nevertheless there remained some scope for development. The influence of humanism and the Renaissance was now coupled to that of the Reformation. As a result of all this, European culture could receive full expression in Hungary.

The century of Ottoman occupation did not produce conditions which favoured the fine arts. What is more, the Reformation was satisfied with fewer churches and, in ecclesiastical art, rejected higher quality figural delineation. However, it was also at this time that the Tuscan-style painting of wooden ceilings and quires in churches began to spread. This was the "flower Renaissance decoration" which was becoming increasingly popular and which also began to find expression in the work of goldsmiths. Unlike its medieval counterpart, the fine art of this period served secular, as well as ecclesiastical, purposes. With the exception of the Turkish-occupied areas, where this type of culture stood no chance, the whole country went over to Renaissance taste. This was manifested primarily in door and window frames carved by Italian and Hungarian masters, as well as in the great diversity of sepulchral monuments.

Large construction projects were planned and supervised by Italian engineers. During this period border castles were provided with modern defences—low, wedge-shaped "Italian" bastions, which served as smaller targets for enemy artillery. Castles designed by Pietro Ferabosco at Pozsony, Komárom and Győr were outstanding as defensive structures. So were the castles of Érsekújvár, Eger and Szatmár, which were designed by the two Baldigaras, Ottavio and Giulio. In the Principality of Transylvania, the fortresses of Várad, Szamosújvár and Fogaras were all rebuilt along Italian lines. The big magnates converted their residences into fortresses with quadrangular or circular corner bastions, suitable for defence purposes. Good examples include the Egervár and Sárvár homes of the Nádasdy family, the Nagybiccse home of the Thurzós, the Martinuzzis' Alvinc residence and the Bethlens' home in Keresd.

Sárvár was also famous for its printing press, established in 1537. There, in 1541, the first book in the Hungarian language was published. This was János Sylvester's translation of the *New Testament*. Books in the vernacular and the printed word generally were among the principal weapons of the Reformation, and this was true for the Counter-Reformation as well. During the sixteenth century, some 850 publications were put out by the twenty printing presses in Hungary.

The Reformation began to spread in the decade preceding the Battle of Mohács, although not without opposition. In 1523, supporters of its tenets were condemned to the stake and some were in fact burnt. After Mohács, however, central authority in the state weakened. Although both King John and King Ferdinand were devout Catholics, the overwhelming majority of the country's population became Protestants. This was possible in Hungary because a very large number of clergy could be presented to benefices independently of the king. Every landlord and every autonomous body, including the free towns as well as the market-towns endowed with this right by the local landowner, could invite a parish priest and be the judge of his suitability.

Initially the German and Hungarian towns employed Protestant preachers but later the magnates and nobles generally followed their example. This was not only because their keep and religious ceremonies were less expensive but because they convinced congregations with their arguments. Another factor was that a fair number of Franciscans—members of the most popular religious order—had supported the Reformation and had converted their adherents as well. Mátyás Dévai Bíró, the first Hungarian reformer (the "Hungarian Luther") was originally a Franciscan, as were András Szkhárosi Horvát and Mihály Sztárai, outstanding poets and preachers who took the part of the serfs. Other former Franciscans were István Kopácsi, the founder of Sárospatak College, and probably even István Szegedi Kis, the pioneer and internationally acclaimed Calvinist theologian. Calvinism first established itself in the market-towns of Eastern Hungary and from these early centres gradually spread through the whole of the Tisza region. The most popular Calvinist leader, Péter Melius Juhász, Bishop of Debrecen, conducted heated theological debates in the

1560s with Ferenc Dávid of Kolozsvár. Dávid advocated Unitarian ideas and was the protégé of John Sigismund.

The Calvinists were saved by István Báthori, who oppressed the Unitarians but simultaneously called in the Jesuits, thereby initiating the Catholic Counter-Reformation. At his court, Báthori provided conditions conducive to a second flowering of Humanism in Hungary. In addition to the historians Ferenc Forgách and Pál Gyulai, the political philosopher Farkas Kovacsóczi and Bálint Balassi—the greatest Hungarian poet of the century —all lived at Báthori's court for some time.

Bocskai and the Heyducks' War of Independence

One of the causes of Hungary's misfortunes was that, owing to a lack of the necessary economic and political preconditions, the country was without a standing mercenary army for the century after king Matthias's death. The latter's "Black Army" had not inspired the establishment of a similarly effective professional force. The absence of a "field army", specially trained and suitable for open battle, was certainly a handicap. To create one would have cost a great deal of money and the Hungarian magnates preferred to direct resources on their own private armies, which they stationed in their fortresses. For the Habsburg emperors, Western Hungary served as a useful buffer-zone which shielded Vienna. They, too, therefore concentrated on fortifying their castles. Without a field army it was impossible for Hungary to drive out the Turkish invader, and this had become obvious. The Habsburgs maintained their hold on Transylvania by employing a ruthless reign of terror but, at the same time, the central part of the country was still occupied by the Turks. Initially, in the early years of the seventeenth century, the Habsburg military leadership wished to suppress the Hungarian Heyducks, whom they regarded as a dangerous element. Later, however, the Habsburgs tried to recruit an inexpensive army from them. A few thousand Heyducks were actually provided with firearms, the intention being to send them against the Turks.

(The Heyducks were peasants who had escaped in great numbers from the areas devastated by the Turks or from oppressive conditions on landlords' estates. Either they took service as mercenaries or plundered the countryside for a livelihood. In the wars against the Turks they distinguished themselves by their toughness. The fact that there was no standing mercenary army meant, though, that only some of them could become regular soldiers.)

The purpose of reorganizing the Hungarian field army at this juncture was to create a force for use, not against the Turks, but against recalcitrant

Hungarian nobles. Habsburg tyranny in Transylvania and in Royal Hungary engendered opposition which needed to be dealt with. In order to obtain money, the Habsburg dynasty, deeply in debt after the war, initiated inheritance and, later, high treason law suits against big Hungarian landowners. Furthermore, to guarantee the spiritual obedience of a country where Protestants constituted the majority, it forced the Counter-Reformation in Hungary, which so far had been spared religious strife. In 1604, General Belgiojoso, the commander of Kassa, occupied the town's Lutheran church on behalf of the Bishop of Eger and further church seizures were also planned. To silence the nobility, a forged Article XXII was appended to the laws passed in 1604. This prohibited the discussion of religion at the Diet.

By this time discontent was running high in both the lower and the upper strata of Hungarian society. The peasantry, oppressed by both the Turks and the Habsburg forces, the free Heyducks, destined either to extermination or serfdom, the Protestant commoners, burghers and nobles, as well as the big landowners whose property rights were under threat—all regarded the Habsburgs their principal enemies.

Insurrection was now imminent and all that was needed was a man to head it. Gábor Bethlen, the young leader of Transylvanian émigrés who had fled into Ottoman territory, chose István Bocskai, the greatest landowner in the territory east of the Tisza river. Bocskai had regretted his previous policy of linking the fate of Transylvania to that of the Habsburgs ánd was now willing to reorganize the Principality of Transylvania with Ottoman help. His activities were, however, discovered and General Belgiojoso set out against him with a large army. Belgiojoso's force included those 5,000 well-armed Heyducks originally intended to constitute the core of a Hungarian field army. Not wishing to kill their own people, the Heyducks joined Bocskai. On 15 October 1604 Bocskai launched a surprise night attack between Álmosd and Diószeg and routed Belgiojoso's German, Walloon and Serbian army, despite the superior strength of the Habsburg general's forces. The panic-stricken Belgiojoso fled to Upper Hungary and Basta's army, which had hastened to Belgiojoso's assistance, was also destroyed in the Heyducks' constant surprise attacks.

Bocskai occupied Transylvania and Royal Hungary. Although the Turkish Sultan sent him a royal crown, he concluded a peace treaty with the Habsburgs at the request of the Hungarian nobility and was himself satisfied with the Principality of Transylvania. The Treaty of Vienna (1606) ensured the right of the Hungarian Diet to enact legislation, guaranteed the power of the officials elected by the Diet and conferred freedom of religion on the Protestants. Bocskai settled some 10,000 Heyducks on his own estates, and later Heyduck settlements grew up there. Afterwards the Princes of Transylvania and the Hungarian aristocracy founded more free Heyduck settlements, the inhabitants of which did not pay tax and did not hold land under feudal obligations. Their sole duty was to render military service. Bocskai also restored the freedom of the Szeklers and thereby procured a large number of free peasant soldiers for the Princes of Transylvania.

Owing to Bocskai's early death in 1606, however, neither the final settlement of the Heyducks nor the implementation of the Treaty of Vienna was assured. Emperor Rudolph stubbornly refused to comply with the wishes of the "rebellious" Hungarians. The Heyducks therefore rose in arms. Intending to elect their own national king, they wished to dethrone the Habsburgs. However Archduke Matthias of Habsburg, who had concluded the Treaty of Vienna, and the Hungarian aristocracy persuaded the Heyducks that they should turn their arms against the Emperor Rudolph instead. With Rudolph forced to abdicate, Matthias was elected King of Hungary as Matthias II. At the Diet of 1608, Matthias put the Treaty of Vienna into effect. Those Heyducks who had not settled permanently joined the young Gábor Báthori and in 1609 gave armed help to him in his acquisition of the Transylvanian throne. This had, however, been due to him as Bocskai had in any case intended him to succeed to it.

Despite the political storms of the first decade of the seventeenth century, Hungarian culture was not entirely without outstanding achievement. The greatest poet of the age, János Rimay, lived at Bocskai's court. So did István Szamosközy, the greatest representative of Hungarian Humanist historiography, Simon Péchi, the Humanist scholar who organized the Sabbatarian sect, and the Calvinist preacher of Kassa, Péter Alvinczi, who worded Bocskai's proclamations and who took issue with the Counter-Reformation. It was at this time that the Jesuit Péter Pázmány began his career as a writer. Pázmány subsequently became Archbishop of Esztergom and converted the greater part of the Hungarian aristocracy to Catholicism. It was also during this period that Albert Szenczi Molnár, Bocskai's foreign propagandist and the compiler of the first Hungarian grammar and dictionary, worked as a linguist and as a translator.

Gábor Bethlen's Struggle to Unify Hungary

Gábor Bethlen was a worthy successor to István Bocskai and strove to continue the latter's work. On Bethlen's banner God's protective arm, holding a sword, stretches out to help the Prince. Bethlen certainly needed divine assistance to achieve his highly important goal: the unification of tripartite Hungary under his own rule, and the re-establishment thereby of a national kingdom.

Bethlen became Prince of Transylvania in 1613 and intervened in the Thirty Years War six years later. Bethlen took the side of the Bohemians, who had rebelled against Emperor Ferdinand II's Counter-Reformation. Since 1608, Transylvania had been in alliance not only with the Bohemians, but with the Moravian, Silesian and Austrian nobility as well. On behalf of the Hungarian estates, Protestant magnates invited Bethlen to support and lead their war of independence against the Habsburgs. Together with his allies, Bethlen besieged Vienna. A counter-attack, however, forced him to withdraw temporarily. In 1620, Bethlen again occupied Royal Hungary and on 25 August the Diet of Besztercebánya elected him King of Hungary. Bethlen wisely postponed the coronation ceremony to await the final outcome of the war. Unfortunately, however, on 8 November 1620 the Bohemians suffered a decisive defeat at the Battle of the White Mountain. Frederick, the king of Bohemia, died in exile and Ferdinand II stripped his country of her autonomy. The leaders of the Bohemian uprising were executed and shortly afterwards the Moravian, Silesian and Austrian estates also surrendered.

These dramatic events naturally enough caused some panic in Hungary but Bethlen kept this well under control. In Europe Bethlen alone dared to continue the struggle against the Habsburgs, thereby gaining time for the forces of Protestantism to reorganize. Although, by the Treaty of Nikolsburg, Bethlen only succeeded in ensuring autonomy for the Hungarian estates, together with freedom of religion, he soon had the opportunity to enter into alliance with the Protestant powers of Western Europe. In 1623 in league with the German Protestants, he launched a new offensive against the Habsburgs. Three years later, in 1626, another followed on the side of the English–Dutch–Danish alliance. However, the abandonment of Bethlen's cause by the Hungarian magnates frightened by the events in Bohemia, frustrated his plans. All Bethlen finally achieved was the annexation to Transylvania of seven counties of Upper Hungary.

Nevertheless, Bethlen won international recognition for his state. Two of the most famous imperial generals, Dampierre and Buquoy, died in battle against him. A third, Wallenstein, retreated from him. During Bethlen's lifetime the enemy never once reached Transylvanian soil. Bethlen led his army of Heyducks and Szeklers in person and no one defeated him on the field of battle. The international renown of the Hungarian hussar dates back to Bethlen's time. The Prince was a politician with an excellent sense of diplomacy; it was he who initiated and organized the anti-Habsburg European coalitions. On the whole, Bethlen acted independently of the Turks—indeed he often exploited them for his own purposes.

At home, Bethlen was the first Hungarian ruler since Matthias Hunyadi to succeed in establishing centralized rule in accordance with the principles of modern absolutism. In his economic policy he followed the principles of mercantilism which were then current. Although he could not abolish the institution of perpetual serfdom that had spread throughout Eastern Europe, Bethlen tried to protect the serfs from the excesses of the land-owners and made it possible for the sons of serfs to attend school. Two decades before Pázmány, he founded a college at Nagyszombat, from where he moved it first to Kassa, then to Kolozsvár and finally to Gyulafehérvár.

After Bethlen's death this famous school settled permanently at Nagy-enyed.

Although it was on behalf of his own Calvinist faith that he founded a college, printing press and library, by the standards of the time Bethlen was extraordinarily tolerant in matters of religion. He recalled the Jesuits—previously expelled from Transylvania—and gave financial support for the Bible translation of the Jesuit György Káldi. Bethlen allowed the Catholics of Transylvania to keep a pontifical administrator and the Orthodox Roumanians were permitted to have their own bishop. Roumanian priests were exempted from obligations and Jews in Transylvania no longer had to wear a yellow star. Bethlen even settled a group of Anabaptists, then persecuted everywhere, in Transylvania.

Bethlen's contemporaries primarily recall his splendid court and magnificent construction projects. Only accounts written at the time have survived to relate the exceptional beauty of Bethlen's palace at Gyulafehér-vár. This matched the Baroque royal palaces of the age not only in decor, but also in the cultural life carried on there. The quality of music was especially high at Bethlen's court and a novelty of the age, the Italian opera, also flourished within its walls.

His loyal associate and subsequent successor János Kemény mourned Bethlen with the following words: "He should either not have been born at all, or he should have lived for ever."

The Luck and Misfortunes of the Two Rákóczis

Gábor Bethlen procured for Transylvania peaceful affluence at home and international renown abroad. This favourable state of affairs still existed when György Rákóczi I was elected Prince of Transylvania in 1630. This ended a brief power struggle which resulted in the ousting of Bethlen's widow, Catherine of Brandenburg, and afterwards that of Bethlen's younger brother, István. Rákóczi owed his succession largely to the Heyducks who, after Bethlen's death, once again found themselves under Habsburg rule. The Heyducks were justly afraid that Palatine Miklós Esterházy, the Habsburg's main representative in Hungary, would curtail the liberties Bocskai had bestowed on them. Accordingly, the Heyducks took up arms against the Habsburg mercenaries sent out to subjugate them.

István Bethlen, the commander of Várad, and Dávid Zólyomi, the Captain-General of Transylvania, rendered military assistance to the Heyducks and in 1631 dispersed Esterházy's army at Rakamaz. The Transylvanian throne was then offered to György Rákóczi, the richest Calvinist magnate of Eastern Hungary. The hope obviously was that he would keep the seven counties of Upper Hungary which Bethlen had acquired but which should have been returned to the Habsburgs on his death. Indeed, this would have served Rákóczi's own interests as large family estates, with Sárospatak as their centre, were located in this area.

Rákóczi was, however, a cautious man. With the help of the Heyducks he had himself elected Prince of Transylvania, but ceded the seven counties to Royal Hungary. In return for this he procured confirmation of the rights of the Heyducks. Rákóczi thereby retained the support of the Heyducks but was at the same time able to conclude peace with the Habsburg monarch who, deeply preoccupied by the complicated situation produced by the Thirty Years War in Germany, did not wish to fight on two fronts. Esterházy was embittered by these developments as his most fervent wish had been to attach Transylvania to Royal Hungary. However, Esterházy's were frustrated not only as a result of Ferdinand II's disapproval and that of the more moderate Archbishop Pázmány's. Also important was the peasant uprising which broke out in 1631 and which was led by Péter Császár. The latter broke out because of looting carried out by mercenary troops recruited for the occupation of Transylvania. Esterházy even had to suffer the humiliation that the peasant insurrection was not suppressed by his incompetent mercenary commanders but by Rákóczi's Transylvanian troops.

An even greater threat loomed over Rákóczi in 1636. Gábor Bethlen's younger brother, István, who had since regretted giving up the throne, received a promise from the Turks that they would re-establish him as Transylvania's ruler. Rákóczi was unperturbed and called the people to arms. At Nagyszalonta his Heyducks routed the Turkish army. The Sultan was forced by a Persian attack and a Janissary rebellion to accept this defeat and recognize Rákóczi's authority.

Having consolidated his position, Rákóczi could now think of continuing Gábor Bethlen's policy of intervention against the Habsburgs in the Thirty Years War. The opportunity arose when Protestant Swedish troops had advanced so far as to almost threaten Vienna. In 1643, Rákóczi entered into alliance with Sweden and in 1644 launched a campaign to occupy Royal Hungary. He was not, however, a military leader of Gábor Bethlen's calibre and his commanders were not particularly good either. Accordingly, imperial mercenaries and Esterházy's Hungarian troops were able to drive him back as far as Kassa. Here the fortunes of war turned. The Transylvanian army not only occupied Royal Hungary, but in 1645 invaded Moravia as well. Outside Brno Rákóczi met with Torstensson, the Swedish military commander. Jealous of Rákóczi's feats, the Sultan ordered him home. Rákóczi was therefore obliged to sign the Treaty of Linz with Ferdinand III. This treaty confirmed the reannexation of the seven counties won by Bethlen and extended freedom to practise the Protestant religion to the peasants as well.

Although György Rákóczi I lacked Bethlen's conspicuous talents as a politician and military commander, he skilfully and steadfastly followed the course set by his great predecessor. Rákóczi did not keep a splendid court, but economized and increased his family's wealth. Nevertheless, he, too, spent a great deal on schools and printing presses. He could do this primarily because his two principal enemies, the Habsburgs and the Turks were occupied elsewhere. Rákóczi therefore had free hand not only in the internal affairs of Transylvania, but also, to some extent, in foreign policy.

György Rákóczi II succeeded his father as Prince of Transylvania in 1648. The younger Rákóczi inherited his father's throne and vast wealth, but not his luck. This was in spite of the fact that at this time the leading politicians of Royal Hungary were friends rather than enemies. In 1648, the Treaty of Westphalia marked the end of the Thirty Years War and the Habsburgs could now turn their attention to Hungary. Their aim was to introduce into the country an absolutist regime on the Austrian model. Also at this time, the reform policies sponsored by the Grand Viziers of the Köprülü dynasty halted the decline of the Ottoman Empire. Now threatened from two quarters, the magnates of Royal Hungary looked to Transylvania for help. The anti-Habsburg faction of Palatine Pál Pálffy and Miklós Zrínyi, the Bán (Viceroy) of Croatia, intended to make György Rákóczi II King of Hungary. However, because of the loyal clergy's influence, after the death of Ferdinand III the Diet of 1655 elected Leopold I as King (1657—1705), Ferenc Wesselényi having become the new Palatine two years earlier.

György Rákóczi II did not pay sufficient attention to the changing of the international status of Transylvania. He became involved in an ill-considered political game. Rákóczi occupied the two Roumanian voivode-ships (a move which had been the ruin of Gábor Báthori). In 1657 he set out to procure the Polish crown, offered him by some magnates. The Swedes encouraged this venture but Rákóczi had not sought permission from his patron, the Sultan. The Ottoman Government sent the Tartars against Rákóczi. On Polish soil these troops took almost the whole of Rákóczi's army prisoner. Although Rákóczi himself fled back with a few supporters, the Sultan stripped him of his throne and forced Transylvania to elect a new Prince. Requesting help from the Habsburgs, Rákóczi tried to put up further armed resistance. Not only did Vienna fail to respond —despite pressure from even the Zrínyis—but even showed spiteful pleasure in watching the demise of Transylvania, the bastion of Hungarian independence. As early as 1658, Ottoman troops sacked Gyulafehérvár and devastated the surrounding countryside. On 22 May 1660, Rákóczi clashed with the Turks at Szászfenes, outside Kolozsvár. He lost this engagement and was himself mortally wounded. In August that year Várad, the Principality's most important frontier fortress, fell into Turkish hands. Having lost part of its territory and having been economically ruined, Transylvania lost its international prestige and ceased to be the defender of Hungarian national independence.

Perpetual Serfdom and Hereditary Aristocracy in the Period of the Turkish Occupation

The seventeenth century was the period of Hungarian independence struggles, although liberty did not flourish for everybody. At the time when the Hungarian magnates and nobles were defending their privileges and autonomy against Habsburg tyranny, and when the upper classes generally were making a tremendous and popular effort to halt Ottoman expansionism, the peasantry in Hungary was going through the gravest trials of its history. Not only were Hungarian town and village dwellers plundered by the Turks and Habsburg mercenaries, but were suffering even more as a result of their own landlords' exactions. By the seventeenth century the system of "perpetual serfdom" had emerged. Under this, the peasants, who were previously free to move and could render their services in either products or money, now became bound to their landlords and, through them to the land. In addition, they were forced to perform labour on the landlord's own farm, the so-called *major* (manor).

This was not a specifically Hungarian development, and not everybody approved of it. Firstly in Poland and later throughout the whole of Eastern Europe, this was how the landowners tried to procure grain for export. The demand for grain was increasing in Western Europe and landowners could use their earnings through this trade to buy Western luxuries. In Hungary, the situation was slightly more tolerable than in the neighbouring countries. Owing to transportation difficulties grain was not taken abroad and it was in land cultivation that labour service was most extensively utilized. Wine and beef-cattle were delicate products and needed high-quality work. Since the landowners did not hire wage-labourers, viniculture and cattle breeding were left to the comfortably-off peasants and to the citizens of the market-towns. This was how Debrecen, Tokaj and the other market-towns became prosperous. The inhabitants of these settlements did not have to render labour service, but paid their dues in money.

Even those suffering from feudal tyranny had a protector: the Reformation advocated not only liberty of conscience, but social justice as well. From the very beginning, Protestant preachers, who largely came from a peasant background, denounced the tyranny of the landlords. Indeed, the Hungarian Calvinist Puritans, János Tolnai Dali, Pál Medgyesi, János Apáczai Csere and György Martonfalvi Tóth were influenced by the English Revolution and condemned the entire serf system. Their opinion was summed up at the end of the seventeenth century by Pál Lisznyai Kovács of Debrecen. In his *Hungarian Chronicle*, Lisznyai writes as follows: "Certainly, that which the Hungarians have learned from the neighbouring Poles, namely that one nation should thus cripple other people of the same nation, that a Hungarian should do this to a Hungarian, that he should cripple a Christian member of that same Christian religion, is against God, is against the Scriptures and is against the law of every learned and Christian republic in this world. Indeed, to do this is sufficient for God to make you, too, the serf of another nation."

This warning was addressed to the Hungarian magnates and nobles, over whom loomed the very real threat of being made serfs of the Habsburgs. That dynasty was then preparing to reconquer the country from the Turks. The danger to the Hungarian upper classes existed in spite of the fact that they had conducted a hard fight, both at home and abroad for the retention of their privileges. Their struggle during this period had also served the defence of Hungarian national autonomy.

The Hungarian nobility was rather large, accounting for 4–5 per cent of the population of the country. (At this time some four million people lived in the territories of Royal Hungary and Transylvania.) The vast majority of nobles were, however, members of the lower nobility who farmed their own land, had only a few cottars and who were no better off than a free Heyduck or market-town citizen. Two thousand well-to–do and two hundred wealthy families owned the greater part of the land and possessed most of the political power. In Royal Hungary rich magnates owned latifundia to which there belonged hundreds of villages and thousands of serfs. Private armies were not unknown. In addition to a few pre-Mohács aristocratic families (the Báthorys, Zrínyis, Csákys, Bánffys, Thurzós, Erdődys, Homonnais, etc.) most nobles rose on the social ladder through service to the Habsburgs (for example, the Nádasdys, the Batthyánys, the Illésházys, the Pálffys, the Esterházys, the Rákóczis, etc.). From the nobles who served them, the Habsburgs created a closed order. While in the Middle Ages wealth and office raised certain magnates to the leading stratum, Ferdinand I created a "hereditary aristocracy". Certain families inherited by the children hereditary titles of baron, count and, in exceptional cases, prince. Members of this hereditary aristocracy came to comprise the upper house of the Diet and established their right to high positions in the State.

Since the royal court was constantly abroad, a significant national cultural centre could only emerge at the Gyulafehérvár court of the princes of Transylvania. In Royal Hungary this cultural function was performed in the castles of the magnates. Built in the Renaissance style, these castles housed not only the owner and his family, but also young noblemen and noblewomen who wished to learn court manners. Also present were soldiers for the defence of the castle as well as numerous domestic servants. Vast numbers of people from all over the country gathered in the castles to attend christenings, weddings and funerals and in this way the castles served to mould political and aesthetic views.

In short, Hungary under Ottoman rule was a country of extremes, where the "perpetual serf" and the "perpetual aristocrat" were separated by a whole world. Yet it was at around this time that danger from outside began to forge a nation out of those living in the country.

Culture in the "Century of Hungarian Decline"

From János Rimay to Miklós Zrínyi, every Hungarian poet—and even the majority of Hungarian politicians, philosophers and preachers—described the seventeenth century as the "Century of Hungarian Decline". The failure of military efforts to expel the Turks, the sharpening of religious conflicts and the fear of being completely crushed between the Habsburgs and the Turks did nothing to inspire confidence in the future. Also, the depression which affected the entire world economy in the form of inflation and marketing difficulties added to anxieties. Contemporaries were concerned about the fate of the country even more when they realized exactly how far Hungary lagged behind the developing states of Western Europe. They acknowledged the superiority of material and intellectual culture in Italy, Germany, Holland and England. However, their despair was overcome by the hope that Hungary's ills could be remedied. By concentrating resources, by learning and by work the decline could be halted and Hungarian culture raised to European standards.

The awakeners of Hungarian national consciousness re-discovered Gábor Bethlen's initiatives. During Bethlen's time, the overwhelming majority of educated Hungarians had worked as clergymen; doctors, engineers, artists and musicians had to be recruited abroad. Bethlen's objective had been to create a secular Hungarian intelligentsia. He hoped to do this in two ways. The first was by sending students to foreign universities where they would learn not only theology, but philosophy, law and architecture as well. The second was by founding a Hungarian college, printing press and library at Gyulafehérvár. Bethlen invited to his capital the German scholars of the age, including Professor Alsted. The latter was a many-sided intellectual who advocated the necessity of practical culture and compiled a Latin-language encyclopaedia to prove it.

Bethlen forebade landowners to prevent the sons of serfs from attending school. In this way knowledge became a means of rising socially. In 1629, Bethlen ennobled those clergymen of serf origin who had qualified for the Church through their erudition. The slogan "to fight with science and arms" in the letter-patent of nobility granted to the sons of these clergymen signified that the recipients would not become serfs if they chose to follow their fathers' profession—or even some secular career.

Gradually, Bethlen's guidance began to produce results—primarily in the development of school education. The first Hungarian college was founded in 1629 at Gyulafehérvár and was the predecessor of the famous Calvinist Bethlen College which eventually moved to Nagyenyed. The Gyulafehérvár college produced a host of outstanding scholars of the calibre of János Apáczai Csere who, following in the footsteps of his master, Alsted, published the *Magyar Encyclopaedia* (Hungarian Encyclopaedia)

—written in Hungarian instead of Latin. This was a synthesis based on contemporary scholarship and came out in Utrecht, Holland, in 1653. Hungarian Catholicism followed suit: in 1635 Péter Pázmány founded a university in Nagyszombat, the ancestor of Budapest's present-day university of arts and sciences. Pázmány's university had a faculty of philosophy and a faculty of law, in addition to one of theology. One of the greatest educators of all time, the Bohemian Jan Amos Comenius, became head of Sárospatak's Calvinist College at the invitation of Zsuzsanna Lórántffy, György Rákóczi's widow. During his four years at Sárospatak Comenius raised the standards of teaching to university standard. In addition, he also wrote numerous textbooks, among them *Orbis Sensualium Pictus* in which he described the world of perceptible things. The book was the first to bring visual presentation into teaching and brought the sciences onto a par with the humanities, which previously enjoyed a privileged status.

Apáczai was the first man in Hungary to spread the teachings of Copernicus and Descartes—the pioneers of modern natural science. He also advocated the ideas of Althusius, the founder of the modern theory of state and the scholar who worked out the principle of popular sovereignty. Althusius praised the English Revolution which had toppled feudalism, thereby paving the way to the spread of liberal ideas. As for the second half of Bethlen's maxim, which related to fighting with arms, a splendid example was to be found in Miklós Zrínyi who, incidentally, was also a poet.

The works of Apáczai and Zrínyi marked the zenith of mid-seventeenth-century Hungarian culture. Just one generation earlier, religious works such as Péter Pázmány's Guide Towards Divine Justice (1613) and Albert Szenczi Molnár's psalm translations (1607) had been the most influential Hungarian literary works. Apáczai's encyclopaedia and Zrínyi's epic poems were, however, secular in both subject and purpose. Through them the seed sown by Gábor Bethlen began to bear fruit.

While at the beginning of the century the struggle between the Reformation and the Counter-Reformation tied down the nation's forces, by the middle of the century a struggle was under way for the very survival of the Hungarian people. Culture also served this cause. Its representatives were imbued with the determination to hold their ground in spite of all difficulties and, with feelings of patriotism and self-sacrifice. The relatives of Apáczai's Dutch wife wanted to dissuade him from returning home from Holland but to no avail. Although in Hungary he was misunderstood and persecuted, Apáczai persevered, exerting himself so much that he died of overwork at the age of thirty-four. Zrínyi lashed out sarcastically at the Hungarian nobility, saying that if the nobles did not wish to do their duty and defend their country, they should emigrate to Brazil. However, Zrínyi only intended to castigate and to warn. "Our noble liberty is nowhere else than in Pannonia", wrote Zrínyi in 1661 in his famous pamphlet *A török áfium ellen való orvosság* (Remedy Against the Turkish Opium).

The Reunification of Hungary within the Habsburg Empire

"Arms, Arms are Desired and Heroic Determination"

The fall of Várad in 1660 sealed the fate of Transylvania. The fertile Bihar areas which the castle had protected now came under Ottoman occupation. The same applied to the areas stretching northwards to Debrecen. The Porte made Mihály Apafi Prince of a diminished and devastated Transylvania. After a few shining decades, Transylvania lost its political significance.

The situation was no better in Royal Hungary. The Habsburgs were still absorbed by their policies elsewhere in Europe and, accordingly, they steered clear of any actions which could provoke the Turks. Although the imperial army lined up for the defence of Vienna every time an Ottoman campaign was launched, it did not intervene in the siege of the Hungarian fortresses.

In the midst of all the vulnerability, devastation and hopelessness, Count Miklós Zrínyi, the greatest Hungarian statesman of the period, rose to eminence. His family was of Croatian origin and it was in the course of the constant struggle with the Turks that the first Zrínyis had moved from near the Adriatic to the Muraköz and Transdanubia, where they became Magyarized. Miklós Zrínyi himself had seen battle at a very early age and was not only a brave soldier but afterwards an excellent military commander too.

Zrínyi made the expulsion of the Turks from Hungary the aim of his life's work. He realized that the Ottoman Empire, once feared by everyone, was no longer its old self. "Certainly, if there were a strong and mailed fist, now would be the time to unbalance the Turks", he wrote. However, Zrínyi was also clearly aware that the Hungarians should conduct this struggle on their own. Hungary would lose her independence if the Habsburgs were to lead the war to expel the Turks.

To shake up an exhausted and apathetic nobility, in 1651 Zrínyi wrote his great epic poem *The Disaster of Sziget*. In this, he celebrates his great-grandfather's heroic death, which occurred in 1566. In a number of military treatises (for example, *A Military Essay; The Courageous Commandeer*), Zrínyi expounded his ideas on organizing an army and on strategy. Meanwhile he proved his bravery and talent as a military leader in endless frontier struggles.

Zrínyi was not yet thirty when he became Bán of Croatia. However, the setting up of a national army, and the organization of a military campaign required national, not local, authority. Accordingly, at the 1655 Diet, Zrínyi made a bid for the office of Palatine. In this he enjoyed the enthusiastic support of the nobility. However, the Habsburg King Ferdinand III did not appoint Zrínyi. It therefore became clear that Vienna did not support the plans he entertained.

Zrínyi was now convinced that the Habsburgs not only disapproved of the expulsion of the Turks, but were in fact obstructing it. In 1656, he wrote *Meditations on the Life of King Matthias,* in which he, the son of a family that had been loyal to the Habsburgs for generations, advocated the idea of a national kingdom. György Rákóczi II was his candidate Zrínyi favoured for the Hungarian throne but the fall of Transylvania meant that such a scheme was no longer realistic.

Zrínyi did not give up. He had a fortress (New Zrínyi Castle) built for the defence of the Muraköz and the southwestern parts of Transdanubia. He did this in defiance of the War Council in Vienna, which feared that the construction of the new castle would serve as an excuse for the Turks to launch a new attack into Habsburg territory. In 1661 Zrínyi wrote his most influential work, *Remedy Against the Turkish Opium.* The pamphlet was a desperate cry, a warning and a determined call to arms: "Behold, I am calling, behold, I am shouting, hear me, Hungarians! Here is the danger, here is the consuming fire... We, who are the descendants of glorious Hungarian race, must go to our death if need be for our wives, our children and our country."

In 1663, the Turks launched another major offensive. The Viennese Court was widely expected to appoint Zrínyi overall commander, but this did not happen. It was only after Érsekújvár, the key to the western part of Upper Hungary, had fallen that he was briefly appointed to this position. In hard-fought battles Zrínyi defended the great isle of Csallóköz and afterwards launched his famous winter campaign during which he advanced along the River Drava as far as Eszék. Here he burned the military bridge built by Sultan Mehmed IV, thereby cutting off Turkish supplies for months. Zrínyi wanted to use this time to recapture Kanizsa Castle, but the Viennese War Council, which wanted peace at all costs, prevented him from doing so.

In 1664, the Court appointed Count Raimondo Montecuccoli to Zrínyi's former command with instructions that the new general should only intervene if the Turkish advance actually threatened Vienna. Montecuccoli stood idly by therefore as Ottoman troops captured New Zrínyi Castle, which was unable to defend itself without help. When, however, the Grand Vizier turned his army in the direction of the Habsburg capital, Montecuccoli blocked his path at Szentgotthárd. In the battle which followed the Ottoman army was driven into the Rába-marshes and the remnants forced to flee. Montecuccoli's victory was complete.

However, the Habsburg commander did not pursue the defeated enemy and a few weeks later the Viennese Court concluded the Treaty of Vasvár with the Turks. It was as though the latter had been the victors in the battle. The treaty acknowledged Ottoman possession of many parts of Hungary, among them Várad, Érsekújvár and New Zrínyi Castle. Nationwide indignation and bitterness compelled Zrínyi to seek contact with Louis XIV of France, an enemy of Vienna. Later the same year, however, Zrínyi was dead. While out hunting, Zrínyi was killed by a wild boar, and this put an end to all his political plans.

In this way, the statesman, poet and military commander Miklós Zrínyi died. Contemporaries were reluctant to believe that he was the victim of a hunting accident and there were rumours that the Court in Vienna had probably hired assassins to murder him.

"Zrínyi's Blood Flooded Vienna..."

As we have seen, the Treaty of Vasvár in 1664 caused profound shock across the whole of Hungary. It became obvious that Vienna was willing to sacrifice Hungary's interests if, in doing so, it could stem the Ottoman advance and thereby win a free hand for its politics in Western Europe. Soldiers in the frontier fortresses were issued strict instructions not to respond to Turkish provocation and not to retaliate for the forays of the Ottoman garrisons. After the fall of Várad, Kanizsa and Érsekújvár, no part of the country could feel safe from the plundering Ottoman troops.

The country was utterly helpless and defenceless. During the reign of Mihály Apafi, the Principality of Transylvania was only a shadow of its own former self, and help could not be expected from that quarter. Neighbouring Poland was preoccupied with its own troubles; no help could be expected from that country either. In this desperate situation even the country's leading dignitaries turned against Vienna and discussed how the country could be saved from total destruction. These prominent figures included Baron Ferenc Wesselényi, Palatine of Hungary; György Lippay, the Archbishop of Esztergom; Count Ferenc Nádasdy, the Lord Chief Justice; Count Péter Zrínyi (Miklós's younger brother and Bán of Croatia), and Ferenc Rákóczi I, the elected Prince of Transylvania. All were Catholic aristocrats loyal to the king. (Ferenc Rákóczi I had been driven from his throne, in fact on account of his conversion to Catholicism and on account of his father's policy.) They were also the largest landowners of Transdanubia and Upper Hungary.

Consultations between these distinguished men were soon followed by conspiracy. The aristocratic plotters were planning an armed insurrection and expected external assistance primarily from the anti-Habsburg powers. They sent a representative to the court of Louis XIV, sought links with the Polish court and established contact even with the Ottoman Government, promising to pay an annual tax in exchange for the Sultan's support.

68

However, the conspirators had neither clear-cut ideas nor concrete plans for the organization of an uprising. Also lacking was a strategy for the more distant future. The plotters considered ambitious schemes to capture Emperor Leopold I, but at the same time did practically nothing to win over the lesser nobility or the peasantry.

After several years of hesitation—during which time Wesselényi and Lippay died—the conspirators decided in 1670 to organize an armed uprising. As leader of this insurrection, Rákóczi summoned the counties of Upper Hungary to arms. The call, though, was not very successful. It now became clear that this conspiracy of aristocrats had no backing either at home or abroad. Alarmed by this, Péter Zrínyi and his brother-in-law Ferenc Frangepán hurried to Vienna, where they revealed everything and asked for clemency. The Imperial army had no difficulty in suppressing the conspiracy. Nowhere was armed resistance encountered.

The Viennese Government believed that it had to make an example of the plotters and put the leaders of the conspiracy on trial. This was done in Vienna where they appeared before a jury made up of foreigners. On the basis of alien legislation, the conspirators were sentenced to death and their property confiscated. In 1671 Zrínyi and Frangepán were beheaded in Wiener Neustadt. Nádasdy was beheaded in Vienna and Mária Széchy, (the "Venus of Murány" and widow of the late Palatine), was stripped of her possessions and locked up in a convent. In case the lesser nobility should think that only the aristocrats would be punished, Ferenc Bónis, a lesser noble, was also beheaded. Ferenc Rákóczi's life was spared—but only in return for the huge ransom of 400,000 forints. In Rákóczi's case, allowances were also made for the merits of his mother, Zsófia Báthori. She was a devout Catholic who had always given extensive help to the Jesuits.

The aristocratic conspiracy provided a good pretext for Vienna to implement its old plan of finally putting an end to Hungary's autonomy. Employing the argument that the country had now forfeited all its rights, the Court suspended the Hungarian Constitution. In 1673, Caspar Ampringen, the Grand Master of the Teutonic Order was appointed Governor of Hungary. Hundreds of nobles were put on trial charged with conspiracy and, although most were eventually released owing to lack of evidence, their property was declared for feint. Some two-thirds of the native soldiers stationed in the Hungarian border fortresses were disbanded without pay and replaced by alien mercenaries.

The country became the "outpost of the Germans" and the reign of terror instituted by the foreign soldiery defies description. Unprecedented taxes were levied on the peasantry which, in addition, had to provide the soldiers keep. The open persecution of Protestants, deemed rebellious, also started. Armed force was used to take away their churches and schools. Calvinist and Lutheran town councils were driven out. In 1674, several hundred Protestant preachers were brought before a summary court, charged with underhand dealing with the Turks and with conspiracy against the Emperor. Those who refused to be converted to the Catholic faith, or to leave the country, were sentenced to death. The death sentences were not, however, carried out. Instead, forty-two of the preachers were driven on foot to the sea and sold as galley-slaves in Naples.

Brutal oppression and persecution forced huge numbers of people to flee. Nobles, former garrison soldiers, town burghers and peasants chose to go into hiding by their tens of thousands, escaping eastwards to the Transylvanian border. There they were safer from alien power.

"Onwards, Kuruc, Onwards!"

The origin of the word *kuruc* goes back to the crusades against the Turks, and derives from the Latin *cruciatus*. During Dózsa's peasant uprising, the name became associated with the anti-feudal peasant wars, and was used in that sense throughout the second half of the seventeenth century... In due course a new nickname was applied to the opponents of the *Kuruc*, the pro-Habsburg party. This name was *Labanc*, deriving perhaps from the German *Landsknecht*. The fugitives gathering along the Transylvanian frontier soon began to form a military organization. In this they were supported by Mihály Apafi, the Prince of Transylvania, who sent Mihály Teleki, the commander of Kővár to supervise them. They attacked the Imperial troops on several occasions, but did not accomplish very much.

The situation changed when the nineteen-year-old Count Imre Thököly became leader of these refugees. The scion of a big landowning aristocratic family from Upper Hungary, Thököly was fourteen when, in 1671 the Imperial forces besieged the castle of Árva. Their purpose was to capture Thököly's father, who had participated in the Wesselényi conspiracy. The elderly István Thököly died during the siege, but his son, Imre, managed to escape to Transylvania. From this time onwards, he was driven by the desire to avenge the injuries done to his family and to his nation. Thököly's passionate make-up was coupled with an outstanding military and diplomatic talent. He had a way with people and was a born commander.

In 1678, the Kuruc army went on the offensive and in a few months drove the Imperial troops (the *Labanc*) out of northeast Hungary. The population received the Kuruc army as liberators and joined up by the thousand. In addition to the nobles and former frontier castle soldiers, the mining towns also joined the uprising soon. In less than two years, the Kuruc troops occupied the whole of Upper Hungary.

Elected commander-in-chief of his army in Hajdúszoboszló at the beginning of 1680, Thököly possessed practically unlimited power. His authority rested on the Kuruc soldiers, among whom he tried to maintain strict discipline. He did not always succeed in this and from the beginning there were many complaints against abuses committed by the troops. Marriage with Ilona Zrínyi, the widow of Ferenc Rákóczi, meant for Thököly a significant increase in strength. Through this marriage, Thököly was able to make the Rákóczi estates serve the uprising. Thököly maintained good relations with the Ottomans and, at the zenith of his success in 1682, he was appointed King of Hungary by the Sultan. Thököly, however, rejected kingly status, taking only the title Prince of Upper Hungary. Thököly was, in any event, more inclined to value links with France than links with the Turks. King Louis XIV of France, who opposed the Habsburgs gladly supported an uprising behind his enemy's back.

The Viennese Government was finally forced to retreat. In 1681 the Diet in Sopron restored the country's constitution (Count Pál Esterházy was elected Palatine) and the freedom of Protestant religion was permitted within certain limits. Vienna sought peace with Thököly as well, promising a complete change in its policy towards Hungary.

However, Thököly and his followers did not trust the Habsburgs, doubting—not without reason—the sincerity of their promises. In any case, they did not consider Vienna's concessions to be satisfactory. Thököly thought that only the creation of an independent national state could resolve the problem and therefore continued the struggle.

Since he was too weak to do this by himself, and as he could not count on the French, who had come to terms with the Emperor, he established increasingly close links with the Ottoman Empire. Thököly overestimated Turkish strength, as did almost everyone in contemporary Europe.

In 1683, Grand Vizier Kara Mustapha marched against Vienna at the head of a huge army. Thököly thought that, in the event of an Ottoman victory, which he felt was certain, he would receive all the territory of the Kingdom of Hungary. Thököly would then organize a vassal, albeit national, state along the Transylvanian model. However, Vienna was succesfully defended by the Polish King John Sobieski, in company with the armies of the German Empire. The attacking forces fled and what seemed likely to be an almost certain Ottoman victory turned out to be a decisive defeat. Recognizing the growing weakness of the Ottoman Empire, Vienna now changed its policy. Emperor Leopold I decided to expel the Turks from Hungary.

Pope Innocent XI established the Holy League directed against the Turks. This was the alliance of the Habsburg Empire, Poland and Venice. In 1684 international armies launched their campaign in Hungary and swept away Thököly's power, which rested on Ottoman support. Ahmed, the *pasha* (general) of Várad, hoped that he could buy peace by handing Thököly over to the Habsburgs and managed to capture him. However, Thököly soon regained his freedom, but his supporters and principality in Upper Hungary were gone for good. Now aware that the Ottomans were unreliable allies, the Kuruc forces went over to the Imperial armies. The Kuruc troops realized that they had a good chance against the Turks and offered their services in the liberation of their homeland. The Court denied

Thököly the opportunity to take part in this great venture and, with only a few hundred followers, Thököly therefore remained in the Ottoman camp. Thököly was eventually compelled to leave Hungary along with the Ottoman troops. By 1685, Kuruc power was confined to the castle of Munkács, which Ilona Zrínyi defended against the Imperial troops for three years.

After two months of bloody siege, Buda Castle was also liberated from the Turks in September 1686. Two years later, the Christian army occupied Belgrade. On the death of Mihály Apafi in 1690, Thököly advanced into Transylvania with an Ottoman and Tartar army and, following a victory at Zernyest, had himself elected Prince. A few weeks later, however, Imperial troops forced him to leave the country forever.

After a few more years of fighting, in 1697 Prince Eugene of Savoy won a splendid victory at Zenta. This sealed the fate of Turkish rule in Hungary. In 1699, the Treaty of Karlowitz was signed. After one hundred and fifty years of subjugation, Hungary, with the exception of the Temesköz area, was finally freed from Ottoman dominion.

"I would Like that our Nation did not Remain in Ignorance"

From the mid-seventeenth century onwards, Baroque culture became predominant in Hungary. Establishing close contact everywhere with the Counter-Reformation, this cultural and artistic trend was propagated primarily by the Jesuits. In Hungary, Baroque culture became inseparable from the strengthening of ecclesiastical and secular authority, along with re-inforcement of an unchanging feudal society. At the same time, the lack of a Hungarian royal court could be felt throughout the period. This would have encouraged cultural aspirations and would have steered them in a uniform direction. Individual aristocratic families had courts of their own (that of the Nádasdys at Sárvár, for example, or that of the Batthyánys at Németújvár) but the influence of these was confined to a certain part of the country. What is more, these separate centres divided national culture rather than unified it.

The new ideals, which originated in the Renaissance, first received expression in architecture. Everywhere, Catholic churches were now built in the Baroque style. The palaces of the aristocracy soon bore marks of the new fashion. Of these the Esterházys' home at Kismarton (Eisenstadt) was to be the largest and most splendid. Simplicity was replaced everywhere by rich ornamentation, which often seemed both ostentatious and extravagant. Interior walls were adorned with frescoes (in the castle of Sárvár murals depicting the struggles between Turks and Hungarians can still be seen today). Ornamental objects of silver and gold were placed on furniture of strong colour and at the large windows were hung Venetian brocade curtains. The late-Renaissance style lingered on in Transylvania, its best example being Miklós Bethlen's palace at Bethlenszentmiklós.

The first significant art collections also came into existence at this time. The silver, gold and jewel collection of Ferenc Nádasdy, the Lord Chief Justice beheaded in 1671, was important even by Central European standards. As for Nádasdy's library, it was so comprehensive that the Imperial library in Vienna took from it 459 volumes which where missing from its own collection. It was during this period that the foundations of the famous Esterházy collection of paintings (on which the collection of the Museum of Fine Arts in Budapest was later based) were laid. Rare flowers and ornamental trees were brought from distant lands to the garden of the palace. A whole book was devoted to describing the garden of György Lippay, the Archbishop of Esztergom.

In the palaces of the aristocracy, a merry social life was to be found. Feasts, hunting parties and family celebrations followed each other in close succession. Court orchestras would provide music. Plays, and even operas, were performed. Prince Pál Esterházy himself composed ecclesiastically inspired pieces of music.

The Catholic Church and the Society of Jesus supervised cultural life in the palaces of the aristocracy. However, Church influence extended far beyond this. The Jesuits and Church generally controlled school education and the education of young nobles. Also under their sway were the university at Nagyszombat, which had been founded by Péter Pázmány, the college at Kassa (after 1674) and the colleges of Graz and Vienna, where quite a few young Hungarians studied. Culture, although ecclesiastically regulated, was, however, closely bound to the old, national traditions.

Literature was also inspired by the nobility and the Church. The poets of the age were, almost without exception, the servants and supporters of an aristocrat. Their task was to celebrate the important events in their masters' lives or to popularize their political principles. The most well-known of these was István Gyöngyösi, who achieved fame for his narrative poem about Palatine Ferenc Wesselényi's courtship of, and subsequent marriage with, Mária Széchy, the "Venus of Murány". Most Catholic literature in the Hungarian language was religious. Alongside it flourished polemical literature and preaching.

The fine arts had little chance to develop amid the conditions of war. The goldsmith's craft was the only branch which produced significant works during this period. Painting began to catch up towards the end of the century. Its finest representative was János Kupeczky, who was born near Pozsony and Ádám Mányoki, who was then just embarking upon his career.

Linking up with Protestantism, intellectual movements of a bourgeois character emerged primarily in Transylvania and Eastern Hungary. The big Calvinist colleges were hotbeds of the new ideas, above all, at Sárospatak, Debrecen and Gyulafehérvár, the latter having been moved to Nagyenyed after the Tartar devastation of 1658. Thousands of Protestant students visited the universities of the Netherlands, Germany and England, where they learned of middle-class aspirations and rational thinking. It was at this time that Puritan ideas demanding a more democratic internal life spread within the Calvinist Church. At the same time, in the wake of Cartesianism, the teachings of Descartes, interest in the secular sciences grew substantially. In 1653, János Apáczai Csere wrote the first Hungarian-language encyclopedia, with a view to leading the Hungarian nation out of ignorance. Apáczai wanted to modernize education in schools and to democratize public life. However, his plans were frustrated by the stubborn resistance of the nobility, which regarded every change as a threat to its privileges. The struggle with the nobility, the ruling class, at this time, greatly embittered Miklós Tótfalusi Kis, the famous printer of the age, and one who had earned European renown. Despite the fact that Western middle-class aspirations could not strike root in Hungary, knowledge of the latest scholarship (including the investigation of the natural sciences) did nevertheless penetrate the country. Under the surface, new ideas slowly began to shape public opinion. Even the modern medical science of the day found its way to Hungary through the works of Ferenc Pápai-Páriz.

After 1670, the Counter-Reformation brutally paralyzed Protestant schools. The College at Sárospatak was closed and its teachers and students had to go into hiding for years. From 1690 onwards, Transylvania also came under Habsburg domination and, accordingly, the possibility of any freedom in Hungarian cultural policy was lost. It was only during the Rákóczi War of Independence that a separate line could exist.

"Our Countrymen are Ready, they only Need a Leader"

After 150 years of Ottoman domination, Hungary's territorial unity was restored. However, the country had to pay a high price for the expulsion of the enemy. The Turkish yoke was removed only to be replaced by Habsburg oppression.

Emperor Leopold decided that the time had come to destroy Hungary's independence and to make the country one of his family's hereditary provinces. Only a year after the recapture of Buda, the Diet was forced to make political concessions. In 1687, it relinquished its right to elect the country's king and rescinded the clause in the *Golden Bull* which permitted the nobility to rebel against any monarch who infringed the nation's rights. Habsburg rule in Hungary became hereditary and the nobles were no longer legally entitled to take action against a king who violated the laws.

74

The long decades of fighting cost a great deal of money, most of which was exacted from the Hungarian peasantry. At the same time, the country, the scene of devastation for a century and a half already, was almost entirely laid waste again. The 60,000–80,000 strong Imperial army, together with all its horses, had to be fed and in this both officers and men regarded local resources as theirs for the taking. The entire population of certain areas fled the forests and marshes and the once prosperous town of Debrecen became impoverished as a result of continual looting. In order to quell nationwide discontent and to acquire more money, General Caraffa, with the approval of his superiors, court-marshalled numerous nobles and burghers at Eperjes. After a summaring trial on trumped-up charges, they were sentenced to death and their property confiscated.

The Habsburgs regarded Hungary as a conquered province. Imperial generals and military contractors received estates the size of counties, while the Hungarian nobility could only get back its landed property after presentation of documents proving ownership and after payment of a certain fee. This sum was for "redemption of arms" a reference to the coat of arms of a noble family, and was laid down by the *Neoacquistica Commissio* (New Acquisitions Commission). All of these measures were designed to strengthen Leopold I's absolutist rule as it was felt that "Hungarian blood, which was inclined to revolution and restlessness" could only be tamed by oppression. The province Jászkunság was mortgaged to the Teutonic Order and the free peasants of the area thereby reduced to serfdom. At the same time, those Serbs who had moved to Hungary in 1689 under the leadership of Arsenije Černojević, the Patriach of Ipek, were granted extensive autonomy. It was at this time that their most important town, Szentendre, north of Buda, began to develop, and during the eighteenth century this became the centre of Serbian culture in Hungary. The Court in Vienna started to settle the depopulated regions of the Great Plain and Transdanubia with Catholic Germans or Swabians, as they came to be known in Hungary. While the Greek Orthodox Serbs acquired complete freedom of religion, the Protestant Hungarian villages were denied it. Another round of enforced conversion began. The country was virtually overrun by various monastic orders—indeed, contemporary folk songs spoke of a "reign of priests".

Devastated and oppressed, Hungary was unable to offer much resistance. Although here and there the peasantry rose up against the foreign mercenaries, their attempts to change matters were easily crushed. In 1697, desperate serfs and border fortress soldiers who had been left without anything to eat launched a surprise attack in the east of the country. They managed to occupy Sárospatak and the castle of Tokaj but, without assistance, were bound to be defeated by the Imperial troops. At this point the people's only hope lay with the young prince, Ferenc II Rákóczi.

Ferenc II Rákóczi was descended from Transylvanian princes. He was the son of Ferenc I Rákóczi, who died after the Wesselényi conspiracy in

1676, and Ilona Zrínyi, the daughter of Péter Zrínyi, the executed Bán of Croatia. At the age of twelve Rákóczi was separated from his mother when she finally surrendered the castle of Munkács to the Imperial troops (1688). In an attempt to make him loyal to the Habsburgs, the Court in Vienna sent the young Rákóczi to Bohemia, where he was educated by the Jesuits. Later, he studied at Prague University, and completed his education in Italy. In Vienna, Rákóczi led the frivolous life of a young aristocrat and in 1694 he got married. Rákóczi chose his bride from the German Hessen-Rheinfels family, which enjoyed princely rank. Through his wife, Rákóczi became related to the King of France. Then the couple moved to his Hungarian estates. The young nobleman dressed in German clothes, had Imperial officers as his friends and was absolutely loyal to the Habsburgs. When rebelling peasants wanted to win him to their cause in 1697, Rákóczi fled from them to Vienna.

However, having become more familiar with Hungary's situation, Rákóczi's enthusiasm for the *status quo* began to wane. His friendship with Miklós Bercsényi, another young aristocrat, was influential in this. So, too, was the realization that everyone was expecting him, the country's greatest landowner and greatest aristocrat, to defend the country. Together with several high-ranking nobles, he organized a conspiracy against the Habsburgs and turned to King Louis XIV of France with an appeal for help. His letter to the French King was intercepted by the Habsburgs and, during the spring of 1701, Rákóczi was captured in his castle at Nagysáros. He was taken to Wiener Neustadt and locked up in the same prison where his grandfather had earlier been executed. Rákóczi's fate was to have been the same, but he managed to escape to Poland. From there, he tried to win support for his cause from France and the other anti-Habsburg powers. Rákóczi's appeal for help was rejected everywhere, none of the countries he turned to would trust in the lonely fugitive.

Rákóczi was staying in the castle of Brezani, on one of the remote estates of a Polish friend, when a peasant delegation from the Tiszahát finally reached him at the beginning of 1703. Headed by Tamás Esze, the peasants informed Rákóczi that "our countrymen are ready, they only need a leader". The young Prince, who had sided with the peasantry in 1697 and who up to then had not even thought of leading an army of serfs against Vienna, heeded Esze's call. Having become convinced that the delegation had reported truthfully, in May 1703 Rákóczi sent into Hungary a banner inscribed *Cum Deo pro patria et libertate* (With God for country and liberty). At the same time he issued a proclamation calling "every noble and non-noble true Hungarian" to arms. In June 1703, Rákóczi himself set out to take command of his armies and start the War of Independence.

"With God for Country and Liberty"

When in June 1703 Ferenc Rákóczi arrived in of the northeastern Carpathians, the frontier district between Poland and Hungary, only a few hundred embittered peasants led by Tamás Esze were waiting for him. As this force proceeded down from the mountains, its numbers swelled daily. After a few weeks, an army several thousand strong had come into being. The nobility, always fearful of the peasantry, took refuge in their castles and resisted the insurgents. It took some time before they saw that Rákóczi himself was committed to the revolt, and the uprising was more than a manifestation of lower-class discontent. In the autumn of 1707, the nobility joined the insurrection and the towns soon followed suit. Tamás Esze's peasant delegation of four years earlier had sparked off a national crusade. By the end of the year, Rákóczi's forces occupied Upper Hungary and the central regions of the Great Plain. In addition, they had advanced not only into Transdanubia but Transylvania, too.

The War of Independence began at a time when the international situation was favourable for it. In 1701 the War of the Spanish Succession had broken out—splitting Western Europe into two camps. Both the French Bourbons and the Austrian Habsburgs made a bid for the rich legacy represented by Spain and her overseas possessions. The maritime powers, England and the Netherlands, supported Leopold of Habsburg, while the Elector of Bavaria and Prince Eugene of Savoy backed Louis XIV of France. Hungary was therefore a natural ally as far as the French were concerned,—indeed Rákóczi's main hope of victory rested on military co-operation with France. After the initial successes of the War of Independence Louis XIV sought contact with Rákóczi, and even gave him money. This was enough only to pay some 5,000 of the 70,000 soldiers who were fighting for Rákóczi at the time. To this extent, French financial assistance was symbolic rather than substantial.

The early years of the war in Western Europe brought successes for France. In spring 1703, the French army was advancing along the Danube towards Vienna while the Kuruc army was heading towards the city from the east. The Imperial Court went through very difficult weeks; had the two armies linked up and captured Vienna, the Habsburg Empire could well have disintegrated.

However, the great hopes of the Hungarians were not to be fulfilled. By the beginning of 1704, the Kuruc forces had reached Austrian border but Maximilian Emanuel, the Elector of Bavaria and commander of the French army, did not move directly against Vienna. Instead, he advanced into the Tyrol, becoming involved there in guerilla warfare. By the time he was again ready to march on Vienna, the English and Dutch armies had already organized themselves. At the Battle of Blenheim Eugene of Savoy and the Duke of Marlborough halted the French advance and knocked Bavaria out of the war. After this, the French were compelled to fall back and plans to link up the French and Hungarian armies therefore came to nothing: Vienna had been saved.

Rákóczi now suggested to Louis XIV that they establish contact on the Adriatic and in Croatia. This scheme was unsuccessful too and Rákóczi came to appreciate that he could no longer really count on French support. Finding himself in a difficult situation, the French King was not willing to commit himself to the Hungarians. Louis therefore did not conclude an alliance with Rákóczi—for all the latter's apparent confidence. Since 1704 Rákóczi had borne the title Prince Elect of Transylvania and, after the Diet of Szécsény in 1705, that of Prince of Hungary.

Rákóczi clearly saw that if the Hungarian cause could not be made a European cause, the War of Independence would become isolated and would stand little chance of achieving its objectives. He was anxious to keep international public opinion informed about the cause and purpose of the struggle and, to counter the hostile propaganda put out by Vienna, he issued a Latin-language paper entitled *Mercurius Veridicus* (Truthful Mercury). In attempts to drum up support, his envoys called on the King of Sweden, visited the kings of Prussia and Denmark and negotiated with the Polish Diet and the Pope in Rome. Rákóczi received words of encouragement from these visits but no material assistance was offered. Foreign governments were generally not prepared to antagonize the Habsburgs on Hungary's account. Rákóczi attempted to win the Turks to his cause— again to no avail. Only Tsar Peter the Great of Russia was willing to commit himself to the Hungarians. Rákóczi concluded a secret alliance with Peter but was unable to derive any military advantage from it. Eventually it became clear that, in her fight for freedom, Hungary could expect no outside help.

In military terms, the Habsburg Empire was by far the stronger of the two sides. Rákóczi made tremendous efforts to organize his brave soldiers, who were unaccustomed to the conventional warfare of the day, into a well-equipped and disciplined professional army. However, the young Kuruc troops were incapable of matching the competence of their opponents. The Kuruc troops lost every set-piece battle against the Imperial forces. They suffered defeat at Nagyszombat at the end of 1704 and at Zsibó in 1705. This was in spite of the fact that in these engagements they outnumbered the enemy. These developments induced Rákóczi to open peace negotiations with Vienna, first in Gyöngyös and than in Nagyszombat. The mediators in these talks were English and Dutch who, as the Emperor's allies, were well aware that the 40,000 Habsburg soldiers fighting in Hungary were very much needed in the Western theatre of war. An end to the fighting in Hungary would mean that these troops could be deployed elsewhere and the country itself made to contribute taxes and arms to the struggle against the French. In addition, the English and Dutch sympathized with the Hungarians, a nation which was also opposed to the

Catholic Counter-Reformation. Negotiations dragged on for months but produced no results. The Kuruc rebels would have been prepared to accept Habsburg hegemony, provided that Hungary's constitutional rights were recognized and guaranteed. They also demanded religious toleration within the country, insisting that this be similarly protected. Vienna, however, refused to accept foreign states as guarantors of the independence of Transylvania, on which Rákóczi had insisted. Although Hungary had become isolated in her fight for freedom, she was, through Rákóczi's efforts, sufficiently strong to reject peace terms which were unfavourable. In 1707 the Diet of Ónod broke internal opposition and dethroned the House of Habsburg. The struggle continued.

"It is my Intention to Bring about my Country's Full Happiness"

Rákóczi fully realized that Hungary was backward in virtually every respect. In his memoirs, he laid the blame for this on the Habsburgs. Nevertheless, even while conducting the war for national independence, Rákóczi attempted to strengthen the state and society by introducing modern reforms.

In his youth Rákóczi had studied the latest French and Italian works on state theory and during his imprisonment at Wiener Neustadt he had also read extensively. From the very beginning Rákóczi strove to establish national absolutism, attempting to weaken the political power of the aristocracy and to improve the lot of the downtrodden. His programme included a promise of freedom for those serfs who joined his army and, while the Habsburgs tried to divide the country, Rákóczi struggled to forge national unity. In order to eliminate religious conflict within the country, he returned the Protestants' churches and schools and ensured equal status for religious denominations. Non-Magyar minority groups which sided with the War of Independence were granted with the Magyar population.

Initially, all of Rákóczi's close associates were drawn from the ranks of the lesser nobility. The nearest to him throughout the struggle was Pál Ráday—also a member of that class. Ráday was first of all Rákóczi's private secretary and later the head of the Prince's chancellery (and director of foreign affairs). The leader of Rákóczi's Court, Ádám Vay, was also a lesser noble, as was Pál Lányi, the Government commissioner responsible for armaments. While in the army, power was exercised by generals from aristocratic families, Rákóczi kept the military leadership out of politics.

The aristocracy, led by Bercsényi took offense at its exclusion from decision-making. The Diet of Szécsény in 1705 witnessed the magnates' first open move to curtail Rákóczi's power. A four-member committee was

79

organized to handle Government business and the Economic Council entrusted with additional tasks. The aristocracy was represented on these bodies but nevertheless Rákóczi retained the power to make the final decisions. The latter served as a pretext for those nobles who opposed him to complain about his total disregard for their privileges. In this they received encouragement from Vienna and infringement of the nobility's rights was the opposition's main grievance at the Diet of Ónod in 1707.

The War of Independence caused serious financial difficulty in the country. Revenues from the Rákóczi estates were by no means adequate to cover expenditure and the collection of taxes was not easy in an impoverished country already under arms. Up until now the nobles had been exempt from taxation but now Rákóczi introduced a law under which this privilege was abolished. The move constituted a violation of the nobility's outmoded rights.

As Hungary's supplies of silver and gold currency were insufficient, at the beginning of 1704 Rákóczi introduced copper coinage. Industry, however, was primitive and backward (even firearms had to be purchased from abroad), and owing to the war, commerce was also paralyzed. The state was therefore unable to protect the value of the new currency. As a result, traders refused to accept copper coins and the soldiers, who were paid in this money found themselves in a constantly worsening situation.

The impact of social antagonisms also affected the army. The landowners tried to keep their serfs out of the fighting. They also attempted to force those who had enlisted to return to the land, placing extra burdens on the families of those under arms. The fighting of the peasant troops suffered accordingly and growing numbers left the army. In December 1708, the Diet of Sárospatak issued a decree which proclaimed the emancipation of serfs fighting in the War of Independence and Rákóczi himself conferred special privileges on several serf villages. These moves, however, were now incapable of reviving morale among the peasants.

In 1708, the Kuruc army lost the decisive battle of Trencsén. The long war had exhausted the country, and economic problems were now compounded by the outbreak of a plague epidemic. Having won the war in the West, the Emperor was now able to send more and more troops to Hungary. Accordingly, the Kuruc forces were gradually compelled to retreat to the northeastern part of the country.

Rákóczi, however, believed that all was not yet lost. He hoped that, through private negotiations, he could persuade Tsar Peter the Great of Russia to provide him with military assitance. At the end of 1710, Rákóczi set out for Russia, making Baron Sándor Károlyi, supreme army commander during his absence. With Rákóczi's approval, Károlyi entered into negotiations with Count János Pálffy, who had been appointed commander of the Imperial armies by Joseph I (1705–11). Rákóczi had intended these talks to be a means of gaining time but Károlyi, who realized that the military situation was now hopeless, signed the Treaty of Szatmár with the

Habsburgs on 29 April 1711. Under its terms, the Kuruc soldiers once again became loyal subjects of the Emperor, who made a number of concessions. An amnesty was promised and Vienna pledged to uphold not only Hungary's feudal constitution but also freedom of religion within the country. On 1 May 1711 the Kuruc forces laid down their arms.

Rákóczi refused to recognize the Treaty of Szatmár, which did not guarantee Hungary's independence and which swept away the social achievements of the war. He went into voluntary exile, first to Poland and later to the French Court at Versailles. From there Rákóczi eventually moved to Turkey—in the hope that the liberation struggle could be restarted from that country. He died in Rodosto in 1735. The diary written in letter form, by his page, Kelemen Mikes, gives a moving account of Rákóczi's last years and the life of those in exile with him.

Settlement and Reorganization in the Eighteenth Century

Joseph I died while negotiations for the Treaty of Szatmár were still under way and was succeded as emperor by Charles VI, his younger brother. The new ruler was the last male member of the family and became King of Hungary as Charles III (1711–1740). Originally, Charles had been heir to the Spanish throne but the prospect of Spain and Austria united under one ruler caused alarm among other European states. In order to preserve the European balance of power against the threat of Austrian hegemony, England and the Netherlands both withdrew from the fighting. The Treaty of Utrecht (1713) confined the Habsburgs to their Danubian provinces. The settlement of Hungary's internal affairs was now vital if Austria was to retain her status as a major power.

After Rákóczi's War of Independence, Vienna dared not continue Leopold's policy of forced assimilation. In theory, Hungary retained her autonomy within the Empire but in practice the supreme organs of the state operated from the Austrian capital and their independence was only illusory. Major issues were decided by the State Council or the Secret Conference, neither of which had Hungarian members. Public administration was entrusted to the newly-organized Council of the Governor-General in Buda, with the Palatine and Governor-General at its head. Since Charles III had no male heir, in 1722 the Diet was forced to accept a law known as the Pragmatic Sanction. By doing so, it recognized the right of succession through the female line of the House of Habsburg. Also accepted was the "indivisible and inseparable" unity of the countries united under Habsburg rule. However, the Pragmatic Sanction at the same time also confirmed Hungary's constitutional autonomy.

81

The 150 years of Turkish occupation and the fighting which took place during this time claimed a heavy toll in human lives. Hungary's population had been 4 millions when Matthias was king, but the figure was now down to 3 1/2 millions. In the meantime, the number of Europe's inhabitants had increased from 80 millions to 130 millions. The devastation primarily affected the Magyar inhabitants of the Great Plain and the river valleys. Some southern regions of the Plain, which had previously been densely populated, were now empty wastes.

The population which had earlier fled to Upper Hungary from the Turks began to return at the end of the seventeenth century. Nonetheless, those areas which had become deserted were re-settled by the Habsburgs. Vienna recruited Catholics in Germany and brought them into the country. This policy to some extent served political purposes, designed as it was to reduce the concentration of Hungarians. The German settlers were provided with newly-built and fully equipped villages and were exempted from tax for years, especially on the Crown estates in the Temes region. In the course of the eighteenth century, the number of Germans from the province of Bánság (known as Swabians) topped the one million mark. It was at this time that the German villages of the regions of Bakony and Vértes emerged, along with those near Buda. These years also witnessed the creation of German blocs in Tolna, Baranya and Bácska counties.

In addition, large-scale spontaneous immigration also took place. The Southern Slavs, under pressure from the Turks, began to move northwards. It was at this time that the Croatian villages of Transdanubia and some of the Serbian settlements of the South came into existence. At the end of the seventeenth century, 40,000 Serbian families fled to Hungary from the Ottomans and were granted extensive privileges by Leopold I. While Leopold had reduced the free Hungarian peasants of Jászkunság to serfdom and did everything to prevent the practice of Protestantism in the Hungarian villages, he granted full freedom of worship and extensive autonomy to the Greek Orthodox Serbs. Roumanian shepherds from Wallachia also came to Hungary in large numbers—fleeing to Transylvania from the tyranny of Turkish-appointed local rulers. Slovak settlers moved from Upper Hungary to the vicinity of Pest and to Békés county.

By the end of the eighteenth century Hungary's population had risen to eight millions. At the same time, however, the Magyars became a minority. In the Middle Ages, they had made up 80–85 per cent of the inhabitants but this figure had now fallen to 40 per cent. A multi-national Hungary had therefore emerged and this development was not unimportant in shaping the country's subsequent history.

The Hungarian aristocracy had previously headed the national movements and now Vienna did everything possible to tie it to the Habsburgs. Aristocratic families moved in growing numbers to Vienna, the centre of the Habsburg Empire, and intermarried with their Bohemian and Austrian counterparts. They seldom visited their estates in Hungary and their contact with the Hungarian people became almost non-existent. The Court was also successful in its efforts to recruit the leading Catholic clergy from those aristocratic families loyal to the dynasty. The Counter-Reformation had brought a new status to the Church, making it attractive to career-minded nobles. Increasingly, the country's upper classes backed the Court's policy.

The fact that the Rákóczi estates were given exclusively to Austrian and Bohemian families also contributed to the weakening of internal resistance. The Diet obediently naturalized these. In Southern Hungary, a large military frontier zone was established and placed directly under the control of the War Council in Vienna. The now defunct Principality of Transylvania remained separated from Hungary. Instead, it was governed as a grand duchy and subordinated to Vienna.

Increased taxation and the necessity of reconstruction work increased burdens on the serfs. The oppression they suffered was almost unrestricted. In 1735, peasants from Békés county joined forces with disappointed Serbian peasants in the Military Frontier zone and staged an uprising in Rákóczi's name. (This is known to history as the Pero uprising after the Serbian captain who led it.) The insurrection was, however, suppressed and the organizers ruthlessly punished.

The fact that Hungary was unaffected by war for three generations meant that the country could be rebuilt. The population doubled and agricultural production started again on the Great Plain. The Baroque townscapes, which can still be seen today, also came into being at this time.

"Our Life and our Blood"

On 20 October 1740, King Charles III died and the male line of the Habsburg dynasty became extinct. Charles III was succeeded by his daughter, Maria Theresa. However, the new ruler's right to the throne was challenged by those powers wishing to expand at the expense of the Habsburgs. Having concluded an alliance with the Elector of Bavaria, Frederick II of Prussia attacked the Habsburg Empire from the north and west. At the same time, the Spaniards and Venetians launched an offensive from the south. In 1741, the enemy was already on Austrian territory and had occupied Prague. It seemed that Habsburg power might well be at an end. In this difficult situation Maria Theresa—who had been crowned "king" of Hungary at Pozsony in June 1741—turned to the Hungarians. On 11 September, the nobility, who had gathered to attend the Diet, offered their "life and blood" for their King, Maria Theresa *(Vitam et sanguinem pro rege nostro Maria Theresia)*. The appearance of Hungarian regiments marked a turning-point in the War of the Austrian Succession. The enemy was driven from Austrian territory and in the treaty in 1742, which ended hostilities, the Habsburgs lost only a part of Silesia. This came under Prussian rule.

In 1757, Maria Theresa made an attempt to recover the territories she was forced to give up fifteen years earlier. In the conflict which resulted, (the Seven Years War) Hungarian troops again fought alongside those of Habsburgs and General András Hadik's hussars even hold Berlin to ransom. The fighting did not achieve its purpose and Silesia remained under Prussian rule. At the first Partition of Poland, however, Maria Theresa obtained Galicia, together with the town of Cracow. Later the Bukovina, which had been under Ottoman Control, was also added to her dominions.

Historians have often wondered why the Hungarian nobility, which only a generation earlier had fought for national independence under Rákóczi, now sided with Maria Theresa. The answer lies in the fact that the world had changed considerably since 1711, the year the Treaty of Szatmár was signed. The Court no longer wished to curtail privileges of the nobility and was prepared to grant to the Hungarian ruling class—almost unlimited exercise of its ancient privileges. This state of affairs suited the Hungarian nobility, which in return was willing to lend its support to the dynasty. Indicative of how satisfied the nobility was during this period is the saying of the time: "Outside Hungary there is no life" *(Extra Hungariam non est vita)*.

Maria Theresa, whose highest rank was "King of Hungary" (her husband, Francis of Lotharingia bore the title "Emperor"), was one of the greatest members of the Habsburg dynasty. Maria Theresa implemented her policies with refined caution and feminine tact. To comtemporaries it seemed that it was guided by benevolence towards, and indeed sympathy for, the country. She re-annexed the thirteen Szepes towns that had been pawned to Poland, together with the port of Fiume and the Banat of Temes, which had been under military administration. In Vienna she organized a corps of Hungarian guards comprising members of the Hungarian nobility and she also founded a Hungarian decoration (the order of St Stephen). Several Hungarians were awarded the Maria Theresa Military Medal. All of this demonstrated that Maria Theresa had broken with the anti-Hungarian policy of her predecessors.

Maria Theresa's aim was to establish a united Danubian empire. Since Hungary constituted the largest territorial unit among her dominions and since almost half of her subjects lived within this, it was of paramount importance that the country be developed and strengthened. This was done not out of love for Hungarians but out of recognition of the Habsburg Empire's interest.

Maria Theresa's measures were already affected by the spirit of the Enlightenment. The aim of these was to bolster the power of the monarchy and the state. Prince Kaunitz, Maria Theresa's Chancellor and chief adviser played an important role in this process. The curtailment of ecclesiastical and aristocratic power, the protection of the serfs, the carrying out of social welfare duties, the encouragement of education and the raising of the cultural level—all served to reinforce central authority. So, too, did those economic measures, often criticized later, which strengthened Austrian and Bohemian industry by means of tariffs while allocating to Hungary the role of agricultural commodities and raw materials supplier.

Naturally, the ruling class was very jealous of its privileges; when Maria Theresa wanted to tax the nobility, the Diet turned against her. After this, Maria Theresa resorted to government by decree. In 1769 she issued a patent regulating the dues and labour requirements for the serfs. It was only in one area that the Enlightenment failed to influence Maria Theresa's policies, and this was religion. Throughout her forty-year reign, non-Catholics remained second-class citizens. They could practice their religion only in the context of considerable restriction and they could not enter State service. Some Roumanians and Ruthenians of the Greek Orthodox faith were forced to join the Greek Catholic Church, which recognized the Pope's authority. However, attempts to force Greek Orthodox Serbs to do the same were unsuccessful. Rather than yield to pressure, many emigrated to Russia.

From Hungary's standpoint, Maria Theresa's reign was a period of consolidation. It was during these years that the country was rebuilt and the devastation wrought by the Ottomans made good.

"Every Nation Became Learned in its own Language"

In the eighteenth century culture was still traditionally in the hands of the Church. The Church controlled the schools, literature and the arts. In Hungary Roman Catholic Church enjoyed a unique position on account of its vast estates and the support it received from the Habsburgs.

Baroque was the dominant artistic style of the age. The monumentality of Baroque buildings, the inner pomp of the churches and the spectacular richness of forms all proclaimed the superiority of ecclesiastical and secular power. During this period, the Baroque cathedrals of the bishops and archbishops were built, together with their elaborate palaces. Also constructed in the Baroque style were the palaces of the aristocracy and the churches of the newly-populated villages. The homes of the landowning classes no longer served defence purposes, but comfort and extravagant tastes. In quite a number there were theatres and concert-halls in which actors and musicians entertained the host and his distinguished guests. The rooms were furnished with expensive furniture and adorned with statues and paintings. The parks around the palaces imitated the gardens at Versailles.

Catholic Baroque left its mark on eighteenth-century painting and sculpture as well. In Transdanubia and in northwestern Hungary, churches were decorated with frescoes which portrayed Biblical scenes. The Austrian Franz-Anton Maulbertsch and István Dorfmeister, who founded a dynasty of artists, were the greatest masters of Baroque painting in Hungary. Murals in aristocratic palaces no longer took their inspiration from the national past, but from classical mythology. Most were painted by Hungarian masters and their quality was often parochial.

The language of scholarship was Latin and the vernacular, which began to flourish in the seventeenth century, lost its prominence. As regards approach and method, however, the eighteenth century saw great progress. A discipline known to contemporaries as *Staatskunde* (this was a blanket term for geography, history and ethnography) underwent considerable development. In his *Notitiae Hungariae* ... (Knowledge of Hungary) Mátyás Bél, the rector of the Lutheran grammar school in Pozsony presents a complete survey of the country, although up to 1742 only five volumes of this work were published. The Jesuit school of historiography, which emerged in the second half of the century (Gábor Hevenesi, György Pray and István Katona), was the first to work on the basis of the modern, critical approach to source material. The Jesuit historians were, however, strongly biased in favour of the Habsburgs.

Most literature in the Hungarian language was in the form of religious works written for the people. Catholic publications were brought out by the Jesuit printing press at Nagyszombat, while Protestant works came out in Debrecen and in the towns of Upper Hungary.

Everywhere the language of tuition was Latin—with the exception of village primary schools. Most Catholic secondary schools were in the hands of the Jesuits. Around 1750, this order ran thirty grammar schools and six colleges, the latter being known as academies. The Jesuits also controlled the university at Nagyszombat. Elementary education they neglected, the teaching of villagers was not their chief concern. The Piarist grammar schools, now increasing rapidly in number, represented a more modern approach in education. At these schools the natural sciences were also taught in addition to the other subjects. Protestants were debarred from education at university level but their colleges (at Debrecen, Sárospatak, Nagyenyed, Pápa, Eperjes and Pozsony) provided a high-quality training in theology and philosophy. The Protestants devoted considerable attention to small village schools, although in these only reading and writing, Biblical stories and, occasionally, arithmetic were taught.

The Government attached great importance to the development of schools. A faculty of medicine was added to the university at Nagyszombat, the mining school at Selmec was awarded academic status and an institute for the training of engineers established in Pest. When the Jesuit order was dissolved in 1773, the Government established from its assets an educational fund for the support of primary education. In spite of these efforts

86

though, the number of rural people able to read or write was very low in Hungary as, indeed, it was elsewhere in Europe. The new cultural trends barely touched the peasantry. However, the peasants did preserve their traditional folk culture, Hungarian language and ancient melodies in a period when the nobility and the middle classes were preoccupied with other things.

In 1772 György Bessenyei's *Ágis tragédiája* (The Tragedy of Agis) was published. This marked the beginning of the Enlightenment in Hungary and of the manifestation in literature of a national awakening. Bessenyei, a member of the Royal Hungarian Guards in Vienna, had become acquainted in that city with the ideas of the French Enlightenment. In his works, Bessenyei advocated certain social reforms and the development of a vernacular culture. "Every nation became learned in its own language", ran Bessenyei's slogan. Things began to liven up first in literature and later in politics. The masonic lodges played a highly important role in this process. The members of these lodges, aristocrats, nobles and even a number of burghers held meetings during which they acquainted themselves with the spirit of the Enlightenment. The view was expressed that social changes were necessary. Within a few decades, Hungarian society was transformed and backwardness in culture, attitude to life and thinking was, to some extent, remedied.

The First Servant of the State

Maria Theresa died on 29 November 1780 and was succeeded by her 39-year-old son, Joseph II. Joseph had become Holy Roman Emperor in 1765, albeit by this time the office amounted to little more than a title. His mother had not allowed him to interfere much in the affairs of the Habsburg dominions. During his long years as heir to the throne, Joseph had travelled extensively in his territories, although taking pains not to reveal his identity. The new ruler had also visited Hungary, and his experiences and impressions thus gained were important. They helped to shape his conception of government and plans for reform.

Joseph II was raised in the spirit of enlightened absolutism. He regarded himself on the one hand as absolute lord of the Empire and, on the other, as the principal servant of his peoples. The goal of his political philosophy, known as Josephinism, was to forge a united and strong empire from its multilingual and vastly differing component regions. He wished to create a state capable of matching the rival European powers. Modernization of government would not, however, be sufficient in itself. Social reforms, designed to eliminate backwardness, would also be needed. Since Joseph believed that the masses lacked the maturity to order their own affairs, he intended to do everything by himself. His ruthless interference provoked resistance even where his intentions were good. His slogan ran as follows: "Everything for the people, nothing by the people."

After his accession, Joseph II immediately embarked upon the path of reform. He wished to strengthen society and the state by reducing the power of the privileged and by allowing the lower classes a freer life. Joseph II refuged to be crowned king of Hungary, thereby avoiding the obligation to observe the privileges of the nobility. What is more, Joseph had the Hungarian Crown, the symbol of a bygone age, transferred from Pozsony to the Imperial Museum in Vienna. He governed by decree and did not convene the Diet. His proclamations regulated the individual and society from the cradle to the grave, and down to the tiniest detail.

Joseph's first measures were aimed at curbing the power of the Catholic clergy—a body which had grown excessively large. He took censorship, in other words, the right to supervise and to veto the publication of printed materials, out of the Church's hands. He restricted the political role of the bishops as well as the Pope's right to interfere in the country. Joseph also dissolved all monastic orders which were not involved in teaching or caring for the sick, using their assets primarily for educational purposes. In 1781, he issued a decree granting freedom of worship to his Protestant and Greek Orthodox subjects, who were now allowed to fill the higher positions in the State. Pope Pius VI personally called on Joseph II in Vienna to persuade him to amend his decrees, but to no avail. Joseph II was a devout Catholic and his policy stemmed not from a lack of faith but rather from practical considerations. The Emperor realized that the State could not do without the expertise and work of the non-Catholics and that creed should not limit the rights of a citizen.

Although his religious policy was welcomed by society at large, Joseph II's administrative reforms created discontent in the ranks of the nobility. In the interests of the Empire's unity, Joseph II abolished Hungarian autonomy. Officials in Hungary were appointed by the monarch and the country was divided into ten administrative units, each headed by a royal commisioner. Even more unpopular as far as the nobility was concerned were Joseph II's decrees aimed at protecting the serfs. Joseph abolished the manor law courts, where the landowners themselves passed judgement on their serfs. Also done away with was punishment by flogging. In addition, freedom of movement was ensured for serfs and the term "serf" abolished officially. At the same time, Joseph II made preparations for the taxation of the nobility. He ordered the land to be surveyed and this was followed by a general census and the registration of estates. The Government's measures gave rise to exaggerated hopes among the peasants. In 1784, the Roumanian serfs on the royal estate at Zalatna, Transylvania, rose in arms. Under the leadership of Horia and Cloşca, the rebellion mobilized some 20,000 serfs against the bailiffs and the landowners. Joseph II ruthlessly suppressed the peasant uprising and, as a deterrent, had its leaders broken on the wheel.

The Emperor's religious and social reforms antagonized the Church and the nobility, respectively, but more general provocations were to follow. In 1784, German was made the official language throughout the Habsburg Empire, and this move turned the entire Hungarian nation against Joseph. As a result of the relevant decree, the language of public administration, jurisdiction and higher education in Hungary changed accordingly. The nation became united in its indignation. Joseph's attempt to Germanize the country contributed appreciably to the subsequent revival of Hungarian literature, the Hungarian language and Hungarian national traditions.

The implementation of Joseph II's reforms became more and more difficult. The Emperor's problems were compounded by other developments. In 1788, Joseph launched a military campaign against the Turks but this was not successful. Domestic opposition increased as a result and the compulsory delivery of produce was sabotaged in many places. In 1789 revolution broke out in France and there was a national uprising in the Austrian Netherlands, a distant Habsburg province. In Hungary the nobility began openly to organize a conspiracy. In 1790, a few weeks before his death, Joseph withdrew all of his reforms with the exception of his decrees on religious toleration, on the monastic orders and on the abolition of perpetual serfdom.

THE DEVELOPMENT OF CAPITALISM IN HUNGARY (1790–1918)

The Impact of the French Revolution and the Age of Reform

"The Line of Habsburg Succession will be Broken"

Although Joseph II revoked most of his decrees, this was not sufficient to calm discontent in his dominions. His death only served to increase ill-feeling and the journey of the Holy Crown from Vienna to Buda in February 1790 was almost a triumphal procession. The Crown was escorted by the private armies of the nobility with the soldiers arrayed in Hungarian national dress. Entire villages turned out for the spectacle and in Győr, the Bishop himself headed the assembled burghers. In Pest-Buda, the cannons thundered and the whole city celebrated. Old Hungarian costumes were taken out, Hungarian dances reappeared at the balls and merry-making occured to the strains of the Rákóczi March.

The country was celebrating a "newly-found liberty". The country organization was restored, former officials returned to their jobs and the land survey documents were publicly burnt. The movement was led by the lesser nobility who believed that the time had come to re-establish the independent Hungarian State. Its leader, Péter Balogh of Ócsa, formulated the lesser nobility's demands. The cornerstone of these was that by refusing to be crowned, Joseph II had violated the social contract between the Hungarian nation and the House of Habsburg, thereby breaking the line of succession. The nation was therefore entitled to conclude a new contract and to elect a new king. The lesser nobility's candidate for the throne was the son of the Prussian Monarch and its most radical members had already established contact with the court in Berlin. These reformists also drafted a new constitution, under which the lesser nobility would play the prominent role. Lesser nobles would enact legislation at the Diet and between Diets, the government of the country would be carried on by a Senate made up of their members. Royal power would therefore become nominal.

The leading groups in the nobility, among them part of the aristocracy, favoured enlightened reforms. Unlike Joseph II, however, they did not subordinate these to Imperial needs, but wished to realize them in accordance with Hungarian requirements. However, the greater part of the nobility thought rather short-sightedly, in terms of its own narrow interests, in other words, the preservation of its privileges. Gradually, the conservatives gained the upper hand. While they were building dreams of an upper-class republic, the serfs and the burghers featured less and less in their plans. There were some who considered unlimited power over their serfs to be natural. As Szabolcs county put it: "Fate has willed it that some be born kings, others nobles and still others servants."

The new ruler Leopold II was the younger brother of Joseph II. Leopold succeeded to the throne at a difficult time. Belgium was on the verge of seceding, the nobles in Hungary were arming themselves and there was discontent in the Polish territories as well. The war against the Turks remained unfinished and the old rival, the king of Prussia, had deployed his troops along the Silesian frontier on the pretext of a military exercise. The Habsburg Empire was again on the brink of total disintegration.

Leopold had previously headed the Dukedom of Tuscany, which he had turned into a state modelled on the ideas of the Englightenment. Like his brother, Leopold favoured reforms, although he favoured a more tactful approach. In Hungary, Leopold convened the Diet and announced that he wished to rule the country in accordance with the constitution. At the same time, he started to isolate the Hungarian nobility's reform movement from possible outside help. Leopold concluded a peace treaty with the Turks and, with some loss of prestige, reached agreement with the Prussian King in the Treaty of Reichenbach. In this way, the Hungarian nobility was denied assistance from the two powers which were in a position to give it support and the Imperial army was freed from foreign commitments. News of the treaties and the fact that Imperial troops were now heading towards Hungary had a calming effect on the Diet. There was no more talk of electing a new king and gradually the demands of the nobility were also dropped. In November 1790, Leopold II was unconditionally crowned King of Hungary. At the same time, Archduke Alexander Leopold, the King's fourth son, was obediently elected Palatine, the chief public officer in Hungary.

Leopold II knew how to scare the nobility. His agents had previously encouraged the peasantry to rise against their landlords. At the same time and also at the instigation of the King's agents, the towns were also demanding autonomy and representation at the Diet. Leopold also used the non-Magyar minorities, whose national consciousness was now awakening. For the Serbs he established an independent Illyrian Chancellery and convened a Serbian national assembly at Karlowitz. In Transylvania, Leopold supported the national demands of the Roumanians. All of these moves made the Hungarian nobility reconsider its position. The influence of the French Revolution was important in convincing the greater part of the nobility that it must forge an alliance with the monarch against the lower classes.

Nevertheless, the Diet of 1790–91 enacted important legislation. It stated again that "Hungary is a free and independent country", which must be governed in accordance with its own laws and customs, and through independent government organs. Freedom of religion, together with Maria Theresa's and Joseph II's serf decrees, was codified.

In the summer of 1791 Leopold believed that the time had come to continue his reforms. This he intended to do not by issuing decrees but legally, by compelling the Diet to act in accordance with his wishes. The creation of a constitutional monarchy was Leopold's ideal. Above all, he wanted to organize the peasantry's representation at the Diet. However, his sudden death on 1 March 1792 put an end to these ambitious plans.

"Let us, Hungarian Citizens, Take the Oath for Liberty or Death"

The accession of Francis I marked the beginning of a new era in the life of the Habsburg Empire and in that of Hungary. Whereas Joseph II and Leopold II wanted to introduce changes inspired by the Enlightenment, Francis was a staunch conservative. At the time of the French Revolution, Habsburg policy was also determined by fear of similar events at home. While Leopold had attempted to "steal the thunder" of the radicals by introducing reforms, Francis was preparing to crush opponents of the existing order. Leopold had wanted the peasantry represented at the Diet but Francis set up a cabinet composed of conservative aristocrats. With the stubbornness of the ungifted, he refused to countenance even minor changes. He established a police state, in which informers operated everywhere. Indeed, even suspicion of sympathy with bourgeois aspirations often brought retribution. To turn attention away from domestic woes, Francis entered into war against the French Republic.

During this time, discontent was growing in Hungary as well. In particular, the intelligentsia, which had finally lost its feudal character and had recently grown strength, gave increasingly powerful expression to its grievances. The bitterness of the intellectuals was, however, now mixed with a growing determination partly inspired by the French Revolution. As regards social background, ideology and opinions, this group was rather heterogeneous, it did agree on one point though, namely, that the existing situation was unacceptable and had to be changed.

The intelligentsia found an ally in that section of the lesser nobility which believed that growing absolutism was detrimental both to the country's interests and to her independence. This part of the nobility was willing to accept certain reforms. Contact between the nobility and the intelligentsia was established primarily in the masonic lodges, where opportunities for discussion were provided.

For a while discontent remained beneath the surface. In the towns, reading circles and clubs were formed where intellectuals could meet and read the *Moniteur,* the official paper of the French Revolution. The most prominent figure among these intellectuals was József Hajnóczy, who had served as deputy sheriff under Joseph II but who, as a non-noble, had lost his job in 1790. Hajnóczy was a man of great erudition who pointed out in print that conditions in Hungary were intolerable and that reform was of paramount importance. However, nobody at this time thought of taking action to change the situation.

All this changed at the beginning of 1794, when Ignác Martinovics became leader of the malcontents. Martinovics had pursued his university studies as a member of the Franciscan order, and afterwards became an army chaplain. He later worked as professor of physics at the University of Lemberg (Lvov). Martinovics was a talented and cultured man, who nurtured immense ambitions but who, at the same time, lacked self-discipline. Not satisfied with his scholarly achievements, he aspired to a political career as well and, in 1791, entered King Leopold's secret service. For appearances' sake Leopold appointed him Court Chemist and Abbot of Szászvár but his real task was to travel through the country and report on the prevailing mood. Martinovics hoped that, by serving the monarch, he could play a leading role in bringing about change in the country but Leopold's death frustrated his plans. The new ruler, Francis I, did not trust Martinovics and sacked him immediately. Soon, Martinovics became the leader of those he had previously reported about to the authorities. These included the group of dissatisfied intellectuals who rallied around Hajnóczy and who wished to see a democratic transformation in Hungary.

In spring 1794, Martinovics established two secret societies. The first, the Society of Reformers, rallied to itself the discontented elements of the nobility. The main goal of this society was to set up an independent republic in Hungary, but at the same time it also advocated moderate social reform. The second was the Society of Liberty and Equality, and was intended to carry on where the Society of Reformers left off. The Society of Liberty and Equality was made up of the Hungarian Jacobins, the advocates of radical transformation. After seizing power from the Society of Reformers, the latter organization would abolish the privileges of the nobility and would introduce the achievements of the French Revolution. Naturally, the Society of Reformers was to be kept in the dark about the existence of its would-be successor. Martinovics appointed leaders to head the secret services. These were Count Jakab Sigray for the Society of Reformers and Hajnóczy, the former hussar-captain János Laczkovics and the young radical Ferenc Szentmarjay for the Society of Liberty and

Equality. The nobility was to have played a decisive role in the first part of the two-stage struggle and the peasantry a decisive role in the second. The conspirators had no clear plans for the period after this revolution and formulation of these would have been difficult considering the level of development of Hungarian society at this time. In any case, the peasants, who had been counted on as allies did not even know about the conspiracy.

After a few months of organizing, the two Societies had some three hundred members between them. In summer 1794, however, the police in Vienna arrested Martinovics in connection with a similar plot. Martinovics revealed the details of the Hungarian conspiracy to the investigating committee. Vienna was not entirely surprised by the plot but nevertheless reacted with panic. The Government put fifty people on trial in Hungary, charging them with high treason. Whoever had seen or read the secret catechism was considered guilty. The code of criminal procedure was tightened and the hands of the defence were tied. An intimidated court passed eighteen death sentences on the accused, of whom seven were actually put to death. Martinovics and the four leaders were executed on 20 May 1795. On 3 June they were followed by Sándor Szolártsik and the young lawyer Pál Őz on the grounds that there was no hope of these two ever reforming their ways. The others were given long prison terms, among them the finest representatives of contemporary Hungarian literature, Ferenc Kazinczy, János Batsányi, László Szentjóbi Szabó and Ferenc Verseghy.

"An example had to be set to make the country live in fear", wrote Kazinczy later. However, the yearning for progress could not be suppressed in the people's hearts. In the ninteenth century Hungarian reform movement continued where the Hungarian Jacobins left off.

The Period of the Napoleonic Wars

By the time the leaders of the Hungarian Jacobin movement were beheaded, Europe had been ravaged by war for years. However, the fighting between the armies of revolutionary France and those of the so-called First Coalition had taken place in Northern Italy and near the Rhine areas far to the west of Hungary. When, however, in 1796 General Bonaparte took over the command of the French forces in Italy, the situation changed. After dealing heavy blows to the Austrians, at the end of the year they were in a position to dictate peace to Vienna. The Habsburgs were on the defensive.

During the next fifteen years, England and Austria attempted to organize coalition against France but these were doomed to military failure. It was during this period that Napoleon scored his greatest victories and became Emperor of the French. The Holy Roman Empire also passed out of existence, this being followed by the formation of the Austrian Empire. Hostilities extended to Central and Eastern Europe (Napoleon occupied Vienna twice) but when, in 1805 the war reached Hungary's western border, the Treaty of Pozsony halted the fighting. In 1809, the French army actually entered the country but even then only a comparatively narrow strip of Transdanubia experienced battle and occupation. Napoleon's decline started only in 1812–13, after the failure of his Russian campaign, and by 1814 he had been defeated.

The French wars lasted for almost two decades and naturally exerted great influence over the political life in Hungary. That small section of the nobility which had been brought up during the period of the Enlightenment together with part of the bourgeoisie and the intelligentsia had sympathy for Napoleon, even when it became clear that, as Emperor, he was not following the democratic course of consistent bourgeois transformation. In this stratum aversion to feudalistic conditions was far more powerful than any disenchantment they felt. Dániel Berzsenyi wrote that "Napoleon had promised liberty, the 'soul of the age' but failed to keep his word. His fall was the revenge of 'humanity's cause'." The poet's words, however, could not diminish Bonaparte's appeal. There can be no doubt also that even at the end of the eighteenth century other sections of the nobility still entertained ideas of enlarging the fights of their class. Accordingly, they attached great hopes to the probable waning of Habsburg power. Their stance did not last very long though. Whereas in private conversations and at county meetings they strongly and sincerely criticized Court policy, sooner or later they realized that they and the Habsburgs shared common interest. The great mass of the nobility from the very beginning had correctly felt that Napoleon's victories posed a serious threat to the feudal order and to feudal privilege. This was the view especially of the tens of thousands of impoverished nobles who, for the most part, led a peasant existence, but also that of the overwhelming majority of aristocrats.

The reaction of the peasant masses to the Napoleon phenomenon cannot be precisely determined, although a certain amount of information had undoubtedly reached them about the affairs of the world. This reached the villages through the accounts of those who returned home from the war, either for good or on leave. For the time being, however, there were no consequences of this awareness.

The changing political attitude of the nobles explains why Napoleon's appeal to the Hungarians in 1809 met with almost no response. In this he offered Hungary the chance of breaking with Austria but the opportunity was allowed to pass. Throughout the Napoleonic Wars, the Hungarian Diets were more than prepared to accede to the Court's every wish, be it the granting of money, produce or new recruits. Indeed, nobles were even willing to play a part in the fighting themselves. Their involvement took the form of uprisings, financed at their own expense, and service with the colours, either on foot or on horseback. The wealthiest undertook to provide fully-equipped soldiers, the number depending on the size of their estates. Many impoverished nobles also volunteered and were equipped out of contributions levied on commoners by the counties. The uprisings of the nobility in 1797, 1800 and 1809 mobilized some 135,000 people but only the last of these actually played a part in the war. This was at the Battle of Győr, where the Imperial army, under the command of the traditionally untalented officers, was seriously defeated by French troops pressing into Hungary from Italy. (This engagement was considered to be important by the French: Győr's German name—Raab—being inscribed on the "Arc de Triomphe" in Paris.) Although they had not received proper training, the insurgents fought courageously for quite a time. However, as in the case of previous uprisings, they were demoralized by the fact that the arms they had received from the army were old-fashioned or substandard quality. The military failure of the nobility's uprising in 1809 shed harsh light on the increasingly weak moral basis of the nobility's exemption from tax. It also contributed significantly greater awareness of the anachronism represented by feudal conditions.

Loyal gestures on the part of the Hungarian nobility, however, did not dissipate lack of trust on the part of Vienna. The Court regarded the uprisings as an attempt to set up an independent nobles' army and not just as a manifestation of solidarity. At the same time, Vienna considered it irreconcilable with the absolutist policy of the day that the monarch should be compelled to bargain with his subjects at the Diet and that the latter should grant his wishes only for something in return. As soon as the Court felt the nobility to be more dispensable (in 1809 Napoleon married Emperor Francis's daughter and in 1813, Napoleon's star began to wane), it began to ignore feudal constitutional forms: excluded the nobles from the business of politics.

From 1814 onwards, Vienna held things increasingly under control. After the fall of Napoleon the Congress of Vienna strengthened the Court's position. The Congress of Vienna based its settlement on conservative and anti-revolutionary criteria and the Holy Alliance, which was initiated by the Russian Tsar and supported primarily by the absolutist Austrian and Prussian monarchs, established the military and political guarantees for the maintenance of this order. No amount of coercion, however, was able to disguise the fact that the new arrangements could not last.

The Period Leading up to the Age of Reform

The collapse of Napoleon's power, the conservative territorial and political settlement in Europe, the establishment of the Holy Alliance by the absolutist powers—all made it superfluous for the Habsburgs to co-operate with the Hungarian nobility according to the rules of feudal constitutionalism.

The Court undoubtedly had good reasons for a more authoritarian approach. After 1800, the only way the Habsburgs could finance their vastly expensive wars was to issue paper money. However, as this paper money lost its value, inflation rose rapidly. To avoid bankruptcy, Vienna was compelled to take drastic steps. In 1811 paper money was first devalued to one-fifth of its nominal worth and a further reduction to forty per cent of this new value occurred in 1816. This was catastrophic for the Hungarian nobility. It meant the ruthless tapping of the modest wealth that class had accumulated from the increased trading made possible by the war. Accordingly, as early as 1812, the nobility questioned the right of the monarch to issue paper money without the approval of the Diet and tried to avoid the consequences of the devaluation.

Vienna, however, did not even convene the Diet after 1812. Instead it reverted to government by decree, dismissing the remonstrations of the counties. Hungary was again flooded by the "informants" of the reorganized secret police. The counties came under growing administrative pressure and in 1822 the King issued a decree under which tax was to be paid in silver money. Although this measure primarily affected the peasantry, indirectly it further curtailed the revenues of the nobility. When, in 1821, Vienna demanded the immediate presentation of a backlog of 28,000 recruits, the majority of the counties openly refused to comply. Vienna found it difficult to counter the increasing resistance, which threatened to paralyze the public administration entirely. It resorted to threats, corruption or even military force where necessary. The poet Ferenc Kölcsey wrote the lyrics of the Hungarian National Anthem on 22 January 1823, at the height of the antagonism. Presenting an evocative image of liberty that cannot flourish "from the blood of the dead", the poet points out the anachronism and weakness of purely historical law in a changed world, thereby indicating the need for new political behaviour.

The time for this soon arrived. Vienna, despite its hard-won victory, had to realize that in Hungary it would still have to rely on the counties for a number of reasons. It therefore could not dispense with them if it wanted to maintain the feudal social order. The convening of the Diet and the suspending of the implementation of the offending decrees were essential for consolidation. Accordingly, the Diet was convened in 1825 after an interval of thirteen years. This was a victory over absolutism for the Hungarian estates and echoed that of 1790, after the death of Joseph II. Even twenty years later, the strong Chancellor Metternich dated the beginning of his troubles with Hungary from 1825. Liberal Hungarian historiography has described this period as the Age of Reform. The original question in the conflict, the legality of the paper money issue, could no longer be disputed and it was less likely still that the victims of the devaluations would be compensated. However, Hungary had, during the Napoleonic Wars, at last entered the mainstream of the European economy and there was now a growing foreign demand for Hungarian grain, wool and even tobacco. This awakened new political demands in the nobility. These were demonstrated by the two main achievements of the Diet—the foundation of the Academy of Sciences and the ordering of renewed discussions on reform. These discussions were to be conducted by a broadly-based committee, which would examine the plans which had been drafted at the beginning of the 1790s, but which then had been shelved by Vienna.

The founding of the Academy of Sciences (thenceforth the name of Count István Széchenyi became inseparably linked with the national reform movement) indicated that a part of the nobility and aristocracy wished to place contemporary science at the service of development in Hungary. The re-negotiation of the reform proposals of 1790 indicated the realization that the country's problems could not be resolved by means of reform. An 81-member committee (the members were delegated by the Diet) discussed the proposals for two and a half years while the whole country looked on. In the end, the whole host of ideas and proposals were summed up in a conservative spirit. Public opinion, however, expected more than this, demanding that the proposals be discussed throughout the country at county level. By summer 1830 there existed numerous proposals and ideas which all aimed at improvement. By the end of the year Vienna had been forced to allow the published findings of the committee to be considered by the counties after all. Only a unifying concept was now missing, around which everything could be organized. This was soon provided and became known of very quickly. On 28 January 1830 Széchenyi's *Hitel* (Credit) was published.

István Széchenyi and the Reform Movement

The fact that during the first half of the nineteenth century Hungary gradually entered the mainstream of European economic life—an irrevocable development—demonstrated to the landowners that in a predominantly agrarian country the expansion of agricultural commodity production offered a good opportunity for augmenting their wealth. At the same time it also revealed the preconditions necessary for this. Intensive cultivation of the land was called for along with animal husbandry of a high order. For these the forced labour of the serf and the expertise of the stockman were increasingly inadequate. It soon became clear that, on the one hand, such work standards could only be demanded of the free wage labourer and, on the other, that the Hungarian landowners lacked not merely the capital needed for the regular employment of wage labourers but more importantly, also that had no access to credit that could make it available. The reason for this was that the landed estates of the Hungarian nobility could not be seized to recover debts. Under the medieval institution of entailment (1351) such estates were inalienable as long as a member of the family in possession was alive. However, capital was vital for the development of the economy, and this was true for industry, trade and banking as well as for agriculture. Credit was needed and this would not be forthcoming while the land remained unavailable to guarantee loans.

Count István Széchenyi was the first to draw attention to the very great importance of all this. In 1825 he offered a year's revenue from his estates to found a learned society, the Academy of Sciences. In 1802, his father, Count Ferenc Széchényi, had donated his collections, thereby laying the foundations of the Széchényi Library and the National Museum. In 1797, Széchenyi's uncle, Count György Festetics, founded at Keszthely the Georgikon, the first agricultural college on the continent of Europe. The young Count István Széchenyi had begun his adult life as an army officer. After the Napoleonic wars, however, he soon left soldiering and started to manage his vast estates. His private life and emotional world were shaped by Romanticism, the predominant philosophy of the age. On economic questions, however, Széchenyi read the bourgeois economists of Western Europe with whose works he became acquainted in the course of his foreign travels. Therefore, when a bank in Vienna rejected his application for a small loan, Széchenyi was able to realize that this shed light on the fundamental problem of the Hungarian economy. Published in 1830, Széchenyi's *Credit* accordingly proposed the abolition of entailment as a first step towards creating credit-worthiness for the Hungarian landowner.

Later on Széchenyi compared the feudal order to a knitted stocking that could be unwound as soon as the first stich was undone. In point of fact, in *Credit* Széchenyi went beyond the abolition of entailment and made further proposals which inevitably pointed towards bourgeois transformation. These included the total separation of the land of the nobility from that of the peasantry, the abolition of the ninth, which was paid in kind to the landowner out of the serf's produce, the disbanding of the guilds, the establishment of a ceiling on municipal prices and the abolition of internal tariffs. Economic and institutional advancement was not, however, to be an end in itself: as Széchenyi saw it, all of this served the prosperity of the nation, which also required "a multitude of educated people".

Széchenyi's approach was a new one in Hungarian politics. Not only did he address problems in a more bourgeois way, but also the reforms he proposed did not involve a deliberate challenge to the Government. In most cases Széchenyi counted on Vienna's benevolence in fact. Admittedly, the fundamental issue, the lack of credit-worthiness was a problem that chiefly concerned the big landowners (in other words, not those strata which had been forced into the opposition). Széchenyi, too, regarded the big landlords —undoubtedly the strongest group in the Hungarian economy—as the possible leading force of the transformation. However, the very fact that *Credit* sought the solution outside the feudal framework was sufficient to prompt sharp attack from several quarters. In 1831 Széchenyi responded —primarily to Count József Dessewffy's *An Analysis of Credit*—by publishing *Világ* (Light) in which he clarified certain parts of *Credit* which could be misunderstood. In the same year Széchenyi wrote *Stádium* (Stadium) in which he put forth twelve concrete laws for a basic programme of transformation. Széchenyi held that the granting of credit must be independent of the social status of the parties concerned. Entailment, which obstructed free trade in land, must be abolished, along with the treasury's right of inheritance after families had died out. The right to own land must be conferred on non-nobles and everyone must be made equal before the law. The nobility (and not just the peasantry) should contribute to the expenses of operating the county administration and of sending deputies to the Diet. Feudal barriers to industry and trade must be removed and Hungarian made the official language of public administration. The Council of the Governor-General, which governed the country from Buda, must be given broader powers (in order to reduce Vienna's interference in the country's internal affairs). Consultations and jurisdiction must be made public. This constituted more than just reform—at least as far as the Government was concerned. No wonder that the censors withheld permission for this book to be published. However, *Stadium* was then printed abroad and smuggled into the country. In November 1833, copies discovered in Hungary were seized. This move came too late though—for at least a decade Széchenyi and his programme became the sole model for reform in Hungary.

Széchenyi was not content to raise the problems of transformation on a theoretical level only. He was in fact the instigator of and active participant in a series of practical economic enterprises. His activities were extensive, ranging from the organization of horse shows designed to promote better blood-stock, the support of shipping on the Danube, and the construction of Budapest's Chain Bridge across the same river. The bridge was built between 1842 and 1848 by a capitalist joint-stock company. Széchenyi was also involved in the Pest Rolling Mill (1846), the first high-performance steam mill in the country. Széchenyi not only organized these modern ventures, but was also one of their largest shareholders. In Pest, he owned valuable residential accomodation, and this increased in value as the city grew in size. By 1848, the greater part of Széchenyi's income came from capitalistic sources and not from feudal dues. To advance his plans at the end of the 1840's he became a member of the Council of the Governor-General, the body which supervised Hungary's public administration. As a member of this, he undertook the state supervision of work aiming to regulate not only River Tisza (to prevent flooding) but also the Danube at the Iron Gate. The aim of these projects was to link the grain producing areas of the Great Plain with domestic and foreign markets. Co-operation with the Government or even just the avoidance of conflicts became more and more unwelcome and by the mid-1840s Széchenyi's popularity also declined. This could not alter the fact, though, that in 1830 *Credit* had provided a convincing analysis of Hungary's increasingly difficult problems as well as definite proposals for solving them. Although Széchenyi did not explicitly say so, what was involved here was the crisis of the entire feudal order, the only way out of which was advancement. This was a decisive realization and its truth was underlined a few months later. In the wake of the 1831 cholera epidemic, a peasant uprising broke out in Upper Hungary and the dreadful events which followed it shed light on the great tensions which had built up in the masses, and which were ready to erupt at the slightest slackening in the social order. This convinced the liberal representatives of bourgeois transformation that they must follow in Széchenyi's footsteps.

"Liberty and Property"

Széchenyi's proposals were, however, only one possible answer to the growing crisis of feudalism in Hungary. In the long run, even the traditional landowning aristocrat, who disposed of the vast revenues from his estates, could eventually hope to become credit-worthy. Széchenyi was a member of the political élite which governed the Austrian Empire. His reform ideas did not include the radical transformation of the existing political order, indeed Széchenyi counted on Government assistance in the realization of his plans. However, the great majority of Hungarian landowning nobles were not satisfied with the answers he gave. New generations of the lesser nobles were increasingly threatened by the fragmentation of their estates and neither their income, nor the size of their properties made major investment possible. These nobles therefore felt that if they wished to exploit effectively the opportunities afforded by the economic boom then occuring, they must take control of the whole state. Once they had done this, the positions of power would be redistributed. More importantly, changes would also be made in the tariff system, the state economic policy which hindered the marketing of their produce. However, this path would ultimately have led to the total annihilation of Habsburg absolutism—a goal that was contemplated in 1790. Just as in the eighteenth-century pro-reform nobles had used the ideology of the Enlightenment to back their demands, so their descendants now applied the ideology of liberalism. This was the ideology which characterized the consolidated Western European régimes emerging after the bourgeois revolutions. In the majority of those reform proposals that cropped up in such great variety during the course of the 1828 debates there surfaced not only anti-absolutist ideas, but also liberal ideas and demands pointing towards bourgeois transformation.

The experiences of the 1831 uprising had made those strata of the nobility which advocated reforms conscious of their need for large-scale peasant support in any conflict with Vienna. With this aim in mind, they worked out a strategy, that of "reconciliation of interests". Under this the nobility tried to create an opportunity primarily for the landed elements of the peasantry, the serfs with small plots, to pay off their feudal dues once and for all with cash. These peasants would then become free and, at the same time, the landowners would acquire a source of money. "Liberty and property"—this was how the poet Kölcsey defined the common interest that bound every inhabitant of the land to his country.

The opportunity to implement reformist plans arose during the Diet of 1832–6. The central issue there was the passing of reform legislation which took account of the conclusions arrived at in the earlier county debates. The advocates of reform made an attempt to develop further the recommendations made by the committees, to make the proposals more liberal in spirit and to enact legislation appropriate to them. However, Vienna succeeded in frustrating the reform hopes. In this it was able to rely on the traditionally-conservative Upper House, the majority of whose members were loyal to the Habsburg, and also on the impoverished mass of lesser nobles. Their representatives in the Lower House could be persuaded to modify the progressive instructions issued to the pro-reform deputies. This victory was not, however, entirely unequivocal.

It turned out that traditional opposition of the nobility to Vienna had taken on a new, totally different, and more dangerous form. At the Diet, there emerged a consciously liberal political grouping which was favourably disposed towards embourgeoisment and which was capable of steadfastly advocating an opposition reform policy. Simultaneously there also emerged new politicians to organize and represent this opposition. Mention can be made of three such figures. First and foremost was Baron Miklós Wesselényi, a Transylvanian aristocrat who entered politics as Széchenyi's friend and follower but who soon turned sharply against the Government. Wesselényi became the most influential and most zealous organizer of the liberal opposition. In a book entitled *Balítéletek* (Misjudgements), he dealt with bourgeois transformation as well as economic and political changes. Kölcsey, a poet, was capable of formulating the central issues of reform with unparalleled lucidity, while the young Ferenc Deák, an excellent tactician, unravelled the internal contradictions of the system and used them to further the cause of reform. Around these leading politicians rallied a large group of opposition youth at the Diet.

Finally, the frequently acrimonious and sharply-worded arguments between the Diet and the Government were brought before the public for the first time. A young Zemplén county lawyer, Lajos Kossuth, reported events at the Diet, and especially the ideas put forward there, in his *Országgyűlési tudósítások* (Dietal Reports). These he published in the form of private letters in order to evade censorship. Kossuth's efforts were not without consequence: more and more people now knew about the important questions of the day.

All of this was, however, too much for Vienna. On 2 March 1835, King Francis I died. He was succeeded by his son, the mentally retarded Ferdinand V. A small ruling clique controlled by Metternich continued to do everything possible to maintain rigid absolutism. In May 1836, a few days after the Diet was closed, the youth leaders were arrested and sentenced to several years imprisonment. Kossuth was prohibited from carrying on with his *Törvényhatósági Tudósítások* (Municipal Reports), in which he wrote about the municipal authorities and local government. When he resisted, in May 1837 he, too, was arrested and sentenced to four years in jail. After his treason trial, which was started in 1835 and lasted four years, Wesselényi himself was sentenced to three years' imprisonment.

The country was again overwhelmed by bitterness and fear. However, this state of affairs could not last much longer.

On the Road to Capitalism

The national and social reform movement scored its first major successes at the Diet of 1839–40. A law was passed under which the serf was entitled to buy his freedom together with his plot of land. A law on bills provided security for creditors, the preconditions for commerce and industry were created in the capitalist spirit and the Jews—formerly without rights—were allowed to settle freely in the towns and to set up businesses in trade and industry. As a result of the reform opposition's persistent and skilful efforts, in May 1840 the political prisoners were released. The blind Wesselényi and László Lovassy, the youth leader who went insane, did not return to political life. The new leader of the movement, Lajos Kossuth, made a triumphant return and immediately became the main spokesman for the opposition.

The opposition's struggle under Kossuth's leadership can be divided into three phases and took place at three different fora. It started on the pages of *Pesti Hírlap* (Pest Journal), a paper edited by Kossuth and which was first published in January 1841. This was the first modern political newspaper in Hungary. It did not merely inform, but also served as a means of agitation and organizing. The paper also had provincial correspondents. Extremely well-informed, Kossuth wrote forceful articles on a wide range of subjects, from the question of poverty, basement flats in Pest, prison conditions and the injustices of soke to pressing economic issues, railway construction and the settlement of the tariff question. He criticized and ridiculed, but at the same time put forward a programme. This advocated the general abolition of the serfs' feudal dues, and the abolition of the privileges of the nobility, including its exemption from tax. The main goal of Kossuth's programme was the creation of a bourgeois middle class thus ensuring the possibility for a constitutional and independent national existence. To this end, it was necessary to pursue a policy of co-ordinating the interests of the nobility, the middle class and the peasantry.

The antagonism which developed between Széchenyi and Kossuth in the 1840's was not chiefly over the primacy of agricultural as opposed to industrial development, indeed not even over the order in which modernization and independence should be achieved. The argument was over "method" and tactics. By the latter, Széchenyi primarily understood the relationship with Vienna. Széchenyi wanted to introduce reforms with the co-operation of the Government and not in defiance of it. Kossuth knew that genuine change could only be accomplished in opposition to absolutism. Ultimately, "method" came to signify conflict between the more moderate, that is, aristocratic path to bourgeois transformation and the more radical, liberal one.

In 1843 the absolutist Government removed Kossuth from his job as editor. This could not, however, stop the opposition movement from making great strides. At the Diet of 1843–4, the Hungarian was declared the official language of the state. In the years that followed, Kossuth organized the reform movement in a new area: economics. He organized a Society for Protection *(Védegylet)*, the aim of which was to organize a boycott of foreign (i.e. Austrian) goods and so encourage Hungarian industry. Kossuth also attempted to establish a Factory Founding Society and a Trade Society, but achieved little practical success with them. In the course of this economic and political struggle, Kossuth developed his plan for an independent tariff area.

During the third phase, in spring 1847, the opposition organized itself into a political party. In response to the conservatives' programme of autumn 1846, Ferenc Deák drafted the "Proclamation of the Opposition". This was inspired by Kossuth and served as the party's programme. Its chief demands were taxation for all social groups, equality before the law, the abolition of serfdom with state compensation, the free sale of the landed estates of the nobility, freedom of the press, the introduction of parliamentary government and a responsible ministry, union between Transylvania and Hungary—all that which was later codified in March 1848.

The opposition party rallied to it some of the country's most outstanding politicians, writers and scholars—a great reform generation that excelled in intellectual prowess, courage and moral integrity. One of its leaders was Ferenc Deák, whose proposal for a new penal code in 1843 was the most progressive at that time. (Naturally, nothing came of it.) Another prominent figure was the writer, scholar and politician Baron József Eötvös. Eötvös's two novels *A falu jegyzője* (The Village Notary) (which unveiled feudal backwardness) and *Magyarország 1514-ben* (Hungary in 1514) (which retold György Dózsa's peasant uprising) had a great impact. Eötvös's circle included the writer Zsigmond Kemény and the historian László Szalay, both of whom were advocates of centralization and capitalism. Count Lajos Batthyány was another outstanding leader of the opposition. He and his cousin, as well as the Károlyis and the Andrássys, patriotic liberal aristocrats and the majority of the lesser nobility—all supported reform.

In the course of the fierce struggles of the 1840s it became clear that the Government in Vienna would frustrate any attempt at genuine change and was opposed to progress and national revival in Hungary. At the same time the conservatives, now organizing themselves into a political party to counter the liberal reformists, could neither provide a meaningful programme, nor produce any results. The pro-government clique gradually became isolated. All of this made things easier for Kossuth and the opposition.

Ultimately, the opposition's success derived from the fact that in the wake of the economic boom of the 1840s a broader and broader segment of society desired modernization and bourgeois development. The landowning nobility, grappling with economic difficulties, the non-noble intelligentsia, the urban and rural lower bourgeoisie, the fledging industrial and agricultural wage labour force and the rising Jewish burghers—all wanted change. The most diverse elements rallied behind Kossuth's programme, all those, in fact, whose existence and opportunities were threatened by the outmoded feudal and absolutist order, and were in serious crisis. Literature, music and the fine arts all gave expression to expectations of radical change. "Young Hungary", a circle of youthful writers headed by Sándor Petőfi, the revolutionary poet, deserves special mention in this respect.

In the autumn of 1847 the last feudal Diet convened in Pozsony at a time of economic difficulty, tensions and a mounting discontent which permeated the whole of society.

New Hungarian Culture in the First Half of the Nineteenth Century

European politics and European economic development played a part in undermining existing feudal conditions and the absolutist political order in Hungary. Primarily as a result of economic development, the demand grew at least for the adaptation of certain modern scientific discoveries for industrial and other purposes. This was despite the fact that the preconditions for independent scientific and technical development, along with money and qualified experts, were still, the most part, lacking. Nonetheless, noteworthy results were produced at Pest University in the agricultural sciences (including botany and zoology), in hydraulics and in medicine. In 1828, Ányos Jedlik constructed the electric motor and in 1832 the Bolyais created absolute geometry. Both of these achievements were highly important contributions to international science. However, owing to backward technical conditions in Hungary, they could not be put to practical use at home. At the same time, however, social sciences and culture developed quickly, as did culture in the broadest sense of the word.

106

The decisive cultural achievement of the time was the renewal of the Hungarian language. This revival had been started at the end of the eighteenth century. In the wake of a new orientation in economy and society, the horizons of the average person began to expand: new objects and phenomena entered his daily life, along with more and more complex relations. The perfection of a new handicrafts industry, changes in agriculture, the first modern Hungarian-language trade books and scientific works —all required that a Hungarian equivalent be found for innumerable new terms. At the same time, in an ever-widening world it became increasingly clear that people were unable to express precisely such things as the more complex and contradictory feelings of love, passion, sadness and joy. Since these were rooted in the more embourgeoised parts of Europe, it is not difficult to see that the renewal of the language indirectly made people familiar with the conditions prevailing in these countries. This was why the renewal of the language triggered off a fierce struggle, and one that lasted for many decades, between those who would have been satisfied with merely increasing the vocabulary and those—led by Ferenc Kazinczy— who, through the renewal of style and human behaviour, wished to introduce a middle-class taste, system of values and world of emotions.

Renewed with tens of thousands of words and expressions, by the first quarter of the nineteenth century the Hungarian language became suitable not only for the expression of the new achievements of economy and science, but also for the adoption of new literary genres. This enabled writers to convey new emotions to their readers, together with the ideals of enlightened and, later, Romantic behaviour. In the early nineteenth-century Hungarian writers and poets (indeed, even some playwrights) were already producing great work. János Batsányi, Mihály Csokonai Vitéz, Mihály Vörösmarty, Ferenc Kölcsey and Ferenc Kazinczy all made outstanding contributions to Hungarian literature. The greatest Hungarian drama to date, *Bánk bán* by József Katona, was also written during this period. These works still reflected the political demands, outlook, historical consciousness and mentality of an overwhelmingly noble readership. Of course, they also bore the stamp of their authors' social origins. At this time most writers came from the lesser nobility, albeit generally from the impoverished strata.

However, cultural change was not confined to the great literary figures and their educated readership. It began to permeate the lower strata of society as well. The rapid spread of literacy was the chief catalyst. Maria Theresa's education decree of 1777 *(Ratio Educationis)* had aimed to organize elementary education for the people and the number of peasants who could read had increased. The 1806 edition of the *Ratio Educationis* made school attendance compulsory for children, although this was not achieved for quite some time. Naturally, not everyone became literate even when they did attend classes but nevertheless a number of people benefited. It was precisely for these strata that the primitively illustrated cheap publications, which started to proliferate at the turn of the nineteenth century, catered. This period also witnessed the birth of the Hungarian-language press in Hungary. The early nineteenth-century Hungarian-language theatre responded to the new requirements of society and started to acquaint even the illiterates with the new models of behaviour and emotion. After the establishment of some provincial theatres (in Kecskemét, Miskolc, Székesfehérvár, etc.), the first Hungarian-language theatre in Pest was opened in 1837. Travelling theatre troupes tried to meet the demand for their services in the provinces. As a result, from the mid-1840s onwards, the more radical mentality and more definite tastes of a rural, small-town and partly non-noble lower middle-class intellectual stratum began to emerge. This stratum, developing during a period of economic upswing, produced figures who began to play an increasingly greater role in determining the course of literature: at this time Sándor Petőfi and János Arany appeared on the literary scene. The voice of literature was brought to a wider and wider readership by several different kinds of literary and cultural journals, while the first popular plays made their highly successful appearances on the stage. Thanks to good translations, the works of not only Shakespeare, Schiller and Molière found their way to Hungarian theatres but also those plays which depicted the modern European middle-class world of the age. The cult of the actor emerged and so did the role of the primadonna.

The first quarter of the nineteenth century brought about a change in Hungarian musical culture as well. Primarily amongst the urban middle class and well-to-do nobility, interest in contemporary European music widened. Vienna's musical culture, now at its height, influenced Hungary as well. On the other hand, it was during these years that a special Hungarian style of music, the *verbunkos,* evolved. This soon became extremely popular—appealing to the nobility and peasantry as well. Traces of its influence could also be perceived in the classical genres of contemporary Hungarian music. Finally, new elements also appeared in musical culture of the broad popular masses. In the wake of intensified social mobility, a wave of new motifs, often originating from distant lands, were added to the previously closed melodies of the village. The new type of folk song appeared. After a quarter of a century of unsuccessful attempts, 1844 witnessed the birth of the first modern Hungarian opera, *László Hunyadi* by Ferenc Erkel (who also composed the music for the National Anthem). *László Hunyadi* was a great success, and not just because of its patriotic theme.

The spread of bourgeois mores brought about the awakening of a demand for, and a receptiveness to, fine art. The number of artists and buyers of art grew. The walls of rural manor-houses were adorned with portraits and engravings and even in peasant homes pictures grew rapidly in number, although these were, for the most part, primitive. In the 1830s, however, sophisticated art also appeared. Its first masters, Brocky and Markó, soon went to live abroad, but Miklós Barabás achieved fame in Hungary

—primarily with his portraits. In addition, Romantic historical painting, which reached its high point only after 1849, was also slowly emerging. Exhibitions staged by the Pest Art Association strove to spread contemporary European artistic taste, as did the first art dealers in the capital. Illustrations in books and periodicals made their contribution to this process. It was during these years that the sculptor István Ferenczy, who had studied in Rome, created the first great pieces of Hungarian neo-Classical sculpture.

Finally, the face of Hungarian architecture also changed in the wake of the modest and periodical economic booms. The growing number of new buildings, primarily aristocratic palaces, urban houses, manors of the nobility and, in some places, even peasant buildings showed the influence of the neo-Classical style, the prevalent contemporary artistic fashion. The same may be said for the churches and, generally speaking, the public buildings built at this time. The great Hungarian architects of the age (especially Mihály Pollack and József Hild) designed public buildings (e.g. the National Museum, the County Hall, Redout) for Pest, which was now the centre of the national economy, culture and the state administration. They also laid out impressive squares as well as entire streets. Attractive neo-Classical building complexes were put up in several provincial towns as well.

The diverse elements of the consciously Hungarian national current thus emerging in culture were integrated by a politically conscious behaviour which by this time had taken its first steps to initiate bourgeois transformation. This behaviour advocated the primacy of the "national" element and from culture it expected the expression and interpretation of what was at the same time a concept and a demand. The demand was difficult to define but it could now rely on historical research—the uncovering of sources and syntheses that occurred from the mid-eighteenth century onwards. Contemporary Hungarian culture could therefore become markedly historical in character. The *National Anthem* and The *Appeal* were poems which were just as much summaries of Hungarian history as the representative works of music and fine art were attempts to interpret the present through history, by means of theme and analogy. It was to meet this demand that Mihály Horváth's great four-volume synthesis on the history of Hungary was written in the years 1842–6.

This close interconnection between culture and politics impared popularity and social significance to the former and penetrating force—the widening of the popular base that understood it—to the latter. This was the decisive precondition for the success of a broad-based political struggle pointing in the direction of capitalist development.

The Awakening of Nations
in the Danubian Region

The process which took place amongst the Magyars at this time, and which resulted in the emergence of the modern Hungarian nation, also occurred amongst the non-Magyar peoples of Hungary. Of course, there were numerous differences in the way this happened.

These differences essentially derived from the social structure of the various nationalities. Only the Croatians resembled the Magyars in the way their society was made up. In any case, contemporaries regarded the Croatians to be different from the rest. The structure of Croatian society was strongly reminiscent of Hungarian society, with its sizeable landed aristocracy, large body of lesser nobles and broad peasant masses. Some of the Croatian peasants were not even serfs but free people who could cultivate their land in exchange for army service in the so-called Military Frontier zone.

In Transylvania, Saxon society was fundamentally bourgeois in character, although feudal privileges had also kept it closed. In Hungary the German urban middle class had already started to assimilate and the peasant masses were not yet affected by awakening nationalism.

The Roumanians, Serbs, Slovaks and Ruthenes were basically characterized by the fact that their nobility, through enjoying feudal privileges, had assimilated with the Magyar nobility and by the fact that Magyarization had already begun to affect their national languages. The bulk were peasants who lived the life of serfs, but there were the urban lower middle-class strata as well. In the case of the Serbs and Roumanians, a small proportion also served as free soldier-peasants in the Military Frontier zone. For the most part, the Serbs became merchants in the royal free towns situated along the main trade routes. They also settled in the southern areas, the Bácska and the Banat. Some were free soldiers in the Military Frontier, the rest free peasants. The Serbian burghers achieved a certain prosperity, especially after the regulation of the Danube at the Iron Gate. That river accordingly became the principal route of trade to the East, at the expense of those which went through Transylvania. This change brought business to the Serbian settlements.

Although numerically small, the intelligentsia, and above all the clergy, played a major part in the life of all the national minorities. In a sense the Greek Orthodox and the Greek Catholic Churches served as national Churches to these peoples. In the case of the Serbs, the Orthodox Church played an especially important role. The privileges granted to this people in 1690 permitted church congresses to be held. These, which were convened from time to time, also served as political fora. The Serbian National Congress held at Temesvár in September 1790 raised for the first time the demand of territorial autonomy for this ethnic group. Also indicative of the political and secular role of this congress is the fact that it was also attended by the Serb officers of the Military Frontier. In 1842, the Congress of Karlowitz elected Josip Rajačić metropolitan. Rajačić was to play an important role later, at the time of the 1848 revolution.

The Serbian intelligentsia was the first to proclaim its secession from the Hungarians, and its belonging to another nation. It believed that this nation had always existed, but that it was asleep and had to be woken up. This way even contemporaries spoke of national awakening and revival.

The first and most important task of this awakening was the creation of the national language, which could be used to address the people, to make conscious their belonging to the nation. At the beginning of this period none possessed a literary national language. The Slovakian Lutherans used Medieval Czech as their literary language, the Catholics used various dialects, the Serbs Russian interspersed with Serb words, which they called Slaveno-Serb. The Croats also used dialects. Towards the end of the eighteenth century Greek Catholic (Uniate) Roumanian priests started to raise the vernacular to the rank of a literary language, and to purge words of non-Latin origin from it. In the case of the Croats Ljudevit Gaj accepted as the Croatian literary language the dialect closest to Serb, that which the serb Vuk Stefanović Karadžić had already raised to the rank of the Serbian literary language. Owing to the conservatism of the Serbian burghers, it was more difficult to attain recognition for the new spoken vernacular as the literary language. Nonetheless, Slaveno-Serb gradually disappeared from usage. After initial experimenting Ľudovít Štúr made the Central Middle Slovakian dialect the literary language of the Slovaks. The languages which emerged at this time have remained the literary language of these people to this day. Only the most backward Ruthenes were incapable of creating their own literary language in this period. Poetry, short stories, novels and plays were written in the new Serbian literary language and the outlines of a national culture began to take shape. In 1826 the Serbs founded *Srpska Matica* (Serbian Mother) in Pest. This was a public education society which later served as a model for other Slav peoples. Primarily concerned with cultivating the Serb language, *Srpska Matica* also published literary works. Also indicative the urban middle class was strong among the Serbs. In 1791, it founded a Serbian grammar school in Karlowitz and another in Újvidék nineteen years later. In 1812, a teachers' training college was established in Szentendre, a major Serbian ecclesiastical centre.

Literary works also dealt with the historical past of the ethnic group concerned, although contemporary historiography also proclaimed the former glory of the nationalities. A good example is the manuscript of the Roumanian Gheorghe Şincai. The Slovak Ján Kollár sang of the great past and sad contemporary situation of the Slavs in an impressive series of sonnets (*Slávy dcera*—The Daughter of Glory) to stimulate their self-awareness. Theories of glorious origins also served to emphasize a historical past. For instance, the Slavs were said to be related to the Scythians and the Roumanians tried to prove their purely Roman origins. The historians of every nationality stressed their people's entitlement to the area where they were now living. During the mid-eighteenth century, Jovan Rajić wrote a history of the various Slavic peoples, dealing especially with the Bulgarians, Croatians and Serbs. He completed this work in 1768 and it was published in Vienna over the period 1791–5. A revised edition came out in Buda in 1823, demonstrating the interest in Serb history which then existed. Rajić, too, believed in the kinship between the Scythians and the Slavs. Apart from this, however, he strove to base his work on original sources, towards which, to some extent, he adopted a critical approach.

The cause of language and literature was also served by the establishment of a separate theatre for the nationalities. Owing to unfavourable conditions, however, for the time being this meant no more than amateur play-acting and travelling theatre companies. The Serbs, too, had theatre troupes which travelled to towns with Serbian populations and which used theatrical performances in efforts to arouse national self-consciousness.

During these decades the cultural development pressed for by the intelligentsia undoubtedly achieved considerable successes, even though it still only reached the urban lower middle-class elements of society. Reference could, however, be made to this cultural development, to its achievements, and to the separate identity of the nationality in question. Moreover, the demand could be raised that the nationalities' languages be granted equal status with Magyar.

The Croatians were in a more favourable position because they had their own feudal institutions—the counties and the provincial assembly *(sabor)*. Croatian deputies also attended the Hungarian Diet. Accordingly, it was the Croatian national movement that first put a political demand—namely the removal of Magyar authority in the areas inhabited by Croatians. Croatian leaders regarded their own people as too weak by themselves it was in the name of all the South Slav peoples that they launched the idea of "Illyrism". This advocated the establishment of a common South Slav State, naturally within the framework of the Habsburg Empire. In 1832, Count Janko Drašković, the Croatian Széchenyi, wrote a work *(Dissertatio iliti razgovor)* in which he also raised social issues.

Although to a lesser extent, the Serbs, too, were in a better position than the other nationalities living in Hungary. This was not just because of the religious autonomy they enjoyed. The fact that they lived for the most part in either the royal free towns or in the Military Frontier meant that the Magyarizing measures of the counties did not affect them. Prior to 1848, therefore, there were no serious conflicts between the Serbs and the Magyars. The prosperous Serbian merchants were also represented in the town magistracies in Southern Hungary, and, indeed, even in the county administrative bodies there. The 1840s witnessed the forming of *Omladina*, the youth organization of Serbian students enrolled at colleges and lycées, which played an important role in arousing political and linguistic consciousness. Major *Omladina* branches functioned in Pest, Pozsony and Szeged. It is interesting from the viewpoint of Serbian national development that, from the early nineteenth century onwards, large numbers of intellectuals and officials originating from Southern Hungary worked in the state apparatus and cultural institutions of the Serbian principality, which existed outside the borders of the Austrian Empire. This embryonic Serbian state was still part of the Ottoman Empire but enjoyed a large measure of autonomy.

On the whole, though, prior to 1848 the national movements were predominantly cultural in character. Their principal demand was the free use of their national languages.

The Bourgeois Revolution

The Outbreak of the Revolution
in March 1848

When in November 1847 Ferdinand V (Ferdinand of Austria) opened the Diet at Pozsony, no one would have imagined that this would be the last feudal Diet in Hungarian history.

Admittedly, those advocates of bourgeois development who appeared in Pozsony to attend the Diet now had higher hopes than ever before. They enjoyed a small, albeit undoubted, majority in the Lower Table and, for the first time, Lajos Kossuth was also present as the chief speaker for the opposition deputies there. His influence in the Lower Table could not be offset by anyone on the conservative side. Although the conservatives still possessed a majority in the Upper Table, here too there were powerful advocates of change, led by Count Lajos Batthyány, the chairman of the opposition party.

This was all to no avail, however. As the months passed the signs grew that once again the liberal opposition would fail to effect a solution to pressing issues, including the most pressing one—the need to abolish serfdom. The Diet of 1840 had made it possible for serfs to purchase their freedom and their plot of land but very few serfs had found the money to liberate themselves in this way. During the early months of the Diet not only conservative resistance stood in the way of tangible results. The fact that the liberals did not act consistently and in concert also played an important part.

Most of the middle nobles were contending with an oppressive shortage of money. These therefore had no alternative but to oppose the idea of liberating their serfs without compensation, at least until they were able to make good in some other way the losses that such a move would involve. In other words, an economic policy which encouraged domestic industry and which rapidly expanded the domestic market would have to be introduced *before* the general liberation of the serfs could take place. Such an economic policy would make the business opportunities of agricultural producers much more favourable, and would boost profitability.

However, the introduction of such a policy was inconceivable as long as the government of the country was not in the hands of the liberal opposition. For their part, the liberals could only contemplate the idea of making a bid for political power if the liberation of the serfs was carried out *first*, so that, in the ensuing power struggle, the peasant masses would side with them and not against them. This contradiction, implicit in the

114

landowners' circumstances had a paralyzing affect on even the best of liberal politicians.

This was the state of affairs until March 1848, when, suddenly, the situation underwent a complete change. In the course of the preceding weeks a wave of revolution had swept half of Europe and soon spilled over into the Habsburg Empire. On 13 March, Vienna became the scene of fervent revolutionary activity, as did Pest, Milan and Venice a few days later. This sudden turn of events created an opportunity for the Hungarian liberals to make an immediate bid for domestic political power, even without ensuring in advance the backing of the peasant masses. Kossuth and his associates availed themselves of this opportunity right away: on 15 March they dispatched a parliamentary delegation to Vienna which returned two days later. The Court had issued a document appointing Batthyány Prime Minister and had promised that the monarch was ready to sanction all legislation drafted by the Diet in the course of the following weeks.

The liberal leaders were, however, well aware that sooner or later they must take steps to win the goodwill of the peasantry. Accordingly, and as early as 15 March, the Diet expressed its support for the liberation of the serfs with the state treasury assuming the entire burden of compensating the landowners. This was a crucial statement to make, as the radicals rallying around Petőfi in Pest soon demonstrated. To exert public pressure on the Diet, they summed up their principal liberal demands in twelve points. These were worded more radically than ever before (e.g. although they demanded the liberation of the serfs, they made no mention at all of any compensation for the landlords). When news of the Vienna disturbances reached Pest, Petőfi and his group also embarked upon the path of revolutionary action. Within a few hours they mobilized the people of the city, as well as the tens of thousands of rural folk who had flooded in to attend the national fair on St Joseph's Day. Without prior permission from the censors, they had the *Twelve Points,* as well as Petőfi's *Nemzeti dal* (National Song) printed, thereby establishing the freedom of the press in a single day. They then forced the Municipal Council of Pest and the Viceregal Council—the supreme body responsible for public administration in Hungary—to grant their demands. Finally, they succeeded in obtaining the release from prison of Mihály Táncsics, the radical politician representing the peasants.

Upon receiving news of the developments in Pest, the Diet stated on 18 March that the serfs must be immediately freed from the obligation of carrying out their feudal services even though the compensation of landowners would not follow right away. Thus the Diet finally settled the peasant question. This extremely important decision at Pozsony was, however, only the first of many which followed each other in close succession and which created framework for transformation. Legislation enacted by the Diet included provision for putting the legislative body on a representational basis, for the creation of a responsible ministry for Hungary's total

115

political independence within the Empire, for the equality before the law of nobles and non-nobles, for the abolition of censorship, for the setting up of a National Guard, for general taxation, the abolition of Church tithes, for reunion of Hungary and Transylvania etc. By enacting such legislation, the Diet made it possible for the millions of people living in Hungary to embark upon the path of prosperity despite their numerous differences of interest and to join forces in creating a bourgeois society.

The Revolutionary Camp and the Counter-Revolution

After the closure of the last feudal Diet, most members of the Batthyány Government set to work convinced that the implementation of the March Laws would be fairly smooth. This was, however, too optimistic an assessment, primarily because it was based on the underestimation of the Crown's counter-revolutionary hopes. For although the Crown had been compelled to retreat in March, it still possessed formidable instruments of power (including the army), and was by no means willing to accept the March settlement as final.

Admittedly, by this time the anti-Habsburg camp in Hungary was far stronger than it had been at the end of the eighteenth century, and, for this reason, the country could no longer be pushed back into its former oppressed state. However, the anti-Habsburg group did not yet wield sufficient power in Hungary to ensure permanently that measure of independence for any government which it could undoubtedly guarantee in March. At the same time, the difficulties which were temporarily preoccupying the Habsburgs concealed, for the moment, the counter-revolutionary threat. From March onwards, the best units of the imperial army were tied down by the struggle for independence waged by the provinces of Northern Italy which were fighting for complete secession. Also, for quite a while, revolutionary mass movements also erupted in Vienna itself. Not even these difficulties made the Crown accept the changes in Hungary as permanent changes. On the contrary: a secret court conference stated as early as 26 March that, although the Crown temporarily had to present a friendly face to the Batthyány Government, as soon as "the time was right" it would have to clamp down on Hungary as well.

The Batthyány Government was already having to grapple with a growing number of domestic problems. The flaring up, again, of the peasant issue presented one of the greatest difficulties. For although initially the peasants were grateful for the abolition of serfdom, afterwards a growing number started to demand exemption from service obligations which were not strictly feudal, obligations incurred after use of land outside their

116

"urbarial" holdings. The demands were often accompanied by militant sabotage movements and attempts to seize land. On the other hand, the Government could make no further concessions to the peasantry that would place additional burdens on the state treasury. For it soon became obvious that, owing to inadequate financial resources, even the repayment of compensation for the abolished feudal services would take far longer than had been expected—something which rather dampened the spirits of the landed nobility. For the time being, therefore, the political leadership of the Revolution rigidly opposed peasant aspirations. This in turn had an adverse effect on the peasantry and again there developed a real possibility that the liberal nobles would sooner or later lose the sympathy and support of the peasant masses.

The rapid sharpening of the nationalities issue was, however, posing an even greater problem to the Government. Although most of the liberal and radical politicians welcomed the news of the March Laws (unlike the right wing of the movement), from the very beginning they demanded that full equality be granted to the country's non-Magyar population. For its part, the Government wished to comply with cultural and religious demands only, and rejected requests to recognize non-Magyars as the sons of separate nations and to grant official status to national languages in those counties where non-Magyars lived. As a result, those nationality politicians who had initially supported the Hungarian Revolution very soon turned against it. Since these politicians immediately gave their backing to the demands of the peasantry, that stratum quickly rallied behind them. This was especially true of those whose situation—for example the Croatian, Serbian or Roumanian border-guards—had not been improved as a result of the liberation of the serfs in March. Moreover, these peasants immediately started to voice national slogans which previously expressed only the sentiments of those politicians claiming to represent them. As a result, the situation deteriorated—rapidly and irrevocably. In June a Serbian uprising occurred in Southern Hungary and during the autumn months Croatians, Slovaks and Roumanians also rose in arms against the Hungarian Revolution.

The deteriorating nationalities situation compelled the Government to start organizing armed battalions for the protection of the revolutions as early as May. This was indeed a pressing need for this.

In the course of the summer the Habsburgs gradually consolidated their position: by early August the Imperial armies had succeeded in suppressing the war of independence in Lombardy. In the meantime, the Crown had also introduced parliamentary government in Austria and made a number of other concessions there. These moves had the effect of winning over the Austrian bourgeoisie which in March had played a revolutionary role and which had also been concerned at the possibility of Hungary's secession. In August, therefore, the Habsburgs were ready to take active steps against revolution in the eastern part of their Empire.

117

The Beginning of the War of Independence

By the middle of August even the most moderate politicians in the Batthyány Government realized that the country would soon be at a crossroads. Up to then only Petőfi and a few other radicals had stressed this. Hungary would either have to relinquish voluntarily the most important achievements of the March Revolution, or would have to undertake the difficult task of defending those achievements, by arms if necessary. However, even at this stage Batthyány made one last attempt at resolving the conflicts. The Prime Minister travelled to Vienna, intending to offer, as a last resort, a substantial curtailment of the Hungarian Government's independence.

In more concrete terms, Batthyány planned to propose the abolition of the separate Austrian and Hungarian defence and finance ministries and their subsequent replacement by common Austro-Hungarian ministries. This would undoubtedly have suited the relative equilibrium now existing between the opposing parties. However, such a compromise was now unacceptable to the Crown, just as, previously, during the promising March Days, it would have been rejected by the Hungarian liberals. Therefore, Batthyány had to return to Hungary on 10 September with his mission unaccomplished. The next days units of the Imperial army stationed in Croatia invaded Hungary. These were commanded by Lieutenant-General Jelačić, the Ban of Croatia, and an officer absolutely loyal to the dynasty.

The liberal nobility, who had been endured to emancipate the serfs only by the hope of achieving self-government for Hungary was now compelled to meet the challenge that presented itself. The Batthyány Government resigned. Power was transferred by the first representative parliament, which assembled in July, to the Committee for National Defence which was more left wing in character than Batthyány's administration. The Committee and its president, Kossuth, started to mobilize the population. Efforts were concentrated on the peasantry, which had become rather disenchanted during the previous months.

To the surprise of many, the mobilization was successful. Only four days after Jelačić invaded Hungary, Parliament passed a resolution abolishing the obligation of the peasants to pay tithes out of their own vineyard produce. It thereby created an unfounded hope amongst the peasantry that if they made a successful effort in defence of the Revolution, they would then receive further concessions. In addition, the fear spread among the people that, in the event of the Revolution's defeat, not only proceeding in the direction charted out by the March Laws would be endangered but also the emancipation of the serfs might be revoked. In addition to these influences, the Hungarian peasants were now also swayed by the zealous national slogans that had previously only affected the leading political stratum. These were suddenly made credible to the peasantry by the fact that the non-Magyars were the first to take up arms against the Hungarian Revolution.

In sum, the mobilization was successful and, on 29 September, the armed forces of the Revolution forced Jelačić to flee at Pákozd. In mid-December, however, the main forces of the Imperial army under the command of Field-Marshal Prince Windischgraetz set out against Hungary. On this occasion the enemy succeeded in capturing, not only Buda and Pest, but also Kolozsvár, in Transylvania. However, this was not the end of resistance: the Committee for National Defence which had moved to Debrecen, continued to organize additional battalions and soon its efforts brought about a dramatic change in the military situation. Under the command of General Bem, a Pole, the Revolutionary army in Transylvania launched a counter-offensive and, having inflicted heavy blows on the Imperial forces from Csucsa through Piski to Nagyszeben, liberated almost the entire territory of Transylvania in three months. At the end of March 1849 an offensive was launched by the main forces of the Hungarian army in the neighbourhood of Eger. Under General Görgei's command, these forces scored splendid victories at Hatvan, Tápióbicske and Isaszeg, and clearing the region between the Rivers Danube and Tisza. After this, they pressed further ahead along the left bank of the Danube, thereby liberating the castle of Komárom, which had been under siege since December and also compelled the enemy to pull back. The Imperial army evacuated Pest without any fighting and had retreated as far as the western frontier by the end of April.

It is, however, certain that, from this time on, the military successes of spring 1849 served not to consolidate the Revolution but, on the contrary, to undermine it. The fact that the Hungarian army succeeded in forcing the enemy to retreat but failed to inflict crushing defeat on him, made stalemate inevitable. Neither side could score a decisive military victory over the other and it followed from this that neither side could force its will on the other. Realization of this gradually convinced the nobility that it should give up the idea of continuing the struggle to protect all the achievements of the March revolution. Instead, it should try to reach a compromise agreement with the Habsburgs and one based on mutual concessions. Previously this view was confined to the right wing in Parliament and to Görgei. It was in vain, however, that the radicals and the more sober-minded section of the liberals warned that up to then Vienna had shown no readiness to negotiate. Attempts at reconciliation were, according to them, bound therefore to produce disappointing results. Most liberals were firmly convinced that the previous successes of the Hungarian army provided an adequate basis for initiating peace talks.

On 2 December 1848 the young Francis Joseph became Emperor of Austria and by early March he imposed an absolutist "constitution" on his peoples, in which he listed Hungary, Transylvania (to be detached from the former), Croatia and the Military Border among those lands of the "Austrian Empire" which only possessed a semblance of autonomy. In response to this arbitrary step the Hungarian Parliament adopted a rather ambiguous course of action. On 14 April it dethroned the House of Habsburg-Lotharingia at Kossuth's suggestion and, under pressure from the Debrecen masses, proclaiming Hungary a totally independent country. Kossuth was elected provisional head of state and given the title Governing-President. On the other hand, Kossuth was deprived of executive power and this was transferred to a new government led by Bertalan Szemere. This advocated the compromise with Vienna—the line of the majority of deputies in the Parliament.

The Fall of the Revolution

The most consistent and devoted advocates of transformation viewed the internal political changes of spring 1849 with growing concern. More and more arrived at the conclusion that another favourable development comparable to that of the previous September could only be hoped for if the Revolution succeeded in enlarging its popular base. The precondition for this, however, was the satisfactory settlement as soon as possible of the unresolved peasantry and nationalities problems. In the ranks of the peasants there were growing signs of disenchantment. This was quite understandable considering that during the months that had elapsed since September two things had become clear. The peasants came to realize that the Habsburgs (who did not wish to incur the wrath of millions of their number) would not, after all, revoke the liberation of the serfs. They also saw that the leadership of the Revolution, comprised as it was of nobles, did not intend to proceed along the path it appeared to be advocating when it did away with the grape tithe in September.

In the course of the spring months, therefore, a number of revolutionary radicals proposed that Parliament quickly encode the abolition of feudal service obligations which still constituted a serious burden for the peasantry. In May and June, Mihály Táncsics, who advocated the most radical steps in this respect, put forth the demand that any land over two thousand *hold* (863 hectares or 2,133 acres) and in the possession of landlords be appropriated and distributed amongst those in need. The majority of liberals, however, rejected any initiatives of this kind—even the most modest ones. The fact that the peasantry's demands remained entirely unsatisfied increasingly handicapped the Revolution.

An even more serious problem was the still unresolved nationalities issue. Indicative of the scope of this were the countless plundered towns and villages in the areas of mixed population and the thousands of civilians who had been ruthlessly killed. Shortly, therefore, not only the radicals but many liberals came to realize that it was necessary to reconcile the nationalities. In April representatives of the governing circles entered into negotiations with Iancu, the head of the Roumanian national movement's left wing and also the commander of the insurgent Roumanian army in Transylvania. In May, representatives held talks with Baron Kušlan, a prominent Croatian liberal, and, at the beginning of June, spoke with Stratimirović, the leader of the Serbian liberals. However, these negotiations were fruitless. In spring 1849 the Hungarian Government gave up its earlier policy and was ready to grant municipal autonomy to the inhabitants of non-Magyar areas but it continued in their refusal to recognize the non-Magyar population of Hungary as constituting separate nations. The liberal leaders of the Hungarian revolution completely disregarded the opinion expressed both by Albert Pálfi, one of the "March Youth", and by Count László Teleki, a leading opposition figure and by now a member of the radical left, that if the Hungarian Revolution wished to prevent a victory by the forces of reaction it would have to recognize the separate nationhood of the non-Magyar peoples and would have to grant them territorial autonomy as well. In this way, Hungary would become a confederated republic.

Finally, in July, the Hungarian Government changed its nationalities policy. Around the middle of that month, Bălcescu, the most open-minded leader of the 1848 revolution in Wallachia and now an exile in Hungary, came to an agreement with Kossuth. This recognized the separate nationhood of the Roumanian people and granted—much to the satisfaction of Iancu—self-government at county level for Roumanians in counties where they constituted the majority. At the end of the month Parliament extended the validity of these concessions to every national minority in the country. By doing so, it laid the foundations, at least in theory, for a sizeable change in the balance of power between the forces of Revolution and those of reaction.

By this time, though, the days of the Hungarian Revolution were numbered. The military developments of the spring made the Habsburgs realize that they could not defeat the Hungarians on their own. However, this realization did not, as the Hungarian "peace party" had expected, prompt Vienna to conclude a settlement on the basis of mutual concessions, but to seek help from "the gendarme of Europe" the Russian army. At Francis Joseph's request, a vast Russian force under the command of Field-Marshal Prince Paskievich invaded Hungary in June 1849. In co-operation with the Imperial troops, now under the command of General Baron Haynau, this force suppressed the Hungarian Revolution. Less than two months after his arrival, on 13 August 1849, the Prince could report to Tsar Nicholas I that "Hungary lies at the feet of Your Majesty...".

The Period of Absolutism and Dualism

The defeat of the Hungarian War of Independence in 1849 was followed by military occupation and bloody reprisals. The sentence passed on the Revolution by the Emperor and his Government was carried out by General Haynau. "I shall have the treasonous leaders hanged...", "I shall have the officers who went over to the Hungarians shot dead. I shall uproot the weed, I shall set an example to the whole of Europe of how rebels should be treated and of how order, peace and tranquillity should be ensured for a century", boasted Haynau. During the dark autumn days of 1849, one execution followed another. On 6 October, Count Lajos Batthyány, the Prime Minister in the first Hungarian government, faced a firing squad. Thirteen generals, veritable heroes, were executed at Arad. The names of Lajos Aulich, János Damjanich, Arisztid Dessewffy, Ernő Kiss, Károly Knezić, Vilmos Lázár, György Lahner, Károly Leiningen-Westerburg, József Nagy-Sándor, Ernő Pöltenberg, József Schweidel, Ignác Török, and Károly Vécsey all serve as a reminder and as proof that Magyars, Germans and Serbians fought together and died together for liberty.

The executions were followed by harsh sentences. Imprisonment in chains and under extremely bad conditions was meted out to many who had participated in the Revolution. Confiscation of property and forced enlistment were also common. In its blind desire for revenge, Habsburg tyranny went well beyond the limits within which some sort of reconciliation could have been possible. If the War of Independence created heroes, then retaliation created martyrs whom the nation never forgot.

After 1849 Hungary was divided up: Transylvania was detached and new provinces were formed under the names of the Serbian Voivodina and the Banat of Temes. The main body of the country was divided into five districts which were first administered by soldiers and subsequently by district főispáns (Lord Lieutenanats) and county chiefs, who were their subordinates. Archduke Albrecht, the Emperor's uncle was placed at the head of the occupied and incorporated country. Real power, was, however, in the hands of the Vienna-based Alexander Bach, the Minister of the Interior. Officials recruited by him, the army of the so-called "Bach Hussars", flooded the country.

Defeated Hungary was thus "pacified" by military occupation and complete—political, administrative and economic—incorporation into the Habsburg Empire. All of this was intended as punishment; Hungary was held to have forfeited her constitutional rights by having rebelled against the Habsburg dynasty. Her treatment was by no means exceptional: this was the sort dealt out to all the peoples of the Empire. It was a bitter ironical saying well-known in the age that the nationalities loyal to the Habsburg dynasty were rewarded with what the Magyars had been punished with: crude tyranny and deprivation of rights. Habsburg absolutism accepted only the emancipation of the serfs and equality before the law from among the reforms of 1848. It abolished every other achievement of constitutionalism and liberty. The national autonomy promised in the 1849 Olmütz constitution was not forthcoming. Indeed, the constitution itself was soon shelved and on the last day of 1851 unrestricted Imperial absolutism was proclaimed.

The young Emperor, Francis Joseph, was the son of the ambitious Duchess Sophie, and a pupil of Metternich and Schwarzenberg. He was raised in an autocratic atmosphere characterized by remoteness from the people and indifference to national aspirations as such. Francis Joseph considered his power to be sanctioned by God. As a ruler, he was mediocre, irresolute and cold, more of a dull bureaucrat, but nevertheless one who was industrious and dutiful. Relying on a large and apparently strong army, a well-disciplined force of civil servants, a strong gendarmerie, police and a whole host of spies and informers, he tried to consolidate a rigidly centralized empire. He wished to Germanize the national minorities within the Empire and to maintain the absolutist government he had introduced. In addition, he also confirmed the privileges of the Catholic Church in the Concordat of 1855.

The vast majority of Hungarians hated absolutism and opposed the Bach regime. Although the Court aristocracy remained on good terms with the Habsburgs, the staunchly conservative group of influential aristocratic politicians were dissatisfied with bureaucratic centralization, the shelving of Hungary's ancient constitution and the spurning of their services. Quite a few nobles, especially the impoverished, accepted office and served absolutism. There was an even larger group of brave patriots who strove to prepare an insurrection. In the years following the defeat, secret organizing started in Pest, Transdanubia, the Mátra area and especially in Transylvania. Counting on Kossuth and his associates, now living in exile, the conspirators were intended to stage an unexpected multinational uprising. However, Austrian authorities discovered these secret conspiracies and executed their leaders. Even harmless social events, such as balls, were banned.

The majority of well-to-do landowners and small gentry, however, chose the path of passive resistance. They retired to their estates, did not enter office, withheld their taxes and wherever possible deceived the authorities. "To despise absolutism, to know nothing of its slaves, as though they didn't live,"—this was the general slogan. "The Austrian should not feel at home anywhere... He should be and should remain alien in this land... Austrians should not be accepted socially... Let them be like plague victims who are shunned by everybody, of whom everybody is afraid."

Passive resistance meant not only retirement from public life, but also a lack of ambition as far as modernization and embourgeoisment were concerned. As a policy, passive resistance was therefore inadequate, considering the grave conditions created by absolutism. The great part of the nation continued to nurture the seed sown by the War of Independence. During 1857, the poet János Arany wrote *A walesi bárdok* (The Bards of Wales). In this, he alludes to a visit by Francis Joseph to Hungary.

> Around him silence which way he went
> In his Welsh lands over the border.

"The Nation shall Endure"

Haynau and Bach failed to ensure "peace" for even a decade. Absolutism proved to be a weak, alien and anachronistic edifice. Its internal base was extremely narrow and rested, leaving aside the obedient bureaucrats and the Court aristocracy, on arms only. However, such a creation was bound to be short-lived in contemporary Europe, where liberal parliamentarism had now already spread and where plans to unify Italy and Germany had implications for the very survival of the Habsburg Empire.

The first blow came from without. On 24 June 1859 Austria was seriously defeated at Solferino by Italian and French troops. Austria lost Lombardy which subsequently went to Piedmont, and the equilibrium of the Habsburg Empire was disturbed. In the wake of defeat, latent discontent and resistance erupted with great force in Hungary and in other provinces. Francis Joseph tried to stem the tide of discontent by sacking Bach, by removing Archduke Albrecht and by promising concessions. These moves did not placate the population, and resistance erupted violently in Hungary. In 1860, the anniversary of the Revolution, 15 March was celebrated for the first time. Students clashed with police.

In this situation the old conservatives, the opposition element nearest to the Habsburg, came out with plans for a moderate new settlement. More importantly, István Széchenyi made his voice heard once more. Having suffered a nervous breakdown, in September 1848 Széchenyi had gone into a mental hospital in Döbling, near Vienna. Recovering from his condition, he was horrified to see the damage done by a decade of absolutism, and the sad fate of his country. When, in 1857, Bach boasted in an anonymous pamphlet about the achievements of "pacification" in Hungary, Széchenyi put pen to paper again. Published in London in 1857, his ruthlessly accurate and ironical critique of absolutism dispelled any notions of its "civilizing" effects. The Viennese police did not overlook Széchenyi's renewed public activity. On 2 March 1860 they searched his quarters at Döbling and threatened him. On 8 April an extremely distressed Széchenyi committed suicide. His death was followed by national mourning and another wave of national resistance.

In the memorable summer of 1860, when Garibaldi's redshirts liberated Southern Italy and when Hungarian patriots already imagined Kossuth's and Garibaldi's legions along the banks of the Danube and Tisza rivers, Francis Joseph was forced to make major concessions. In the October Diploma, which was based on the plan of the conservatives, he granted a constitution to his peoples. In this he attempted to temper absolutist rule with a certain measure of constitutionalism. The October Diploma set up an Imperial Council with a very restricted sphere of authority and with a number of appointed members. The Emperor wished moderate centralism by promoting limited provincial autonomy and to placate the Magyars by partially restoring the pre-1848 system. This attempt was, however, doomed to failure. By far the greatest section of the Hungarian public wanted more than this, demanding the restoration of the 1848 achievements. At the county meetings and during the re-election campaigns of officials this sentiment received expression.

The Austrian bourgeoisie was not satisfied with the October Diploma either. It demanded more constitutionalism but, at the same time, stronger centralization as well. The February Patent was, accordingly issued in February 1861. This increased the size and sphere of authority of the Imperial Council but simultaneously strengthened centralization as well. The new constitution triggered off even greater protest in Hungary, especially at the time of the national elections which took place in early spring.

From the Diet which convened on 6 April 1861 Vienna expected acceptance of the new constitution and the election of deputies to the Imperial Council. However, the Diet was imbued with the spirit of 1848. Francis Joseph had not been crowned King of Hungary and the majority of deputies did not recognize him as the country's legitimate sovereign. They accordingly wished to reject the Emperor's rescript by means of a simple resolution. This party faction was led by László Teleki, an outstanding politician and friend of Kossuth. (Teleki had, in fact, been captured abroad when he met his lover at Dresden but had been released in Hungary.) The group rallying around Ferenc Deák recognized Francis Joseph as the *de facto* ruler and wanted to respond to the rescript with a traditional address. In the days leading up to the voting, Teleki committed suicide. Some of his followers interpreted this as a symbolic warning that they should give their support to the address idea, which left open the way for a compromise.

Deák's two addresses were legal and political masterpieces in defence of the 1848 constitution. "Your Highness", one of them ran, "as King of Hungary... [You] cannot abolish any part of our sanctioned law arbitrarily, without the country's consent." The inviolability of Hungary's independence and constitution was closely connected with the recognition of the right of succession. "We cannot sacrifice the country's ... constitutional independence... to any consideration or any interests, and we insist on it as the fundamental condition of our national existence."

The full restoration of the 1848 achievements was unacceptable for Vienna, which insisted on her policy of integration. The Diet was dissolved in August 1861 and absolutist government restored. Solemnly remonstrating against the coercion and the breach of legality which had taken place, the deputies broke up peacefully. Legal resistance did not develop into revolutionary insurrection. Unfavourable developments internationally also played their part in this. Italy did not launch a new war against Austria and Hungary could not count on foreign assistance. Kossuth, who organized opposition abroad, and who led the Hungarian exiles, had himself recommended that negotiations be rejected. At the same time, the landed nobility also feared the peasant movements which strengthened at the time of reconsidering vassal duties. It was also worried by the reorganized national movements of the non-Magyar peoples and growing demands for autonomy. The leading stratum which organized Hungarian resistance became isolated both inside and outside the country.

The landed nobles therefore indeed had no choice but to return to passive resistance and to playing a waiting game. Again, it was Deák who provided guidance in a warning he delivered when the Diet was dissolved: "If need be, the nation shall endure..., for that which force and power take away, time and good fortune may restore, but that which the nation... itself relinquishes, to retrieve is always difficult and always uncertain."

Lajos Kossuth in Exile

After the defeat of the War of Independence, the Ottoman Government offered refuge to Kossuth and several thousands of his followers. Protection was, however, more personal than political. Kossuth and a small group of his supporters were first settled in Sumla, in what was afterwards Bulgaria. Later, in spring 1850, Kossuth was sent to Kütahya in Asia Minor following demands for his extradition by the Russian and Austrian governments. Almost completely isolated from the outside world, Kossuth worked on the organization of a new uprising and a new democratic constitution. Finally, in September 1851, the American fregate "Mississippi" freed him from banishment—a gesture symbolic of European and American public sympathy.

The hero of popular liberty was given a rapturous welcome in Italian, French and English ports. His arrival in London, Manchester and Birmingham occasioned tremendous support to be shown. His tour of the United States, between December 1851 and July 1852, brought even more

126

celebration and admiration. At the memorable New York, Philadelphia and Boston receptions Kossuth was called "The Demosthenes of the Modern Age", "The Hungarian George Washington" and "The Greatest Man since Jesus Christ". In the figures of Washington and Kossuth the people saw the champions of Western and Eastern liberty respectively. At the beginning of January 1852, the Senate and the House of Representatives received Kossuth, the first Hungarian to be honoured in this way. In a Ciceronian speech to the Congress, Kossuth pleaded for active support of the United States in the attainment of Hungarian liberty. This bold dream could not be realized at this time, however, and the White House offered Kossuth no more than courteous words. Nonetheless, during his six-month trip through America, Kossuth won enormous popularity and substantial financial support.

In his early years of exile Kossuth regarded the reorganizing of the uprising and the continuation of the War of Independence as the main priorities. He settled in London and maintained close contact with Mazzini and the other leading European revolutionaries. From London he controlled secret conspiracies in Hungary. He did not realize—contemporaries rarely see at once changes in the historical climate—that the time for revolutions and uprisings was over for many years. Only a string of failures and serious losses could make him realize that he must wait for the right moment, the moment when Habsburg absolutism was shaken both at home and abroad. This came at the end of the 1850s, when the Franco–Austrian War erupted in Northern Italy. This conflict filled exiled Hungarian politicians with new enthusiasm. In 1859 Kossuth, László Teleki and György Klapka formed the Hungarian National Directorate, a kind of a government-in-exile . Kossuth concluded an agreement with Emperor Napoleon III of France by which, in exchange for French support, they would organize a Hungarian legion in Italy. Kossuth, Teleki and Klapka would then signal for an uprising in Hungary, but only when French and Piedmontese armies actually appeared on the country's soil. However, after two important French victories (Magenta and Solferino), the war suddenly ended—without the unification of Italy and without assistance being given to Hungary, Italy was now in ferment. Kossuth therefore moved first to Genoa and finally to Turin to be near the scene of decisive events.

Large numbers of Hungarian officers and soldiers participated in Garibaldi's campaign to liberate Southern Italy in 1860. They fought courageously against the Neapolitan troops in defence of Palermo and the skirmishes outside Naples. István Türr was promoted to the rank of general and became one of Garibaldi's deputies. At the same time Kossuth concluded a military alliance with Cavour, the Piedmontese premier who was leading the drive to unify Italy. In the summer of 1860, external help appeared to be a realistic proposition. Moreover, revolutionary organizing and resistance were, under Kossuth's supervision, making considerable progress in Hungary. The following year, however, brought disappointment. The war against Austria failed to materialize, Cavour died and in the end the Hungarian Legion was disbanded.

During the third phase of his activities in exile, Kossuth invested his hopes not in the promises of the Great Powers, but in the association of the smaller Danubian peoples. After Klapka, Teleki and others had conducted talks with Roumanian and Serbian politicians, in 1862 Kossuth published his plan for a Danubian Confederation. Under this, Roumania, Serbia, Croatia and Hungary would establish a confederation in which foreign affairs, defence and the economic matters would constitute common affairs. A confederate council would be responsible for these and would be accountable to a common parliament. "Unity, understanding and fraternity among Magyars, Slavs and Roumanians—this is my most fervent desire, my most sincere advice. This offers a happy future for all of these peoples." However, under the international and domestic political conditions then prevailing, the fine plan was incapable of implementation.

Since Kossuth's utopia did not offer a realistic alternative, the majority of Hungarian leaders gradually came to accept the idea of reconciliation with Austria on the basis of a compromise agreement.

In 1866, Prussia challenged Austria for hegemony in German affairs. The early and impressive victories of the Prussian army raised hopes in Kossuth of military assistance from Prussia and hopes of Austria's disintegration. After the conclusion of peace, however, he devoted all his energies to prevent a compromise between Austria and Hungary. In a series of studies, articles and letters Kossuth argued that for Hungary to link her fate with a Habsburg Empire doomed to extinction would be tantamount to national suicide. "Hungary shall be the stake at which the unrelenting logic of history will burn the Austrian eagle." Even at the last moment, in May 1867, Kossuth entreated his one-time friend, Ferenc Deák, to reconsider and not to commit the country to an arrangement which offered no prospects for a future.

After the Compromise of 1867 Kossuth gradually retired from active politics. He delved into botany and astronomy, arranged his papers, and consoled himself with history. Kossuth's once-fervent desire to accomplish things vanished on the southern slopes of the Alps and on the shores of the Ligurian Sea. There he searched for thyme and cudweed. From time to time, Kossuth spoke out for independence and liberty. "The hand of the clock does not regulate but indicates the passage of time", he said. "My name is a clock hand, it indicates the time that shall come... if fate holds a future at all for the Hungarian nation. That future is a free homeland for the free citizens of Hungary."

After forty-five years in exile Kossuth died in Turin on 20 March 1894. His burial turned into a great national demonstration, indicative of the contemporary trend.

The Compromise

Although the revolutions of 1848 were defeated in Central Europe, the revolutionary process forged ahead irresistibly. Two things gradually became clear. The first was that the consolidation of absolutism, which blocked the path to all progress, was impossible and the second that its overthrow by means of revolution was similarly unlikely. This was borne out by the unification process then taking place under dynastic leadership first in Italy and afterwards in Germany. Especially important, though, was the Russian Tsar's suppression of the Polish revolutionary uprising of 1863 while a liberal and sympathetic Europe merely looked on. Austria, too, felt the need for change, but neither the semi-constitutionalism introduced in the western part of the Empire, nor the feeble attempts to win over the "reliable" nationalities produced the desired result. Austria became increasingly isolated internationally, and her credit and finances fell into disarray. Moreover, Hungary, the resisting "province", could in no way be integrated into the Imperial edifice. Slowly, the idea established itself in Viennese political circles that some sort of agreement must be reached with the Hungarians if the Empire was to remain intact.

The willingness to consider a compromise also grew amongst the ranks of Hungarian political leadership, the landed class and the bourgeoisie. The fate of Poland served as a serious warning, as did the menacing possibility of German unification. A Germany united under Prussian leadership and directed by Otto von Bismarck could swallow up the western half of the Empire. In such an event Hungary would be caught up between two great powers, Germany and Russia. The prominent politicians of the age were very aware of Hungary's geographical position. The country could be crushed between Germany and Russia, the former pursuing its "Drang nach Osten" policy and the latter expanding westwards under the banner of "Pan-Slavism". Deák and his supporters believed that it was not only impossible to overthrow the Habsburg Empire given the circumstances, but that such a development was not even desirable. It was preferable to remain within the framework of a constitutional Monarchy reaching agreement with its ruler, rather than to fall prey to two expansionist powers as an independent, but weak, state.

In Turin, the exiled Kossuth drew radically different conclusions from the balance of power at this time. His view was that the Magyars should reach a compromise with the national minorities rather than with the Great Powers or the Habsburgs. He formulated his conception in a draft for a Danubian Confederation, a draft previously mentioned. Although ideologically important, this plan was both utopian and unfeasible at the time. Not only was it opposed by the Great Powers, but even those whom it most directly concerned lacked enthusiasm. Hungarian public opinion, and even most of Kossuth's supporters, rejected it.

129

Meanwhile, the economic situation acquired importance. The markets opened up as a result of railway construction and the desire to participate in the Great European boom also prompted the leading stratum to opt for an agreement. Certain aspects of the settlement reached between Austria and the national minorities, such as the winning of the Roumanians in Transylvania, induced the political leadership to seek such a solution. The liberals who rallied around Deák in Hungary therefore welcomed initiatives for a compromise which came from Austrian liberal deputies and then from the Court itself. During the several months of secret negotiations, Deák formulated the conditions of such an agreement, which at a suitable moment, at Easter 1865, he made public in his famous article. If Vienna would recognize the territorial unity of Hungary, recognize the 1848 laws and appoint a responsible Hungarian government, he was willing to concede that foreign affairs and defence questions were common to both Austria and Hungary and would be handled accordingly.

As a sign of goodwill, Francis Joseph suspended the February Constitution of 1861 and convened the Hungarian Diet for the end of 1865. It was while the Diet was assembled that war broke out between Austria and Prussia in June 1866. Bismarck intended to use Prussian troops to drive Austria out of Germany before unifying that area and subordinating it to Berlin. On 3 July, Austria suffered a grave defeat at Sadowa (Königgrätz) and was forced to make peace on Bismarck's terms.

The defeat at Sadowa was of decisive importance from the point of view of the Habsburg Empire. Deeply shaken, it could now only restore its equilibrium and authority by reaching agreement with Hungary. Finally, after much wrangling and numerous modifications, Deák's proposals were accepted. The Empire was to be transformed into a dualist state with two centres, Vienna and Budapest. Common foreign and defence ministries were to be set up, as well as a common finance ministry to defray their expenses. Two separate governments and parliaments were also to come into being. The Compromise (*Ausgleich*) was born. Common affairs would be supervised by delegations seconded by the two parliaments. The tariff and commercial alliance between Austria and Hungary, as well as the charter of the Empire's bank, were to be reviewed by both governments and both parliaments every ten years. The Austrian Empire would now become the Austro–Hungarian Empire.

On 17 February 1867 Francis Joseph appointed a responsible Hungarian government headed by Count Gyula Andrássy, the former exile condemned to death in absentia in 1851. After lengthy debates, on 29 May Parliament passed the Compromise bill into law, and with a large majority. Kossuth's numerous warnings were in vain. He regarded the Compromise as "the death of the nation". Hungary would become attached "to the tow-line of alien interests". In May 1867, Kossuth wrote in his famous *Cassandra letter* that the Compromise would turn Hungary's neighbours into her enemies and would "make impossible the satisfactory solution of the nationalities question...". Kossuth added, ominously, that "...European complications which clearly threaten would make our country the target of rival ambitions".

The leading stratum, together with the majority of the middle class, did not listen to Kossuth. They welcomed the Compromise and the reconciliation it brought about. On 8 June, Francis Joseph and his wife Elizabeth, herself sympathetic to the Hungarians, were crowned with great pomp in the presence of numerous aristocrats and prelates at the Matthias Church in Pest-Buda. By a curious irony of history it was Andrássy, the hussar colonel sentenced to death in 1851, who placed the Hungarian Crown on the head of Francis Joseph. The latter had signed Andrássy's death warrant and was now dressed in the uniform of a hussar general. The celebrations were extensive.

Austria–Hungary—An Empire of Contradictions

The Austro–Hungarian Empire was vast: it spread from the Swiss Alps to the snow-capped mountains of Brassó, from the Dalmatian coast to the Polish Carpathians, indeed even beyond, to the onion-shaped domes of Lemberg. Its area exceeded 600,000 square kilometres and its population was 35 millions at the time of the Compromise and 50 million when the First World War broke out. As regards size and population it was the third biggest power in Europe but in political influence it ranked either fifth or sixth. In Austria–Hungary public institutions were "imperial", "royal", or "imperial and royal". In German this last phrase was *kaiserlich und königlich,* abbreviated to *k.u.k.* Robert Musil, a prominent writer on the Austro–Hungarian Empire, spoke of 'Kakania' and a historian who knew it well, Heinrich Benedikt called it "the empire of contradictions".

On the surface, Austria–Hungary appeared to be a constitutional state. There could be discerned within its territory modest signs of progress, good roads, attractive cities, schools and barracks, a bureaucratic apparatus to keep watch over its citizens and a large army on which vast sums of money were lavished but which nevertheless remained the weakest among those of the European Powers. The Empire embraced eleven nationalities: within its closed frontiers, Germans, Magyars, Czechs, Slovaks, Poles, Ukrainians, Roumanians, Serbs, Croatians, Slovenes, Italians and a dozen other small ethnic groups, including Yiddish-speaking Jews, multilingual gypsies, Armenians, Bulgarians and Serbo-Croatian Muslims. The Austro–Hungarian Empire was indeed a modern Babel of peoples and the more educated these peoples became, the less they understood each other.

131

The State was officially called the Austro–Hungarian Monarchy, although it was commonly referred to as Austria, a practice the Hungarians continually complained about. They held that the Empire was the alliance of two independent states in which a united Hungary stood opposed to "His Majesty's other countries". These other countries, admittedly, did not have a collective name. They were not referred to as "Austria" because the Czechs, Poles and Southern Slavs would have resented this. However, the leading Austrian circles did not use this term either, as this would have implied giving up the idea of a united empire. Thus, Cis-Leithania, the non-Hungarian part of the Empire, was named "kingdoms and provinces represented in the Imperial Council". The two parts matched each other, said Musil, "like a red, white and green coat matched black and yellow trousers; the coat was all right on its own, the trousers however were only half of a black and yellow suit torn apart in 1867". With some sarcasm we could say that this empire was the only creation in world history that "died of its ineffability".

The Empire thus consisted of two states, with two governments, two parliaments and two separate public administration systems. The two halves of the Empire often frustrated each other's aims and paralyzed each other's measures, although they could not interfere in each other's "internal affairs". The unity of the Empire was represented by its ruler, Francis Joseph, and the common ministers—the ministers of foreign relations, defence and finance. Not burdened by too many duties, these ministers also governed Bosnia-Herzegovina after its occupation in 1878. The common ministers did not constitute a government, they were only responsible for their own portfolios, and primarily to the Emperor-King. The separate "Austrian" and Hungarian governments had little influence over foreign affairs, and still less over the army. The common ministers could not exert any constitutional influence over internal affairs in either half of the Empire. The final decision on important matters always rested with Francis Joseph, commander of the army, and appointments remained his prerogatives. Despite heated public debate the Habsburg dynasty for the most part preserved its former absolutist power. For although Austria–Hungary had a liberal constitution, it was "governed in a clerical spirit". Although "every citizen was equal before the law, not everyone counted as a citizen". Parliament made ample use of its liberty and because of this it remained closed for most of the time. By declaring a state of emergency, it was possible to govern by decree. However, "every time absolutism was acclaimed, the Crown ordered the reinstatement of constitutional government".

Serious antagonisms were placing the Empire's socio-economic structure under growing strain. Despite the flourishing of capitalism, a powerful aristocracy survived. Leading aristocrats possessed landed estates the size of half a county and had an army of inspectors and farm servants to run them. The material and spiritual assets of the Catholic Church also remained intact, as did its political influence.

132

In Hungary, public administration continued to be very much the preserve of the nobility. The impressive cities of Vienna, Budapest and Prague, with their famous universities, clinics, stores, motor-cars and railway transport contrasted sharply with the results of centuries of backwardness and oppression in rural Galicia, the Bukovina, Upper Hungary, Transylvania and Dalmatia. The countryside contained millions of landless destitute people, large numbers of whom were compelled to emigrate.

The nationalities issue was at the root of most antagonisms within the Austro–Hungarian Empire. Of the two ruling nations, the Austro–Germans were in the better position and Austria was economically superior to Hungary. Fifteen provinces of Austria enjoyed a certain degree of autonomy. The Poles had the most privileges, while the Czechs were the best off materially, although they, too, were subordinated to Austrian hegemony. In 1868 the Hungarian ruling class reached agreement with Croatia. Under this, the Croatians were granted a large measure of autonomy and a parliament. The other nationalities had even fewer privileges and now became subject to increased political and cultural oppression. The structure of the Austro–Hungarian Empire was thus characterized, in addition to the survival of the bastions of absolutism and feudalism, by a system of hierarchical dependence amongst the nationalities. This facilitated the application of the "divide and rule" principle of government. Nonetheless, tensions generated by national tensions undermined the apparently solid edifice of the Dual Monarchy from the very beginning.

At the time of the Compromise, and afterwards as well, the plan for a confederative settlement, which would have suited the national structure, was also raised. In 1871, the Hohenwart Government drafted a plan for a Czech compromise. Under this, Bohemia would have been granted equal status with Austria and Hungary in a trialistic arrangement. The scheme was, however, opposed by Austrian leading circles, Hungarian leading circles and the German Chancellor, Bismarck. Nothing came of the proposals.

This multi-national and many-faceted empire could have been the experimental laboratory of history had not its leaders, who insisted on national and class oppression, frustrated every attempt at serious change. It was their intransigence which eventually brought about the collapse of the entire system.

A Hungarian Minister at the Ballhausplatz

Count Gyula Andrássy was the descendant of a prominent aristocratic family and was fortune's darling. He was just twenty-five when the Revolution of 1848 appointed him to head Zemplén county. He participated in the War of Independence and was present at the Battle of Schwechat. Andrássy was promoted colonel when Kossuth sent him to Constantinople on a diplomatic mission. Having been forced into exile, he spent a number of years in Paris where he lived affluently and in the limelight. The fact that he had been hanged in effigy in 1851 made Andrássy even more appealing in high society. This handsome aristocrat, who was a brave soldier, a courageous horseman, and a captivatingly witty cosmopolitan, became popular everywhere he appeared. His rich family eventually procured him an amnesty from the Emperor, making his return home a possibility.

In 1858, Andrássy came back to Hungary and in the years of constitutional experimentation he entered public life as an advocate of compromise and as a supporter of Deák. He enchanted his associates, the Imperial couple, and even Deák himself with his appealing manners and diplomatic skills. It was not without reason that Deák recommended Andrássy for the post of prime minister. It was in him that Deák saw "the providential statesman given us by the Grace of God". What exactly did Deák mean by "providential"? Andrássy was certainly a skilful politician and diplomat, although many contemporaries considered him a man of remarkable talent rather than a genius. Certainly, he owed a great deal to his family background, his rank and his patriotic past. However, Andrássy's greatest asset was that he was able to win the confidence and sympathy of the Imperial couple who lived in the cold atmosphere of the Hofburg. One could also describe as providential the qualities which awakened a deep affection in the young Queen towards Kossuth's one-time officer, this "fine hanged man". The day after Austria's defeat at Sadowa, Elizabeth recommended to Francis Joseph that he appoint Andrássy Foreign Minister, or at least Hungary's Minister, "for what is now most needed is that the country calm down".

As head of the Government, Andrássy lived up to the highest expectations. He achieved territorial unity for the country, reincorporated Transylvania and the Military Frontier and set up a separate Hungarian army. The establishment of the army was a great achievement twenty years after the War of Independence, even though it differed vastly from its predecessor of 1848–49. Insignia and banners were changed, but its equipment and combat-readiness were greatly inferior to those of the "common" Imperial and Royal Army. The Andrássy Government hammered out the compromise with Croatia and organized public administration together with a judiciary. It also gave financial assistance for the promotion of railway building and for the development of the economy.

Important legislation is linked with the name of the scholar and writer Baron József Eötvös. The Nationalities Act of 1868 declared that, politically, Hungary's citizens belonged to the "united Magyar nation". That is to say, it did not recognize the national existence and right to autonomy of the non-Magyar peoples. Yet this act was a liberal piece of legislation by contemporary standards. It guaranteed the nationalities free use of the mother tongue at the lower levels of litigation, public administration and education. It also ensured their freedom to organize culturally and politic-ally. The Public Education Act of the same year made elementary schooling compulsory and placed it under state supervision. However, the Act did not make any changes in the nationalities' right to education in the mother tongue, or in their right to use their own languages.

At the same time the Government suppressed the peasant movements on the Great Plain and in Transdanubia. Worker leaders who had demon-strated in favour of the Paris Commune (1871) were put on trial, charged with treason. The Government also dissolved circles of democrats, disci-plined those army associations which adhered to the spirit of 1848 and even wanted to forbid in public life any praise of the exiled Kossuth. It helped to strengthen a liberal system that protected the interests of the landowners and the upper middle class and, by doing so, helped to consolidate the Austro–Hungarian Empire.

In 1871, the German Empire was proclaimed in the Hall of Mirrors at Versailles. German unity posed something of a threat to Austria–Hungary and in this sensitive situation Francis Joseph made Andrássy the Mon-archy's Foreign Minister. Formerly, Andrássy's appointment was attri-buted to his pro-German stance. The facts, however, indicate that An-drássy did not like Bismarck at all during the early 1870s. The Hungarian minister, who nurtured the foreign policy tradition of 1848, regarded tsarist Russia to be the principal enemy. At first, Andrássy considered that his main task was to push Russia into the background. Bismarck, on the other hand, wished to bring her into European affairs.

Andrássy initially tried to win England as an ally, but failed. Having comprehended, however, the realities of the European balance of power, he decided that a different policy was necessary. Alliance between the emperors of Russia, Germany and Austria, all bastions of the conservative order—represented the only guarantee of the Monarchy's security. András-sy moved to the Foreign Ministry in Vienna and followed in the footsteps of Metternich and Beust. He realized more quickly than his predecessors that there was nothing for Austria–Hungary in the West. Her nationalities policy and her expansionist ambitions all pointed towards the Balkans.

Originally, Andrássy had not opposed the aspirations of the small Balkan peoples for autonomy, provided these aspirations did not undermine the *status quo* and lead to Russian supremacy in the area. One by one the peoples of the Balkans now rebelled against Ottoman tyranny and, in spring 1877, Russia took up arms to help them.

In the Russo–Turkish War of that year the Sultan's crumbling empire suffered total defeat. By the Treaty of San Stefano (1878) Russia acquired Bessarabia and most of the Caucasus. Bulgaria acquired not only full independence but also an Aegean coastline. Andrássy's hour then struck: he succeeded in creating a united front of England, Germany and France, all of whom were unhappy at the prospect of excessive Russian influence in Southeast Europe.

Andrássy scored his biggest success at the Congress of Berlin in 1878. The Great Powers cut down Russia's annexations and reduced Russian influence in the Balkans. To counter that which remained, they commissioned Austria–Hungary to occupy Bosnia and Herzegovina, two Southern Slav provinces formerly under Turkish rule. These territories were the Empire's first territorial gains since 1815, and even though their actual occupation was accomplished only after serious losses and considerable fighting, they did represent a conquest. Andrássy was quick to capitalize on the favourable turn of events and to consolidate the Monarchy's international position. In 1879 he concluded a defensive military alliance with the Germans. Under this, the Dual Alliance, as it became known, Germany was obliged to render military assistance to Austria–Hungary in the event of a Russian attack on the latter.

Thus, Andrássy partially—with modest success—accomplished his foreign policy goals to counter-balance Russian expansion in Southeast Europe. The price he had to pay was rather high. Hungarian public opinion was averse to the occupation. Anti-Slav sentiment had obliterated memories of the one-time Ottoman occupation of Hungary and gave rise to a wave of sympathy for Turkey, which permeated even the House of Deputies. On the other hand, the Dual Alliance was not looked on favourably by ruling circles in Vienna and this feeling of antipathy found its way to the Burg as well. Popularity at the bottom and confidence at the top, ebbed.

Andrássy signed the German treaty on 7 October 1879. Francis Joseph dismissed him the following day.

"Let Sleeping Dogs Lie"

Hardly had the "cold-hearted man", the Imperial administrator of Bihar county died, his sons swore an oath to revolution and the War of Independence. The Baradlay family of Mór Jókai's gripping novel was modelled on the real-life Tiszas. The elder son, László Tisza, died on the battlefield at Mór, while the younger son, Kálmán, who had a poorer physique, served the revolutionary government to the very end. He endured the vicissitudes of exile, joined the great remonstrations against the persecution of Protestants and participated in the struggles to re-establish constitutionalism. Nobody would have thought that this gaunt, nondescript Calvinist, whose spectacles and full beard made him look much older than he was, would one day become a party leader.

Tisza owed his position in politics to a number of misfortunes and national afflictions. After his uncle, László Teleki, committed suicide, Tisza became a leader of the opposition at the Diet of 1861 and subsequently a leader of the national resistance. He did not join Deák after the conclusion of the Compromise, regarding the concessions it involved as too many, and their resulting unpopularity too great. "If we accept the Compromise", he said in March 1867, "I believe that we shall be happier and shall have fewer difficulties. We, who live in our country today, shall enjoy greater liberty, but we ourselves will have made the re-establishment of a legitimate independent Hungary impossible." Tisza was not against the Compromise itself, but, rather, the terms under which it was agreed. As the leader of the left-centre faction in Parliament, Tisza issued a party programme, the "Bihar Points", in 1868. In these he called for the abolition of the delegations and the common ministries. He also demanded the establishment of an independent army, together with entirely independent finances and commerce for Hungary.

Tisza and his party did not remain on the opposition benches for long. Growing internal opposition in the years following the Compromise, the demands of the nationalities for equality, threatening developments in the Balkans, continual deficit and serious financial difficulties—all undermined the governing Deák Party. Things were made worse by the fact that this was not a true political party, rather an alliance of factions which shared political power. After Andrássy's move to Vienna, Eötvös's early death (1871) and the retirement of the ailing Deák, the party started to disintegrate. When the situation became serious enough to undermine the entire dualist system, Tisza came to the rescue. His party merged with the Government party in spring 1875 and Tisza soon became Prime Minister. Tisza was accused by contemporaries of having "shelved the Bihar Points" and of having become a renegade. Tisza rejected these charges, saying that it was his patriotic duty to take control of the country at a time of crisis. There was some truth in what his opponents said, but Tisza's response was more than an attempt at self-justification. To Tisza, "country" meant the estates of the landed nobility and "patriotic duty" signified the protection of the Dualist system which could best preserve the existing political order and which, according to Tisza, also ensured the survival of the Hungarian people.

As Prime Minister (1875–90) Tisza showed excellent tactical skill in surviving crises and in avoiding those pitfalls that would jeopardize the Dualist system. At considerable sacrifice to the country, he put state finances in order and renewed the Compromise in 1877 and 1887. Despite strong public opposition, he also supported the occupation of Bosnia-Herzegovina. How could he do all this in a multi-national country where the population was predominantly made up of peasants and where the inhabitants were strongly opposed to the Government?

Kálmán Tisza's name is linked with the establishment of the political system of the dualist state. The franchise had been extremely limited ever since the first settlement in 1848 and was dependent on property and educational qualifications. Yet, as far as the system was concerned, the number of peasants and lower middle class people entitled to vote was too high. To prevent supporters of the opposition from being elected to Parliament, Tisza cleverly altered constituency boundaries, introducing "electoral geometry" to favour the Government. Canvassing in return for public administration posts, the bribing of voters, corruption, getting people drunk and intimidation were all features of the electoral process. By the time the House of Deputies convened, the Government party always had a majority among the 413 members. However, it was not enough that the Government party could outnumber all the others in the Lower House. Government deputies had to be moulded into an obedient squad. Tisza knew how to do this. By means of kind words and strict discipline, appointments and patronage generally, Tisza put the Government party under obligation to him. Deputies followed their leader, "Tisza General", like bodyguards: contemporaries referred to them as "Mamelukes" for this very reason. In addition, Tisza gave jobs to sons of the impoverished landed nobility, employing them at State, county and municipal level in an ever-expanding public administration system. By demanding a certain degree of professionalism from these employees, he strengthened public administration and therefore the Government. In the provinces, Tisza set up the gendarmerie and established a police force in the capital.

What, then, was the purpose of parliamentarianism? Why was there such emphasis on constitutionalism? Would not absolutism have been a more appropriate political form? The answer is that constitutionalism was quintessential in Austro–Hungarian dualism, and the product of the struggle against Habsburg absolutism. Constitutionalism protected Hungary against Vienna and at the same time legalized the domination exercised by the leading Hungarian political strata over Magyars and non-Magyars alike. "Every country has an ideal crucial to its existence. Hungary has… survived primarily through adherence to her constitution." This ideal will be embodied in "the monumental building to be constructed for the two houses of Parliament", said Tisza in 1883, when the money for the new Parliament was voted.

Intolerant nationalism strengthened under Tisza's term as prime minister—on both a social and governmental level. Tisza closed down the Slovak Cultural Association, crushed the autonomous political movements among the nationalities, put the leaders of these on trial and developed an educational policy of Magyarization. As a liberal politician coming from the ranks of the nobility, Tisza was insensitive to the need for a social welfare policy, demanded by the new times. He regarded the labour movement as the work of "callous" agitators, but at the same time was convinced that the semi-feudal dependence of farm servants on their landlord was natural. For Tisza this represented the age-old relationship between master and servant, something he attempted to conserve by legislative means as well.

No major reforms were introduced during Tisza's term of office. *Quieta non movere*—Let sleeping dogs lie—this was Tisza's principle of government. During the 1880s, that "happy time of peace", this principle seemed to work well in practice also.

There was one, and only one, question that Tisza was unable to handle —that of the common army. The Imperial and Royal army constituted a state within the state. It still treated Hungary as a conquered province and showed scant respect for the country's national tradition and independence. Public opinion, which was slowly adapting to Dualism, could not come to terms with the presence of the domineering soldiery. Incidents involving the officers of the Imperial and Royal army were everyday occurrences and kept the public in a state of constant tension. It was in such an atmosphere that at the beginning of 1889 Tisza put forward new proposals for the Hungarian army. In addition to increasing its strength, the various points would have curtailed the Parliament's right of control and would have prescribed a German-language examination for officers.

The proposals provoked a general outcry and were followed by innumerable demonstrations. In the end the government was compelled to make modifications but, in spite of this, it lost its prestige. In a matter of weeks, the year 1889 revealed how superficial and fragile this decade of peace had been. Kossuth, living in seclusion in Turin, sensed "the spontaneous pulsation of national aspirations". To manifest themselves as history, all they required was a slightly favourable climate. "When all is said and done, the great historical problems cannot be suppressed. They must be resolved", wrote Kossuth at the beginning of 1890.

In March, Kálmán Tisza fell from power.

"We're Heading towards the Land of Liberty..."

The most peaceful years of the "happy time of peace" arrived: noisy campaigns for election to parliament, extravagant festivities, frenzied business enterprises, spectacular company crashes, notorious games of cards, gallant adventures, secret duels. The upper class was enjoying the post-Compromise boom. Why worry about the twelve-hour day of tens of thousands of workers and the unspeakable destitution of a few million farm servants and day-labourers? Who cared about a few dozen workers who occasionally met in a workshop corner or in poorly-lit pubs to organize and set up societies. Only the police in fact, and with exemplary meticulousness. Having completed his apprenticeship, a worker either travelled abroad for a time or took a job. If he joined a relief society on beginning work he was immediately subject to their attention. The guardians of law and order were afraid of workers who had just returned from foreign countries. They might have learned a trade certainly, but they also have become acquainted with ideas—very dangerous ideas as far as the vigilant police were concerned.

139

Prior to the Compromise, only a few dozen harmless associations existed. These rendered certain asistance to a worker or his family in case of the former's illness or death. In a constitutional system the organizing of workers could not be held up and associations specializing in self-help and self-education proliferated. Those which, under the cover of "self-education" and "assistance", were also involved in politics and the protection of workers' interests, were called trade associations. After the Compromise, these served as the basis for the development of the working-class movement. Founded in 1868, the General Workers' Association was the first umbrella organization for these associations and workers' circles. The General Workers' Association co-operated closely with its German and Austrian counterparts.

According to its first charter, the aim of the General Workers' Association was "the intellectual advancement of the working class, the safeguarding of its material interests and its development with a view to enabling the worker not only to become a useful inhabitant of the state, but also to become one of those citizens capable of enjoying its liberal constitution". It wanted to lead the working-class army of slaves out of "the Egypt of the labour wage", and take it to the "Promised Land". Ferdinand Lassalle was the guiding star at this time. Before long, the Hungarian sections of the First International were set up, the teachings of Marx became known and social democratic organizing started within the Association.

In a few years the General Workers' Association had increased its strength in Budapest and in the major industrial towns of the provinces. Mihály Táncsics, the renowned democrat and member of Parliament, joined the Association, as did a number of intellectuals concerned about social problems. The activity of the Association was especially intensive at the time of the Paris Commune. It organized successful strikes and demonstrations and staged a funeral procession after the defeat of the Communards. For this the Government put the leaders of the Association on trial for "high treason". Those tried were Károly Farkas, an iron worker and one of the organizers of the International, the printer Antal Ihrlinger, András Essel, an iron worker, the journalists Viktor Külföldi and Lajos Szvoboda, a university student. Newspaper editor Zsigmond Politzer and twenty-two others were also charged with the same offence. Although only Politzer was sentenced, the General Workers' Association's activity was paralyzed. The organization dissolved in 1872.

After the defeat of the Paris Commune a campaign was launched against socialist workers and labour organizations throughout Europe. In Hungary, undercurrents of the movement survived in the few trade associations that maintained a low profile, while socialist ideas were advocated by the labour press. In 1873, the *Munkás Heti-Krónika* (Workers' Weekly Chronicle) and in 1877, *Népszava* (People's Voice) was published. The economic depression of 1873 and the lengthy recession which followed also handicapped the movement, which picked up again only towards the end

140

of the 1870s. In this a major role was played by Leó Frankel, one of the Hungary in 1876 and who became one of the organizers of the labour press. An experienced revolutionary and a trained Marxist, Frankel clearly saw the tasks that lay ahead—linking the economic and political struggles and expanding the movement's size. Together with his associates, he founded the General Workers' Party of Hungary *(Magyarországi Általános Munkáspárt)* in 1880. This was essentially a social democratic party, although because of a goverment ban, it was unable to adopt such a name. The party's programme openly formulated the socialist goal: the socialization of landed estates and all means of production, the abolition of the capitalist system of wage labour and the liberation of the workers.

The General Workers' Party of Hungary did not accomplish great feats, indeed, circumstances were not conducive to this. The 1880's still characterized by peace and the Tisza Government took care lest unruly working-class agitators should disturb the tranquil life of the propertied classes. The working class itself was still going through its formative years, its numbers barely topped the 100,000 mark, and the better-paid skilled workers constituted the majority of those organizing.

At the end of the century, the strengthening of the socialist movement was facilitated by three factors. Firstly, industrialization in Hungary had speeded up during the previous two decades. The capital especially, and the areas near it, underwent rapid industrial development and there was a corresponding growth in the industrial population. In a matter of a few decades Budapest was encircled by factories, whose chimneys emitted thick clouds of smoke. Secondly, the 1880s witnessed a slump in agriculture and, accordingly, the situation of the agricultural population deteriorated substantially. Poverty, unemployment, the hopelessness of life on the land—all made people receptive to socialist ideas that permeated the village as well. Thirdly, the socialist movement generally was making progress through Europe. In many countries socialist parties were formed at national level. In the summer of 1889, on the 100th anniversary of the French Revolution, the representatives of the socialists convened in Paris to form a new international organization. Once again the Marseillaise was heard in Paris, with socialist wording. This time Vienna, Prague and Budapest echoed in unison:

> Capital shall not dominate us.
> He who lives in the past shall be lost.
> We are heading toward the land of liberty.
> Justice is our goal...

The Age of Founders

Hungary was founded several times. It was founded by King Stephen I after the Magyar conquest of the Carpathian Basin and by Béla IV after the Mongol Invasion of 1241. Modern Hungary was founded by the generation of Széchenyi, Kossuth and Deák. They were followed by new founders, with spades, industrial tools and business sense. This last group founded banks and factories, bult railways, towns and water-mains. The half century that followed the Compromise was the age of founding.

Between 1867 and 1918, the dualist period, Hungary's population rose from 15.4 millions to 21 millions. Arable land increased from 25 million hectares to 27 million hectares. Vast areas of land were reclaimed, the Rivers Danube and Tisza were regulated and the Marsh of Ecsed and other swamps were drained. At the beginning of the period a quarter of arable land remained fallow, at the end only 8 per cent. Since the area of arable land grew by one-third and since average yields rose between two and three-fold, harvests trebled. Wheat yields rose from 14 to 42 quintals, potato yields from 8.5 to 50 millions and those of sugar beet from 2.3 to 16 millions. As the country consumed only half of the grain produced, between 15 and 20 million quintals were exported annually by the turn of the century. Increasingly, grain was sent abroad in the form of fine, albeit gluten-rich, flour. The expansion and prosperity of the milling industry in Hungary was based on this enormous grain production. In the 1870s, Budapest's milling industry was the largest of any city in the world and was overtaken only at the end of the century by those of Minneapolis and Cincinnati.

New tools and machines helped the work of agriculture. Completely new machinery was introduced in treading-out, the use of the threshing machine became widespread and a great many new machines were introduced in land cultivation and harvesting. Examples were the stell plough, steam ploughing and various small machines.

During the decades of prosperity, Hungarian agriculture was strong enough to stand up to competition from overseas grain, although farmers had been badly hit by two decades of falling prices. It also survived the phylloxera attacks which destroyed excellent vineyards at the end of the century and reduced the grape harvest to a quarter of what it had been previously. This crisis was overcome at the beginning of the twentieth century when new vineyards were planted. To halt the decline of the profitability of grain, intensive livestock breeding was started. During this period the cattle population rose from 4.5 million to 6.2 million head, in spite of the fact that the exports of cattle for slaughter rose by between two and three-fold. More importantly, the grey longhorn Hungarian cattle kept outside all the year round were, for the most part, replaced by the red-speckled breed, which produced much good milk. As a result, there was an enormous growth in the quantity of dairy produce. During these decades Hungary's stock of pigs doubled, topping the seven million mark in good years. Pig killing in the winter became a national custom, indeed something of a festivity.

The upswing in agriculture was helped by improving communications and credit facilities. The chronic shortage of credit and poor transportation about which Széchenyi so bitterly complained in 1830 now became a thing of the past. While at the time of the War of Independence there were only two railway services, one to Vác and one to Szolnok, and while even in 1867 trains ran only to Vienna, Debrecen and Arad, between the Compromise and 1913, the length of track increased from 2,200 kilometres to 22,000 kilometres. Freight carried rose from 3.5 to 72 million tones, the number of railway passengers from 3.5 to 200 million. While at the beginning of the period only some sixty modest credit institutions functioned with a total of 700 million crowns, prior to the First World War a network comprising 5,000 institutions and with over 13,000 million crowns at their disposal was established. Five major banks played a key role in the Hungarian economy.

The numerous disadvantages of the common tariff zone and the powerful competition of Austrian and Czech industry notwithstanding, the process of industrialization accelerated in Hungary. As one would expect from the country's natural resources, the food industry—especially the milling industry, the sugar industry and distilling—prospered most. Machine production was on a par with that of the other areas of the Austro–Hungarian Empire. Hungary's progress was especially impressive in the most modern branches of production—the electrical and chemical industries. In these Hungary started at the same time as her Western neighbours.

Let a few facts and figures speak for themselves. After the Compromise, before new businesses started to mushroom, there were 170 industrial joint-stock companies and a few hundred private firms in Hungary. Their employees numbered less than 100,000. By the end of the century as many as 2,700 industrial plants were registered with 300,000 workers and with an output worth 1,500 million crowns. The ensuing decade and a half witnessed even more dynamic development: 5,500 plants operated before 1914, with 600,000 workers and producing an output worth 3,300 million crowns. At the beginning of the period, machinery developing 9,000 horsepower was employed in industry. By the end of period, machinery in developed 900,000 horsepower, a hundredfold increase. Industrialization made especially great strides in Budapest, with its trams, railway stations, huge factories, smoke, and labour force. The population of the suburban Újpest, Kispest, Erzsébetfalva and Csepel factory districts—districts which had been just farmland before—rose from a quarter of a million to over one million in the course of half a century. Manual workers accounted for over 40 per cent of these.

Hungary's national income multiplied three times during this period and, at 2.5/cent the average annual growth rate was significant even by international standards. It indicated that Hungary, once a backward agricultural country, had become a fast-developing agrarian-industrial state.

What were the social factors behind this great leap ahead? Mention must first and foremost be made of the leading liberal stratum which recognized the necessity and usefulness of modernization and encouraged the evolution of the capitalist system. Gábor Baross, who founded the Hungarian State Railways, thereby establishing modern transportation in Hungary, was one of its members. Secondly, there was a large group of excellent businessmen and entrepreneurs who operated on a large scale. These men were not sentimental philanthropists. They ruthlessly exploited and oppressed the workers but nevertheless achieved something. Haggenmacher established the beer industry and, to some extent, the milling industry; Hatvany Deutsch the sugar industry; Manfréd Weiss the Csepel factory and Goldberger the best textile complex in the country. Engineers, technicians, inventors, innovators and a large number of devoted experimenters made substantial contributions to advancement. Special mention must, in this relation, be made of András Mechwart, the brilliant chief engineer of the Ganz factory; Tivadar Puskás, the inventor of the telephone exchange; Károly Zipernowsky, Ottó Bláthy and Miksa Déri, the inventors of the transformer; Donát Bánki, the inventor of the turbine; János Csonka, who invented the carburetor and hundreds of others.

Last, but not least, credit for this great boom must go to those industrial workers, agricultural workers and peasants who were compelled to accommodate themselves to capitalist labour discipline, who learned trades, who became familiar with materials and who really got to know what work meant. It was from their expertise, diligence that modern Hungary was built.

The Decline of Romanticism

During the hectic period of the Age of Reform and the Revolution, and then in the difficult years of absolutism, the national consciousness and the public mood was in complete harmony with Romanticism. The poems of Petőfi, the paintings of Barabás and Madarász, the operas of Erkel (*László Hunyadi* and *Bánk bán*) appropriately expressed the struggles of the War of Independence, joy and sorrow. The doubts that arose after the defeat and a search for the meaning of human existence were formulated in *Az ember tragédiája* (The Tragedy of Man), a profoundly philosophical play written by Imre Madách in 1860. Even János Arany, who belonged to the popular-national tendency, drew on Romanticism for inspiration in those epics and ballads he wrote in this period.

1867 marked an end to the revolutionary period. The greater part of the leading classes became reconciled to the Compromise, and moved into the historicizing public buildings of Austro–Hungarian Dualism. The sober epoch of founding and construction had arrived. József Eötvös, the distuinguished writer, thinker and Culture Minister, laid the foundations of a capitalist educational system. Ágoston Trefort, Eötvös's successor, continued his work in this field. The number of elementary schools rose from 13,000 to almost 17,000 during this period. Standards improved substantially. The number of teachers doubled, while the proportion of State and village schools rose from 3.5 per cent to 28 per cent of the total number. While in the period of the Compromise, over half the 1.1 million children of school age received no schooling, in 1914 this was true for only 10–15 per cent of the 2.5 million eligible to attend. The number of secondary school students also doubled. At the beginning of the period Hungary's only provincial university was enlarged, and prominent politicians and scholars of the period established the modern college network. The medical and arts faculties of Budapest University earned a high reputation in Europe. Budapest's Technical University was founded in 1891. A year later the university of arts and sciences in Kolozsvár was set up and at the end of the period the universities of Pozsony and Debrecen. These years also witnessed the founding of the Academy of Fine Arts (1872), the Academy of Music (1875) —not to mention the colleges of law and veterinary science, the museums, and the libraries, along with the string of Budapest and provincial theatres which followed in the wake of the National Theatre opened during the Age of Reform.

In sum, cultural standards rose substantially—the proportion of illiterates dropped from two thirds to one third of the population. Yet the content of culture changed only very slowly. In poetry, the popular-national trend established by Petőfi and Arany was continued in the work of untalented epigones, while the novelist Mór Jókai popularized and wrote Romantic works. His novels *A Rab Ráby* (The Strange Story of Rab Ráby), *Egy magyar nábob* (A Hungarian Nabob), *Kárpáthy Zoltán* (Zoltán Kárpáthy), *Az új földesúr* (The New Landlord), *A kőszívű ember fiai* (The Baron's Sons), *Az aranyember* (The Man with the Golden Touch), *Fekete gyémántok* (Black Diamonds) gave expression to the finest patriotic and heroic virtues. These virtues included a passionate love of liberty, unselfishness and chivalry. Jókai's novels were naturally laced with innumerable anecdotes, cheerfulness and patriotic grief. Jókai achieved unprecedented popularity. He was more than just a writer, editor and politician: he was a representative of the nation, its great story-teller and educator for half a century. There were many fine and noble things, in this period, as well as a great deal of self-deception. It was a period which would have benefited more from sober self-awareness than from Romanticism.

Jókai's most outstanding successor, Kálmán Mikszáth, also started out by writing short stories and exciting tales in the romantic tradition: *Tót atyafiak* (The Slovak Yokels), *A jó palócok* (The Good Palots), *Szent Péter esernyője* (St Peter's Umbrella), *Beszterce ostroma* (The Siege of Beszterce).

145

In these works, the plot is woven around an anecdote and there is a great trick in the middle of everything. Later, however, Mikszáth's anecdotes became increasingly bitter and turned against a decaying and profligate gentry. The short stories and novels written by Mikszáth at the end of the century often portrayed, in a satirical vein, the decline of the once-powerful Hungarian noble.

Romanticism also flourished on the stage, and not only at the National Theatre. In those theatres where the popular play scored its great successes, Romanticism was also well established. The sympathetic portrayal of life for ordinary people tended towards romantic idyll, even in the late works —*The Gypsy* (A cigány), *The Foundling* (A lelenc) and *The Old Discharged Soldier and his Son the Hussar* (A vén obsitos és a fia, a huszár)—of those who started this, Ede Szigligeti and József Szigeti. In the 1870s, the popular play turned into a song-and-dance peasant "musical" which smoothed over the set-back in the embourgeoisment of the peasantry and presented a spectacular bogus folkishness of sorts. The only thing that could be said for this genre is that Lujza Blaha, "the nations's nightingale" rose to through it. In fame and fortune she was on a par with the great tragic actresses of the day, Mari Jászai and Emilia Márkus.

For three decades, the famous historical tableaux of Viktor Madarász, Bertalan Székely, Mór Than and Gyula Benczúr evoked patriotic enthusiasm for Hungary's historical past and did so with great artistic force. However, even in painting the appeal of Romanticism slowly began to wane. It was no accident that the great popular painter of the post-Compromise period was Mihály Munkácsy, who used naturalistic techniques and whose genre paintings—*Condemned Cell, Linen-Shredders*—and whose religious and historical tableaux—*Christ before Pilate, Milton*—contained some impressive realistic elements. In his late works—*The Entry of the Magyars, Ecce Homo*—not even Munkácsy's brillant painting skills can conceal the empty theatricality of late romanticism. The truly modern painter of the *fin de siècle* was the then almost unknown Pál Szinyei Merse, who in his great paintings—*Picnic in May, The Nightingale*—discovered air, light and colours almost contemporaneously with the masters of French Impressionism.

Ferenc Liszt, the great genius of the age, worked until the mid-1880s. His *Hungarian Rhapsodies*, Hungarian portraits and the *csárdás* made Hungarian melodies known the world over and pointed ahead to the appearance of folk music in formally composed works. Ferenc Erkel was still active at the beginning of the period, although his new operas, *György Dózsa* and *György Brankovics* did not attain popularity. Musical life stagnated at the end of the century and Hungarians found it difficult to choose between Western-type musical culture and recently-written, pseudo-Hungarian folk songs.

Late nineteenth-century Hungarian culture presents a varied picture. The important achievement of mass education and the establishment of a network of cultural institutions notwithstanding, there were signs of stagnation and decline in many areas. Admittedly, men of great talent such as Jókai, Erkel, Munkácsy, and, especially, Liszt, introduced and maintained high artistic standards. However, the class that fostered culture, the one-time landed nobility, was decaying—along with national Romanticism. The Romantic sun still shone, but the evening hours had already arrived.

By the end of this period Budapest, Hungary's capital city, had grown into a big metropolis. It had a sizeable middle-class population, an intelligentsia with a European horizon. It also had a working class. These strata were no longer satisfied with the antiquated tastes and empty culture of a nobility which looked to the past.

The Millennium

Around 1890 important developments started to affect the history of this peaceful era. The strong Prime Minister, Kálmán Tisza, fell from power, and opposition in the country began to grow. In Hungary the Social Democratic Party was formed and socialist ideas penetrated to the remote villages of the Great Plain. Bloody riots broke out in Békés and Csongrád counties, the "Stormy Corner" of the southeastern region. The towns of Orosháza, Békéscsaba and Hódmezővásárhely were all caught up in these disturbances. The landless and destitute, for example, day labourers and harvesters, demanded higher wages, better conditions and rights. These people formed socialist organizations and swore an oath of allegiance to the red flag. The Government's first response was to declare a state of emergency on the Great Plain and to use coercion. However, it also tried out a more sophisticated approach. As Finance Minister, Sándor Wekerle started to put the state's monetary affairs in order. In 1892 Wekerle became Prime Minister but continued with his earlier work. Adopting the gold standard, he stabilized the Austro–Hungarian Empire's uniform currency, the Crown. (One old forint was worth two crowns, and one American dollar 4.935 crowns.) These years witnessed the last revival of the Hungarian liberal traditions dating from the Age of Reform. In spite of fierce opposition from Francis Joseph, the Viennese Court, influential conservatives and leading churchmen, the Wekerle Government was able to enact important liberal legislation. Civil marriage was made possible and state registration of births, marriages and deaths introduced. In addition the free practice of religion was guaranteed, as was the equality of Judaism with other faiths.

Wekerle was a talented economic policy maker, and a popular politician at that. So was Dezső Szilágyi, a Liberal Justice Minister of great erudition. The same held true for Albin Csáky, Minister for Public Education. Also highly thought of was the railway-building minister Gábor Baross, who died in 1892. Nevertheless, the Wekerle Government remained in office for only two years. At the burial ceremony of Lajos Kossuth on 2 April 1894, the true feelings and discontent of the nation were expressed in no uncertain terms. At the same time the Roumanians also revealed their grievances to the world when the stundents of Bucharest University proclaimed the suffering "the case of the Hungarian Roumanians was suddenly spotlighted in two *causes célèbres*. In 1896 the students of Bucharest University published, in Roumanian, German, French, English and Italian, a 'memorandum' on the grievances of their kinsmen in Hungary... The Court of Kolozsvár sentenced the principal author of this, a certain Aurel Popovici to four years' prison..." (Macartney). Even conservative grouping, political party and religious denomination now turned against Wekerle. His permissive and liberal policy had become generally unacceptable and Francis Joseph himself was dissatisfied. The equilibrium of the system had been upset. On January 14 1895 Baron Dezső Bánffy was appointed Prime Minister.

In 1896, the thousandth anniversary of the Magyar Conquest of the Danube Basin was celebrated. The festivities for which the country had been preparing for a whole decade, took place with great pomp but also served to restore balance and to obscure problems.

In 1896, the country looked back on a millennium full of struggle. Situated between stronger peoples and at the crossroads of Europe, her very survival had often been in jeopardy. Hungary's position among states, peoples and cultures had always been peripheral and this had led to oppression. Despite all the vicissitudes of history, though, the Magyars had fought simultaneously for survival, acquisition of European culture and acceptance for their own. At the end of the nineteenth century, however, Hungary could look back on a period of peace characterized by economic development, hectic construction work and fine cultural achievements. The nation could indeed commemorate with pride the thousand years of its history, and its half century of capitalist development.

The organizers of the celebrations, though, overplayed this pride, as did the authorities, official institutions and the press. The events soon turned into boasting on an enormous scale. *Fin-de-siècle* nationalism used the Millennium to popularize Hungarian state power and in stone, iron and words, to perpetuate the illusion of a Hungarian Empire.

At midnight on New Year's Eve, 1895, bells rang out simultaneously throughout the country. Every town and every village, no matter what its size, greeted the anniversary year. In April, Parliament, at a festive session, commemorated the Magyar Conquest of the Carpathian Basin, giving thanks to Providence, to Prince Árpád and Francis Joseph for himself, for their gracious contributions. On 2 May, the king amid great splendour and the presence of the chief dignitaries of the Austro–Hungarian Empire, opened the Millennary Exhibition. The present-day City Park was designed and laid out especially for the occasion. The exhibition was certainly impressive and demonstrated Hungary's great material and cultural progress, as well as her relative affluence. The effect of the exhibition was heightened still further by a large number of important construction projects put under way. The Great Boulevard was opened to traffic, the first electric underground railway on the continent of Europe was put into operation and the Francis Joseph Bridge (today's Liberty Bridge) was inaugurated. At the same time reconstruction work started on the Royal Palace in Buda and on Heroes' Square, where the millennary memorial column and the Museum of Fine Arts were built. One splendid celebration followed another. A thanksgiving service featuring Liszt's Coronation Mass was held in the Matthias Church. During this a festival address was delivered by the Prince-Primate.

On 8 June, homage was paid to the anniversary of King Stephen I's coronation. This in particular was a grand affair. The representatives of the counties and towns appeared with mounted escorts, along with members of the aristocracy in Hungarian gala-dress. Together with these belonging to institutions and associations, this body proceeded through the streets of the capital, Budapest, with flags and insignia. In the newly-completed House of Parliament on the Danube embankment, Dezső Szilágyi spoke of the significance of King and Nation coming together. This, in his view, would serve as an eternal guarantee of the ancient freedom and unity of the Hungarian people.

Later on, Francis Joseph, accompanied by the Serbian and Roumanian kings, ceremonially opened the newly improved Iron Gate. The Iron Gate is the name given to the ravine which then marked the common border of Austria–Hungary, Serbia and Roumania. Through this ravine flowed the Danube and navigation here was perilous before the Hungarian Government improved conditions. The Court and the diplomatic corps spent most of the year in Budapest, where the annual meeting of the delegations was also held. It did indeed appear as though the idyllic empire of King Matthias had been revived. However, the bright lights of the Millennary celebrations were extinguished in the autumn and in the New Year everything continued where it left off. The year 1896 witnessed stormy parliamentary elections and political battles, along with the strengthening of the working-class movement. The next year there followed strikes among the harvesters and growing agrarian socialist activity on the Great Plain and in the region east of the River Tisza. From this emerged the first programme for the distribution of land among the impoverished peasantry. These developments did not go unheeded. The rural socialists were hauled off to prison by the gendarmes and the leaders of the industrial labour movement expelled from the capital by the police. The socialist press was banned and legislation enacted to prohibit strikes among the harvesters.

The poor, the workers and the national minorities hated the firm-handed approach adopted by the Bánffy Government. They put up strong and resolute resistance to its oppressive measures. The parliamentary opposition also disliked Bánffy's brutal policy, and had itself suffered harsh treatment at his hands. Parliament toppled Bánffy at the end of 1898.

Hungary entered the twentieth century with a whole host of unresolved social and national issues. By this time, the entire Habsburg Empire was undermined by the existence of potentially explosive contradictions.

Nations and National Minorities under Dualism

Ever since the Middle Ages, members of seven peoples, Slovaks, the Ruthenians, Roumanians, Germans, Serbians, Croatians, Magyars as well as scattered minorities had lived side by side in Hungary. We have already seen how the good-neighbourly coexistence of these peoples and their common alliance against the Turks came to an end with the spread of Habsburg power. The Habsburg Empire was multi-national and dominated by a German ruling class centred in Austria. From the eighteenth century on, however, nationalism began to develop in Europe. The national consciousness of its peoples began to grow, and national culture began to flourish. With time even the small peoples wished to establish independent national states of their own. These developments had serious implications for the Habsburg Empire. Conflicts between these peoples sharpened in the period 1848–49—the time of the revolution in Hungary. With the Austrian victory, the common adversities of the non-German ethnic groups brought some sense of community between them. However, the problem remained unresolved even in the years of Austrian absolutist rule.

The Compromise of 1867 created a new situation. The main reason why the leading Hungarian circles entered into alliance with the Habsburgs and Austria's ruling circles were to preserve their territorial assets and political power intact. The Compromise also served to maintain their domination over the non-Magyar minorities living in Hungary. During the negotiations which led to the Compromise, and even more so after its enactment, the political leaders of the non-Magyars protested against an agreement which only took account of Austrian and Hungarian interests. True, in 1868 the Hungarians passed the Nationalities Law designed to protect the non-Magyars of the country and in the same year agreement was reached with the Croatians who were to enjoy limited autonomy within Hungary. However, the Nationalities Law was largely ignored and it was from only many years afterwards that the Hungarian landlords and the Hungarian public accepted the slight concessions to Croatia. The other nationalities continued to express their discontent repeatedly. Their main grievance was that the legislation enacted after the Compromise failed to recognize their separate national identity and grant the autonomy and political rights which followed from this.

The question, said Mihajlo Polit, the Serbian liberal, is not whether we are entitled to draw up petitions in Serbo–Croatian, Slovak, Roumanian, or, say, German, but whether "on the basis of self-rule, the villages, towns and counties bear the stamp of individual nationalities". In other words, autonomy for the minorities should be the aim and that no citizen "be alien in his own homeland". Under the consolidated dualist system, the political parties of the national minorities could achieve little success. Although the minorities were allowed to use their mother tongue and were permitted to develop their economic and cultural associations, dominant Magyar nationalism was increasingly asserted in education. After several years of unsuccessful efforts, the parties representing the national minorities declined. The first to do so was the Roumanian and, in the 1870's the others followed. These parties lapsed into passivity, confining their activities to cultural work and keeping alive the national idea.

The last quarter of the nineteenth century, however, saw significant changes in the economic situation and social structure of the national minorities. Modern capitalist farming methods, along with modern transportation and banking facilities, reached the central and southern grain producing regions of Hungary. At the same time, concomitants of industrialization and civilization generally also arrived. By the turn of the century the mountainous eastern periphery and Transylvania had been penetrated. In the twenty-five years up to 1914, even these outlying areas witnessed an expansion of their railway network. Industrial concerns were set up and banks increased three or fourfold both with regard to number and capital available. From the point of view of both economic and political development, special mention must be made of the Slovak Tatra region, the Roumanian Albina and Victoria areas and the network of credit co-operatives among the Serbian minority. New industrial settlements and industrial regions flourished in the Slovak-populated districts of Upper Hungary, in the Bánság and in Southern Transylvania.

As a result of economic development, the middle class among the national minorities became stronger. In the more backward areas a middle class came into being for the first time. The growth of this class brought with it the beginnings of embourgeoisement for the peasantry and an industrial working class came into being. In spite of considerable development, Roumanian and Ruthenian society remained overwhelmingly agrarian in character: the proportion of these people employed in industry, commerce and transportation was below eight and five per cent of active earners respectively. Only 4.5 per cent of Roumanians and 1 per cent of Ruthenians lived in towns. Embourgeoisement in Slovak, Serbian and Croatian society was more advanced. Only 70 to 75 per cent of their populations worked in agriculture, while the proportion of these peoples employed in industry, commerce and transportation rose to 15 and 20 per cent. Literacy was higher among these peoples and the intelligentsia played a more important role. Only the Serbs had a sizeable landowning class and an affluent middle class. The Slovaks had a comparatively developed middle class. Only the

Croatians possessed a complete social structure. Since it lacked a big landed aristocracy and gentry, the society among the nationalities was more democratic than Magyar society. Their middle class was less inclined to adopt gentry values and stood closer to the people, the lower middle class and the peasants. At the same time the bourgeoisie among the national minorities was not the chief enemy and oppressor of the peasantry and working-class elements in these ethnic groups. This distinction belonged to the big Austro-German landowners and capitalists in general and to their Hungarian counterparts in particular. This meant that forging a democratic national unity to oppose the Government and ruling circles generally was easier for the nationalities then for the Magyars, themselves.

The great economic changes, the structural transformation of society and the deepening crisis of the dualist system created, around the turn of the century, favourable conditions for the national minorities' struggle. As early as the 1890s' the so-called Memorandum Trial (1894) involving the leaders of the Roumanian National Committee, gave rise to considerable controversy. This and the congress of the national minorities held in Budapest during 1895 indicated not just the revival but also the strength of feeling among the non-Magyars. At the beginning of the twentieth century, every nationality party cast off its passivity and once more became involved in political life. Behind this change of approach lay hidden a change of generation and the participation of new classes in politics: church and moderate bourgeois leadership positions were taken over by more democratic and secular-minded elements. Above all, the nationality parties now strove to broaden the popular base of their support and to win over their own working masses. Accordingly, in their new programmes they laid stress on economic and social reform and democratic political rights. The demand for national independence was not emphasized and, in any case, this seemed a remote goal in the early years of the twentieth century. The desire to transform the Austro–Hungarian Empire into a confederation lost prominence and nowhere was there any open mention of secession.

In the Slovak movement, the staff of the journal *Hlas* (Voice) represented orientation towards the Czechs—an ethnic group under Austrian, not Hungarian, rule. The journal supported Pavol Blaho and Vavro Šrobár, while Milan Hodža came forth with a Democratic Peasant Party, and Andrej Hlinka with a Catholic People's Party programme. At the time of its revival, the Roumanian National Committee was led by Aurel Vlad, Alexandru Vaida-Voievod and Teodor Mihali. However, the writer and poet Octavian Goga and the outstanding politician Juliu Maniu increasingly took over this role. The Radical Party, which was popular amongst the Serbs, followed Jaša Tomić's popular-peasant line. Of these parties, those of Hodža and Tomić co-operated with the forces of Magyar democracy. Formed in autumn 1905, the Serbo-Croatian coalition proposed alliance and actually maintained good relations with its Magyar opposition counterpart. However, when the latter came to power in Hungary, and continued the nationalist line of earlier governments, the situation changed. When in 1908, Austria–Hungary annexed Bosnia-Herzegovina, (an area populated by Serbs) the new rulers in Hungary supported the move. Magyar hostility to an autonomous South Slav state based on independent Serbia was therefore openly revealed.

Whilst the middle-class nationality parties were unable to reach even temporary agreement, there was close co-operation between the workers and peasants of the various ethnic groups. The Slovak, Roumanian, Serbian and Magyar working people fought shoulder-to-shoulder in István Várkonyi's Agrarian Socialist Party against their common oppressors. Movements were organized to seize the land and to provoke strikes among the harvesters. In Hungary, unlike Austria, the unity between the Socialist Party and the trade union movement did not disintegrate, even when separate Slovak, Roumanian and Serb sections and agitation committees were formed within the framework of the Socialist Party in the early years of the twentieth century.

During this period, national minority culture underwent great development. Above all, literacy and basic general education became more widespread. Cultural associations such as the "Matica Slovenska" performed important and progressive work. After the banning of the latter the local associations, e. g. the Roumanian "Astra", and the Serbian "Matica Srpská" carried on. They successfully cultivated the languages and literatures of their respective peoples, studied their national history and encouraged national theatre and the national folk arts. The national minority newspapers were similarly effective: before the First World War there were fifteen Roumanian, fifteen Serbo-Croatian and thirteen Slovak daily newspapers as well as several literary and scientific journals published within Hungary's borders. Thanks largely to this extensive cultural activity, the cultural level and national consciousness of the national minorities strengthened. They became prepared for the time when the World War created the preconditions for national independence and union.

The Face of Hungary

The Millennium was largely the occasion of the Hungarian upper classes, while common people played an almost negligible part in the celebrations. The society which entered the twentieth century in a festive and optimistic mood was, as regards fundamental social relations and employment structure, capitalistic. Hungarian society had taken on an essentially bourgeois character, although the remnants of feudalism survived in the form of the aristocracy and gentry. In this society the main line of division lay between the upper class and the people, but here also existed a perceptible difference between the historic upper class and the newcomers to it.

At the apex of the social pyramid stood the aristocracy, made up of rich landowning magnates endowed with the title of Prince, Count and Baron. Through division and bestowal of noble rank, the number of families bearing these titles showed considerable increase during this period, although earlier the figures had been 3, 91 and 113, respectively. Of these, six hundred families possessed an estate of over 600 hectares (roughly 1,500 acres). One hundred and eighty-four had an estate of over 6,000 hectares in size (roughly 15,000 acres), and such large estates were called latifundia at this time. This aristocracy still occupied a leading position in political life, in the army, the diplomatic corps and as honorary directors of large firms. The aristocracy was isolated from other social classes. Living in remote country houses or in town residences, the aristocracy sought entertainment in its own clubs, married from among its own members and, as a class, loyally supported the Habsburg dynasty. Situated nearest to it in the social hierarchy was the affluent landed gentry, which comprised some one thousand families. Below this group and made up of some five thousand families, was the lesser gentry class, possessing over 100–150 hectares (250–375 acres) of land per family. This lesser gentry class was also very much part and parcel of upper-class Hungarian society at both national and county level. These landed classes together enjoyed the greatest social prestige and members of these families filled the important positions in government and public administration.

However, most of the landed gentry lost part, and sometimes all, of their estates during this period. The gentry members who were unable to keep abreast of capitalistic farming practices found it difficult to make their estates pay and left agriculture. Lagging behind in the process of embourgeoisement, they took jobs in public administration. In fact, gentry recruitment to these positions was so great that this class became the backbone of the bureaucratic apparatus required by capitalist Hungary at that time. The gentry was also prominently represented in the intelligentsia, and it determined the character and outlook of these bodies. The gentry outlook combined the conceit of the nobility and a powerful historical consciousness. Also present were patriotic feelings, which increasingly changed to nationalism and the love of liberty of the first Reform Generation turned into conservatism. The anti-democratic attitude of the landowners, was also a feature of it, together with a value system which stressed the merits of landowning, agriculture, political activity, government and public administration. Also favoured were intellectual occupations. However, all forms of service to the public, such as business and trade were out, and still more so was manual labour.

The large section of middle-class and, later, lower middle-class elements was of German and other national minority origin. These people comprised the majority of white-collar workers and intellectuals at the beginning of the twentieth century and they aped gentry outlook and way of life. At the end of this period the numbers of earners in these occupations exceeded

300,000 and, with family members included, the size of this milieu was one million. Not only their political influence, but also their very numbers made this grouping an important factor in Hungarian society.

It was during this period that the wealthiest and most influential part of the middle class (the small group of bankers, manufacturers and big entrepreneurs) caught up with the big landowners at the top of the social pyramid. By origin, most were not ethnic Magyars, for such an entrepreneurial middle class could not have emerged in the feudal society, still existing in the backward and agrarian Magyar areas. Typically, the entrepreneurs came from the ranks of Jews who had settled in Hungary in the first half of the nineteenth century and partly from those of the German entrepreneurs and technical experts who came to Hungary between 1800 and 1900. Some were the Magyarized descendants of Greek, Serbian and Armenian merchants who had emigrated to the country in the eighteenth century. The enormous wealth of these people was abundant compensation for their lowly origins. Under the reign of Francis Joseph, several hundreds of these families were given gentry status and about fifty—among them twenty-eight Jews—were raised to the rank of Baron. Most bought estates, palaces and ancestors for themselves and their offspring. They therefore became genuine Hungarian aristocrats who donned Hungarian gala-dress and wore the sword of honour on festive occasions.

The upper middle class therefore assimilated with the traditional leading classes in public life and in upper-class society, in its business activities, it preserved its bourgeois virtues, of which ruthless acquisition and accumulation were just as much part as a rigorous work ethic, an excellent business sense and entrepreneurial risk-taking. Outstanding industrialists and bankers included Zsigmond Kornfeld, Leó Lánczy, Manfréd Weiss, Sándor Hatvany Deutsch, Henrik Haggenmacher, Leó Goldberger, the Fellners and the Brülls and their associates. These men substantially contributed to the modernization of the Hungarian economy, to the development of a modern banking system and to large-scale industry in Hungary.

The largest section of the middle class consisted of merchants, small manufacturers, factors and university graduates. During this time, the number, wealth and landed property of this section increased also. This was true not only in the capital, Budapest, but in commercial and industrial centres in the provinces as well. These members of the middle class procured important positions for themselves, although their power to influence important political and economic decisions remained limited.

What was it, then, which held together this "middle class", composed as it was of such vastly heterogeneous elements? One important trait uniting the various sections was their separation from the working people and from the middle strata of the non-Magyar nationalities. Consequently, they all had a vested interest in maintaining the dualist Hungarian State and social system. This, however, was insufficient in itself to unite them, in the same way that middle-class wealth and affluence was.

155

Some sort of rank, position and a certificate of secondary-school education paving the way to an army career were the preconditions for admission into the Hungarian middle class. To these had to be added a particular outlook on life and an ostentatious manifestation of traditional patriotism. Finally, the middle class was held together by an increasingly uniform way of life which, according to the succinct description of a contemporary, featured a flat with three rooms, home-cooked and freshly-served midday meals, a free railway pass and domestic servants. These, as well as a good education for the children, were the status symbols of middle-class life.

The mass of lower middle-class earners, which numbered almost a million, belonged also to bourgeois society. Although they were still addressed in a deferential manner, they were no longer respected accordingly. The term lower middle class covered strata which differed widely with regard to occupation, income and social status. The lower middle class ranged from the prosperous artisan working with assistants to the grocer and shoemaker and from the poor junior clerk to the junior officer. Within the lower middle class, a line of division was clearly discernible between the real petit-bourgeois with his own workshop, store, house and perhaps small plot of land or vineyard and the transitional strata who made a living by doing manual work. The rift widened between the assimilated retailer and small manufacturer strata on the one hand and the *déclassé* elements, victims of capitalism on the other. The remaining guild members and the bottom strata of the lower middle class constituted the rest of this particular social grouping, which was conservative in outlook.

Lacking a consciousness and value system of their own, these latter elements were without structural cohesion.

Below the lower middle class were situated the workers and poor peasantry, the broad masses of the people, several million strong.

The Life of the Poor

Who were the poor of Hungary? Those who had no land, no wealth, nor secure livelihood, those who made a living out of other people's stubble —this is how Lajos Kiss, an expert on the life of those people, saw it. In 1900, the poor in Hungary comprised two million day-labourers and farmhands, as well as some 500,000 dwarfholders whose tiny plots did not provide them with a proper means of subsistence. The hundreds of thousands of smallholders who owned bad-quality land and who possessed no livestock or machinery were also included in this category.

At the end of the nineteenth century, the time of the Great Agricultural Depression in Europe, the life of the poor was made extremely difficult by low grain prices and a growing tax burden. Some smallholders tried to improve their situation by raising livestock, but this required the work of the whole family. Another alternative was co-leasing, on slowly deteriorating terms, with the young son or daughter working as a day-labourer. In the course of the last quarter of the nineteenth century, there developed pressure which drove the poor of the villages to labour day and night from early spring until late autumn. On the other hand, these people were without work in the winter, a state of affairs occasionally alleviated by fatty food if the larder was full and aggravated by hunger if it was empty.

The external conditions of the peasant life-style changed slowly and very gradually. In the more prosperous regions of Transdanubia and the Great Plain dried mud was slowly replaced by brick as a building material and tiles superseded thatch and reed for the roof. Otherwise the form of the peasant dwelling did not basically change. The chimney, which was connected to the stove, constituted a major innovation. The kitchen thereby became free of smoke and, as a result, fit for habitation. The iron cooking stove also came into common use in this period, transforming both the heating and cooking situation. From this time on, the former living room, which had always been overcrowded, lost its ordinary function and became a room used only on special occasions. The kitchen took over as the centre of family life, serving all sorts of purposes from cooking to sleeping and as the place for neighbourly chats.

Eating habits also changed. In addition to wheat and rye bread, (both were consumed according to region and nationality) along with girdle-cake and polenta, potatoes became the staple food of the masses. Previously mutton was the type of meat most commonly eaten but after the soil was allowed to lie fallow and with the decline of cotton production, pork took its place. This was because pigs could be raised on small plots of land. Although pigs yielded less meat, they produced more lard, bacon and smoked sausage for the poor. At the turn of the century only the poorest did not slaughter pigs.

The monotony of work eased by important holidays. On such occasions the village people put on their best clothing, their folk costume. In the nineteenth century loose white linen clothing was replaced by colourful folk garments, above all the embroidered peasant cloak, embroidered shirts, jackets, skirts and headdress. Naturally, in the course of time items of commercially produced clothing also found their way even to the remotest village; the cotton skirt, dungarees and the jacket-type coat are just a few examples. However, the objects and practices of more urban interior decoration and dress were characteristic of the ordinary working day. Festive occasions brought forth the "folk" dress and articles for personal use which so conspicuously indicated peasant status. The second half of the nineteenth century witnessed the emergence of the most beautiful regional folk cultures: the Matyó, Kalotaszeg, Kalocsa, and many others.

The sharp contrast between the more urbanized everyday existence of the peasant and his consciously-preserved folk culture was not merely an ethnographical curiosity but was indicative of the duality of the peasant way

157

of life, its growing stagnation and crisis. The majority of the smallholder peasants did not become capitalist entrepreneur farmers in the same way that those *déclassé* elements, which were unable to find work in industry immediately, did not become integrated into the ranks of the workers.

The great mass of the rural proletariat was made up of seasonal workers, harvesters, navvies and farm servants. Their number topped the 2 million mark at the beginning of the twentieth century and, counting the members of their families, the figure was 4 1/2 million. The farm servants were usually bound to estates by contracts valid for several years, although these often meant life-long commitment. The estates had a regular force and contracts could be renewed repeatedly if the farm servant's work and conduct found favour. The farm servant's remuneration consisted of some cash, payment in kind and a small plot of land. Farm servants' duties were innumerable: the working day for these people lasted from sunrise to sunset, and the livestock had to be looked after on Sundays and holidays as well. The farm servant's wife had an obligation to express gratitude to her husband's employer by performing several weeks of unpaid work as well as various minor services. Farm servants were not allowed to leave the estate without permission, were not allowed to receive guests and were under the supervision of the inspector and the estate bailiffs. For the farm servant, work began in early childhood as assistant to the swineherd and ended, at best, as headman of the farm. Over the centuries there evolved a closed hierachical society which was as conscious of and as sensitive to differences in position as the high aristocracy itself. At the bottom of the hierarchy stood the day-labourers, followed by the drivers, first of the oxen, then those of the horse-drawn carts. Above them came the liveried coachmen, the most prestigious of the three groups. The husbandmen came next, with the horseherd and the shepherds at the top. The artisans, blacksmiths, cartwrights and machine operators constituted a separate caste; they were addressed as "sir" and did not mix with the farm servants.

The "people of the puszta" (a reference to a book on the subject by Gyula Illyés) lived in great poverty and backwardness, eating, working and speaking frugally. They mostly lived in stable-like huts and, from the early twentieth century on, in farm servants' quarters shared between two or four families. It was only after 1900 that servants' quarters of better quality were built. Those contained a separate room for each family but the kitchen was shared. The furniture consisted of plank beds, straw mattresses and a chest. The staple diet of farm servants was carrots, onions, bread, polenta and bacon, with some meat and pastry on holidays.

Harvesting and threshing were done in teams, called harvester gangs, which were recruited especially for the summer. They were hired for two to three months and received one tenth of the harvested crop in payment. By the early twentieth century, however, this had dropped to one eleventh or one twelfth. Crammed into a few months, the harvesters' work was extremely difficult. In the rest of the year, they were lucky if they could

158

work for a few weeks as day-labourers, doing mowing, construction work and wood-cutting. As a migrant worker, the harvester was not closely attached to the estate and the steward. His life was more insecure and more subject to hardships than that of the farm servant but he was also freer. The harvester's thinking was less limited than that of the farm servant and his spirit of enterprise greater. It was primarily these rural day-labourers who went to do seasonal work in the towns, it was they who settled in the suburban factory districts and they who set out to seek their fortune in other lands.

At the end of the nineteenth century, emigration from Hungary gathered momentum. In the twenty-five years prior to the First World War, some two million people, mostly smallholders and agricultural labourers, left the country. Initially their purpose was just to save up money to buy land in Hungary, and a quarter of this number did in fact return to their homeland. Some acquired land, others purchased houses. But a million and a half people emigrated for good, mostly to the United States and Canada. Only one third of these people were, however, Magyars. The rest were Slovaks, Ruthenians, Germans and Croatians. Emigrating Hungarians tended to settle in clusters, the majority in the vicinity of Ohio, Michigan, Cleveland, Detroit and Pittsburg, where they went to work in the mines.

A new world, a new homeland, a new language, a new culture and a new way of life—all brought considerable affliction for the first, pioneer generation of Hungarian emigrants. Understandably, they tried to stay together, sought the community they had been accustomed to, cultivated their mother tongue and preserved their love of the homeland.

Landslide

On 8 October 1905, express messengers from Vienna carried top secret orders to the army corps at Pozsony, Budapest, Kassa, Temesvár, Nagyszeben and Zagreb. Troops were to have occupied the Hungarian capital and key points in the provinces. But why did Emperor Francis Joseph want to wage war against the Hungarian half of his Empire?

The crisis dated back to January 1905. Count István Tisza's Liberal Government lost the election and thirty years of liberal rule came to an end. The opposition parties gained a majority in Parliament and formed a bloc hostile to the Prime Minister. These parties demanded concessions which were unacceptable to the Crown. From this arose a Cabinet crisis. Tisza no longer possessed a majority in Parliament while the Emperor would not permit the victorious opposition parties to form an administration in which the Party of Independence was dominant. The constitutional machinery of Dualism became paralysed.

More distant causes of the crisis go back to the end of the nineteenth century. As Prime Minister, wealthy landowner and bank president Kálmán Széll could ensure only a a few years of calmness (1899–1903). The crisis between the Crown and Hungary stemmed from the old question of the army. When the Széll Government introduced its Army Bill early in 1903, the national opposition issued its programme demanding that the language of command in all Hungarian units be Magyar and that the Hungarian national coat of arms be included in the insignia of Imperial and Royal army. When these demands were rejected, the opposition restored filibustering in Parliament, with the result that parliamentary business would be obstructed. This tactic was so effective that the Budget could not be passed and, in May 1903, the country entered a state of constitutional vacuum known as *ex lex*. In autumn 1903 Francis Joseph in his Chlopy address, warned the Hungarian opposition in no uncertain terms. He declared that he would tolerate neither the undermining of the common army's unity, nor infringement of his own royal prerogative. When this resulted in the fall of yet another Hungarian cabinet, Francis Joseph asked Count István Tisza, known for his firmness, to form an administration.

The son of the powerful Prime Minister Kálmán Tisza, István Tisza was brought up in a period when liberalism was already in decline and when power was there to be exercised, not fought for. From his father he inherited political ability, from his uncle, Lajos Tisza, his title and from his family upper-class conceit. At the turn of the century the Government Party was in search of a leader and determined to make István Tisza a politician. Tisza, a devout Calvinist, believing in his vocation, regarded himself as a political Hercules who would restore law and order and clean the Augean stables of decadent parliamentarism. From 1903, Tisza dealt firmly with obstruction in Parliament. After temporary successes, however, in November 1904, a minor parliamentary "coup" left him isolated. Most members of his own party opposed his coercive methods and throughout the country the opposition, whom Tisza constantly provoked, demanded his sacking.

It was such a situation—made worse by alarming news of the Russian Revolution of 1905—that elections took place in January, bringing such heavy defeat to the Government Party.

Things were made more difficult still by the fact that, in the midst of the political turmoil, working people also launched a struggle. Their aim was to improve working conditions which had deteriorated during the economic depression of the previous few years or so. "The entire country was veritably shaken to the core ... the workers in workshops, factories, and on building sites are downing their tools," wrote *Népszava*. After Russia, there was a landslide in Hungary as well during the spring and summer of 1905. Huge strikes, one staged by over 20,000 workers in the capital, took place. Then, in the summer, a harvesters' strike broke out and extended to Southern Transdanubia. These developments as well as other demonstrations, helped to make the situation explosive.

160

Under these circumstances the country could not be left without a functioning government and consolidated political rule. For lack of anything better, in 1905 the Emperor-King Francis Joseph appointed his favourite soldier, Géza Fejérváry, to be Prime Minister. Fejérváry had previously been Minister of Defence and was commander of the Royal Hungarian Bodyguard. The Lower House protested immediately and there was a public outcry in the whole country. After Fejérváry's unconstitutional government suffered defeat in parliamentary vote of confidence, Parliament announced that the traditional form of national resistance dating from feudal times would be put into effect. This meant that the counties should not collect taxes, should not give their annual complement of recruits and should not carry out orders issued by the unconstitutional government. In the summer of 1905 a national resistance movement was launched by the conservative landowners and the clergy, who had suffered under liberal rule the officials, imbued with the gentry spirit, supported this.

Hard pressed, the Government accepted a proposal by József Kristóffy, the Minister of the Interior, to counter national resistance by introducing electoral and social welfare reforms. By doing this, the Government could expect support from the Social Democratic Party, the organized worker masses which were several hundred thousand strong, the radical intelligentsia and the national minority politicians. On 15 September a huge demonstration took place outside the Parliament building. 100,000 Budapest workers demanded the right to vote and the freedom to organize trade unions. In response, the national opposition planned to resent its own demands on 10 October, the day Parliament was to reconvene after its adjournment. It was out of fear of the consequences that the Ministry of War in Vienna issued its military orders. Those had been prepared in advance and were to be executed in the event of insurrection.

Nothing, however, happened on 10 October. Although the leaders of the opposition coalition remonstrated loudly they called on their supporters to preserve constitutionalism and to support peaceful efforts. They denounced excesses through which the radical popular elements had shown their fighting spirit. The upper-class opposition ostensibly wished to negotiate a compromise solution. Their willingness to negotiate a settlement was increased by the events of the Russian Revolution, by the Tsar's "October Manifesto" granting universal suffrage and by the Moscow uprising in December. Also persuasive were the demonstrations which took place in Vienna at this time and finally led to the introduction of further electoral reform in Austria. At first the leaders of the coalition withdrew some of their demands and said that they would be satisfied by the acknowledgement in principle of the justice of Hungary's army demands. When, however, Francis Joseph dissolved Parliament by military means in February 1906 and threatened to introduce absolutist rule, the opposition leaders came round to view that the Crown's position on this would have to be accepted.

In April 1906 the Coalition concluded a secret pact with Francis Joseph in which it capitulated totally. The opposition undertook to form a government on the basis of the 1867 Compromise agreement and relinquished its demands for military and other national concessions to Hungary. It undertook to renew the Compromise with Austria when it expired and in fact did so in 1907. The opposition also undertook to introduce democratic electoral reform, but it never carried out this promise.

The Cabinet crisis of 1905–6 was resolved with apparently no results, for neither national concessions nor democratic reform were achieved. Yet, there was a result of sorts, namely that the opposition's real nature became clear. Its capitulation to Francis Joseph and its ensuing four years in power showed that the landowners and gentry middle class belonging to it were actually no different from the old Government Party. They manipulated the people by means of traditional national slogans, and were just as undemocratic and just as chauvinistic. Neither the oppressed nor the national minorities of the country could expect anything from this opposition. One positive result of the crisis was that the forces of democracy, the real national and social opposition of the system, became more organized, gained in strength and achieved a certain degree of cohesion.

The Beginnings of the Labour Movement in Hungary

The Hungarian working-class movement had become an organized force by the turn of the century. In its early days it survived intense persecution, especially under the ruthless Bánffy Government (1895–9). During this period almost a hundred workers were killed, several hundred imprisoned or deported from the capital and numerous trade associations and rural workers' circles were dissolved. However, it was precisely during these years that the workers waged their most steadfast and most difficult struggle. In 1897 miners staged a huge strike in the industrial region of Resica and Anina, while 10,000 brick-factory and construction workers did the same in Budapest. In 1897–8 there were harvest strikes and a wave of unrest in the Nyírség, in the counties east of the River Tisza and to the southern part of the Great Plain. April, 1904 witnessed the first railway strike in Hungary: the entire railway network was paralysed and the army had to be called in to deal with the situation. In 1905, a wave of strikes swept through the country and in 1906 extended as far as Miskolc, Temesvár, Fiume and Nagyvárad.

The organizing of the workers into trade unions took place rapidly. Unions were formed in each occupation and trade, and a Trade Council was set up in 1899 to act as an umbrella organization. Both the Trade Council

162

and the unions were under the leadership of the Social Democratic Party and this leadership consolidated at around the turn of the century. The SDP leadership comprised Ernő Garami, Jakab Weltner and Dezső Bokányi. From 1908 onwards, the former teacher Zsigmond Kunfi increasingly emerged as the most influential leader in the party. The SDP leadership steadfastly advocated revolution as the party's ultimate goal, together with the need for a socialist society. Although the SDP leadership stressed the revolutionary character of the movement, in practice it wished to follow the path of reform—adapting a centrist line between the right-wing revisionist and the left-wing revolutionary trends of the international working-class movement. The right to vote was the SDP's chief demand. Other demands were civil rights, equality between nationalities, the abolition of privileges, the nationalisation of Church land, mines and forests and the abolition of entailment.

This programme was geared to conditions in the advanced Western capitalist countries. Although it succeeded in winning the support of the Hungarian workers, it failed adequately to grasp the two issues fundamental to Hungarian development, the agrarian question and the nationalities problem. The Hungarian Social Democracy rejected the idea of distributing the land as it felt that this would be counter to the scientifically confirmed tendency for the means of production to concentrate into large units. The leadership of the party maintained its rigid position even when the movements among the peasantry openly demanded land for the millions of rural poor. "The people need bread, not land"—was a slogan during the early years of the twentieth century, but one that was more suited to self-justification than winning over the poverty-stricken peasants.

The programme of the Social Democratic Party did not openly declare its position on the issues of whether Hungary should be a republic and on demands for greater concessions to the country from Vienna. Also vague were the issues of self-determination for the nationalities and the plan to establish a federation, which had already been accepted in Austria. The program did, however, mention "total autonomy", "the election of all bodies and officials" and "the abolition of all inherited offices and titles". This wording used had the effect of leaving a number of things unclear. It was uncertain whether Emperor Francis Joseph himself would be included and whether "total autonomy" referred to that of the Hungarian State or to self-determination for the national minorities. Not only did the programme ignore these fundamental issues of Hungarian political life, but the SDP did not in practice tamper with these sensitive problems either. In point of fact the SDP directed its entire effort towards achieving universal suffrage with secret ballot. It subordinated every other goal, plan, desire, and even the economic struggles of the workers (which it organized and encouraged), to this.

Although neither the SDP programme, nor the labour movement took up the problems related to the highly topical issues of democratic transformation and national self-determination, the ideas of socialism exerted considerable influence on the masses, shaping their consciousness in the process. In the face of the official liberal nationalist and right-wing conservative political and conceptual system, it created a socialist counter-culture. This was characterized by worker solidarity, new ideas, socialist literature and theatre, music, singing and community spirit in socialist associations. This counter-culture attracted hundreds of thousands of people, although membership of the organized movement did not exceed 200,000 even during its most successful period. The working-class movement exerted particularly great influence over the radical intelligentsia which emerged at the beginning of the twentieth century.

Young sociologists, lawyers and political publicists founded the journal *Huszadik Század* (Twentieth Century) in 1900 and a year later the "Social Science Society". Their aim was to investigate Hungarian society, to discover the causes of Hungary's backwardness and to identify the direction leading to development. The Society organized in-depth discussions and launched the sociographic series *Magyarország felfedezése* (Discovering Hungary). It exposed, one after the other, the grave consequences of large estates and the rule of the big landed aristocracy. These were shown to be poverty for the vast majority of the people, the anti-democratic nature of the political system and the unjust oppression of the national minorities. This radical group also founded the most radical group of freemasons, the Martinovics Lodge, and encouraged the forming of the Galileo Circle. The Galileo Circle organized extra-mural education for the workers and tried to encourage a revival of intellectual life. Oszkár Jászi was one of its leading intellectual figures and alongside him stood his learned associates, Pál Szende, Gyula Rácz and Ervin Szabó, the last of whom broke with Social Democracy.

The group emerged in an organized form in June 1914, shortly before the outbreak of the War and under the name of National Bourgeois Radical Party. Its programme included the abolition of feudal remnants, land reform, human rights, an independent tariff zone, the guaranteeing of the country's interests and equality for the national minorities. As belated advocates of the Enlightenment, the Radicals accepted the socialist idea to be their distant goal and co-operated with the working-class movement. Together they arrived at a new interpretation of patriotism. "Where there is justice, there is the homeland!" They believed that the idea of national autonomy, which had been hijacked and reduced to a slogan, should be linked to the programme of social revival. They reformulated the idea of "country and progress", as it had been known to the Age of Reform. By "country" they understood the country of the whole people and by "progress" they understood social advancement. This is why they came to be known as "the Second Reform Generation".

At the end of the first decade of this century, leftists disappointed by the conservative nationalist leaders of the Party of Independence, joined the

Radical group. These people aspired neither to a political career, nor to a ministerial position, but genuinely represented the tradition of 1848. Their leader, Gyula Justh, was an old warrior for independence. It was he who made the historic transition from the coalition of landowners, gentry officials and clergy to the idea of popular patriotism and left-wing ideals. This change of direction was also made by the young aristocrat, Count Mihály Károlyi, who entered the political arena in the 1910s and soon became the leader of the Independence politicians.

From the left-wing Independence politicians, socialists and radical intellectuals the Hungarian national democracy slowly and belatedly emerged. This occurred too late for the First World War and its consequences to be averted. Nevertheless, it was still in time to give prospect for renewal to the sober and progress-minded elements of the nation.

A Peacock Takes its Perch

"A peacock takes its perch upon the county hall—
A sign that freedom comes to many folk in thrall."
Let the proud, frail peacock, whose feathers daze the sun,
Proclaim that to-morrow here all will be undone.

(Endre Ady; translated by Sir Maurice Bowra)

Hungary was a colourful country at the turn of the century. It was open to foreigners and foreign influences and, accordingly, its culture was rich and complex. The Millennary memorial monument, the reconstructed Royal Palace and the enormous neo-Gothic Parliament building all excluded national tradition. In 1896 also the first *Art nouveau* palace, Ödön Lechner's Museum of Applied Arts, was inaugurated. At this time too, Simon Hollósy, together with his students, founded a new school of painting at Nagybánya, and the Comedy Theatre, the home of modern European acting, was opened. As Hungarian society restructured itself, with the process of embourgeoisment making substantial progress, so its scientific and artistic life became more complex. Alongside the traditional romantic and popular-national neo-Classical culture of the nobility there emerged in it new middle-class urban and popular trends. It was in the field of literature that the simultaneous stratification and ferment in cultural life were shown most clearly.

At the highest level, the national tradition was continued by the elderly writer, Kálmán Mikszáth. However, in the novels he wrote during the first decade of the twentieth century (*A Strange Marriage* and *The Black City*), the anecdotic and cheerful tone of the narrative was increasingly replaced by a bitter and sharp criticism of society. The national tradition was diluted by Ferenc Herczeg to make it suitable for a lower middle-class readership.

It was Herczeg who invested the declining gentry with middle-class qualities and who popularized them in his short stories and plays appearing in
the journal *Új Idők* (New Times). The novelist Géza Gárdonyi brought
national tradition closer to the people, primarily in his fine historical novels.

Edited by József Kiss, the journal *A Hét* (The Week) was the first
publication for the middle class and the big city. The quiet break with the
tradition of the nobility became increasingly obvious in the works of writers
who sympathized with the urban poor and the oppressed. This was especially so in the work of Sándor Bródy, a writer who paved the way for a
new literature. Ferenc Molnár and Jenő Heltai, both good story-tellers and
playwrights, stood closest to the spirit of Budapest's middle class.

Although Ferenc Molnár did not concern himself with the serious problems of Hungarian society and was not alarmed by the premonition of
impending disaster, he did, with refined irony, shed a revealing light on the
upper-class world of his day. In addition he was a great master of stage and
his plays brimmed with sparkling wit. Although less talented perhaps, Jenő
Heltai was a warmer personality than Molnár.

In poetry, though, traditionally the outstanding genre of Hungarian
literature, neither the representatives of the popular-national tradition, nor
those of the new urban taste produced anything of outstanding quality.
A revolutionary change in literature was brought about by the radical
democratic intelligentsia, which made its mark with the appearance on the
literary scene of Endre Ady. Ady was an outstanding poet of the twentieth
century and his significance is not confined solely to literature. Not only
did Ady renew the subject-matter and language of Hungarian poetry, but
he also radically transformed its relationship to the people and the nation.
Ady formulated the new national ideal of the radical reform generation. In
his poetry, he exposed the hitherto hidden depths of the Hungarian common people. In his poems, the language, voice, suffering and rebellion of
the Protestant preacher can be heard, along with the bards of the fortresses
and the soldiers who lived in hiding.

Endre Ady was the poet of the Hungarian soul and at the same time, the
prophet of Hungarian destiny. By means of his work, faith and actions Ady
soon rallied behind him friends and enemies alike. Ady represented a
watershed in the Hungary of the Habsburg Empire. Around him gathered
the innovative, creative spirits and around him Ernő Osvát and Baron Lajos
Hatvany built the literary journal *Nyugat* (West). *Nyugat* later attained
great fame and the outstanding writers and poets of the period belonged
to its circle. They were joined by a friend of Ady's, Zsigmond Móricz, who
revived popular narrative prose. Other members included the poet Mihály
Babits, a master of form inclined to intellectual exclusiveness and whose
art was remote from that of Ady. Mihály Babits carried on the legacy of
János Arany. Another *Nyugat* writer was Dezső Kosztolányi, the poet so
receptive to Western Impressionism. Others included Árpád Tóth, the
poet with a quiet voice who sympathized with the people; Gyula Juhász,

who united tradition with rebellion; and Frigyes Karinthy, a satirist with a philosophical frame of mind who also possessed a sense of the absurd and the grotesque. The *Nyugat* circle was joined by thinkers who were far removed from the materialism of the radical left. They included Dezső Szabó, Béla Balázs and the greatest philosopher of the age, György Lukács. Lukács was initially an idealist and was also won over by Ady to the concept of a new, progressive Hungarian spirit.

The musical tradition of the Romantic era was continued at the beginning of the twentieth century by Jenő Hubay and was later modernized by the talented young musician, Ernő Dohnányi. The activities of the Opera and the Philharmonic Society refined the musical taste of their educated audiences, which were drawn from a narrow section of society. The majority of the middle class and the lower middle class were ardent operetta lovers. Their favourites included the Viennese waltzes of Johann Strauss, the *Gypsy Baron* and later Ferenc Lehár and his witty and animated work *The Merry Widow*. Soon Victor Jacobi, Jenő Huszka and Imre Kálmán produced indigenous Pest operetta and the *Csárdás Queen,* which has reigned supreme ever since. The nobility, whose taste was becoming increasingly middle-class, preferred the Hungarian-style singing of popular tunes, the sentimentally composed songs of Lóránd Fráter and Pista Dankó and the melancholic, sometimes lively music of the gypsies, which made it so easy to cry and be merry. This soon gave rise to the creation of the so-called popular play which dealt with peasant life in the nineteenth century and which contained songs composed for the purpose. Another work which resulted was *John the Hero* whose lyrics, written by Jenő Heltai, were set to music by Pongrác Kacsóh.

The distinction between a Western-style musical culture and the Hungarian custom of singing popular songs was lessened by two young musicians and scholars, Béla Bartók and Zoltán Kodály. The two Hungarian geniuses of this century, Bartók and Kodály started out from national romanticism but soon discovered the pure source, the genuine, ancient pentatonic folk song. The two men went on study trips to collect long-forgotten and neglected Magyar, Slovak and Roumanian folk songs which they adapted to modern European music's new form of expression. Bartók's opera *Bluebeard's Castle,* his music for the ballets *The Wooden Prince,* and *The Miraculous Mandarin* raised an archaic popular genre to the realm of subtly composed music. Like Ady's poetry, Bartók's music gave expression to the complaints and humanism of the twentieth century individual represented in the suffering Hungarian people. The works of Bartók and Kodály triggered off a huge offensive by artistic and political conservatism but nevertheless they became the foundation of new Hungarian musical culture.

The turn of the century also marked the beginning of an entirely new epoch in the history of Hungarian art. Admittedly, the start of this new era was not accompanied by the appearance of new artistic geniuses but nevertheless work of considerable value in fine arts was produced. As in literature, music and the theatre, in fine arts, too, there was a three-part division of culture and taste. The circles committed to tradition rejected innovation, even Pál Szinyei Merse's early Impressionism. Even great masters such as Gyula Benczúr and Bertalan Székely were not receptive to new developments. Innovation in a middle-class vein was represented by the Nagybánya School and above all by Károly Ferenczy in his pictures. These were inspired by French Impressionism and were imbued with a sense of light and air.

The "Art nouveau" of the turn of the century inspired the painting of János Vaszary and especially József Rippl-Rónai, the outstanding artist who was brought up in Paris. From the circle of artistic innovators, a small avantgarde group, known as "The Eight", broke away. "The Eight" rallied painters who shared the markedly Constructivist vision of Károly Kernstok. Many eventually broke with traditional forms of expression and moved on to abstract trends.

There were, however, two exceptionally talented artists at this time. Tivadar Csontváry Kosztka and Lajos Gulácsy could not be placed in either of these categories. Both painted a magical reality that was behind and beyond the visible world. Full of symbols, Csontváry's Biblical scenes sought lost community and identity, as did Gulácsy's dream world, Naconxypan, and its timeless and other-wordly inhabitants.

During this period Hungarian scientific life also enjoyed a revival. Having learnt from the achievements of German and, later French and British scholarship, the social sciences developed rapidly. The same was true for legal and historical scholarship—both traditionally popular in Hungary—and also for linguistics and literary history. A new development occurred, however, when the natural sciences took root. The name of Loránd Eötvös became famous not only for his invention of the pendulum used in geological research, but also for his theories on the measurement of gravity and magnetism. Alongside Eötvös, and partly under his guidance, there emerged the first great school of mathematicians, hallmarked by the names of Gyula Kőnig, József Kürschák and, later, those of Lipót Fejér and Frigyes Riesz. These schools produced great mathematicians and physicists such as János Neumann, who made a substantial contribution to number and set theory, and Leó Szilárd and Jenő Wigner, who did outstanding work in nuclear physics. This period witnessed the emergence, alongside the world-famous medical school in Vienna, of the Budapest School of Medicine. This followed in the wake of excellent doctors such as Frigyes Korányi, János Balassa, Endre Hőgyes and others.

It appeared as though abundance of great talent in all fields of art and science was Nature's way of compensating for the centuries of mediocrity. The early twentieth century witnessed the rallying of some of the finest intellects, writers, artists, and scholars of the country. "In the struggle waged with intellectual weapons the victory is already theirs," wrote Endre

168

Ady in 1907, "The time will come when it will be theirs in the political struggle as well. That time will be the renaissance of Hungary."

And that time did come, although not as had been envisaged by Ady and his associates before the First World War. Many of Hungary's outstanding intellectuals, artists and scholars died during the war and many became crippled for life. The loss of the war and the failure of the two subsequent revolutions broke the spirit of most of these people, forcing them either into exile abroad or into oblivion at home.

On the Road of War

The political crisis of 1905, which was accompanied by fierce class struggles and national resistance across the country, clarified the political situation to some extent. After thirty years the national opposition finally gained power—but nothing changed. This was despite the fact that the Party of Independence, which won the most seats in 1906, had for decades been the bearer of national desires and hopes. The Constitutional Party had promised national reforms and the Catholic People's Party social ones. These were not, however, forthcoming from the new Wekerle Government which was in power from 1906 to 1910, and which was based on a coalition of these parties. Admittedly, the landowners were given the high agricultural tariffs they had been promised and the middle class sizeable financial support for industry. Also a new code of regulations was drafted for officials and their pay raised. In addition, nationalist public opinion was encouraged by a new Magyarizing education act. Nevertheless, important national reforms, the establishment of Magyar as the language of command in the army, the creation of an independent tariff zone and the introduction of universal suffrage, were never implemented. Universal suffrage had even been agreed to with Francis Joseph in 1906 but this made no difference. In the autumn of 1907 the Wekerle Government renewed the economic Compromise with Austria. This was the last time this was done and for Hungary the terms agreed to in that year were unfavourable.

The Cabinet was studded with big names. They included Count Gyula Andrássy Junior, scholar, writer and party leader; Count Albert Apponyi, a talented speaker; Ignác Darányi, an expert on agriculture; Count Aladár Zichy, son of the founder of the People's Party; and Ferenc Kossuth, the son of Lajos Kossuth but disappointing in comparison with his famous father. The traditional Independence opposition's period in office shed true light on the nature of Hungarian politics. The real alternative to the traditional Liberalism was not the conservative nationalism which this opposition represented, but radical democracy.

The peasantry and the lower middle class now began to realize this. In 1906, András Áchim formed his Peasant Party at Békéscsaba and, for the first time a political party linked the issue of political democracy with the demand for land distribution. It was in vain that Áchim was stripped of his seat in Parliament, it was in vain that he was harrassed with libel suits and personal attacks. The popularity of his party spread rapidly among the peasantry in the "Stormy Corner" *(Viharsarok)* and the Great Plain. In 1908, four hundred settlements delegated their representatives, which included a number of non-Magyars, to the party's congress in Cegléd. This congress, which witnessed the unveiling of a statue of the great peasant leader György Dózsa, adopted a programme demanding the distribution of big landed estates of over one thousand hectars in size. Finally, upper-class Hungarian society would tolerate Áchim no more: in May 1911 the two sons of Endre Zsilinszky murdered Áchim on the grounds that he had insulted their family.

In Transdanubia, István Nagyatádi Szabó founded the National Independence and "48 Smallholders'" Party, commonly referred to as the Smallholders' Party. This party adopted a more moderate platform than Áchim's Peasant Party. It did not entirely reject the big landed estates, but it did call for the abolition of entailment, for a more equal distribution of land and for suffrage. Although Nagyatádi Szabó's organization was less radical than Áchim's, also tended towards democratic transformation.

Within the Party of Independence, Gyula Justh and his left-wing supporters gave voice to their disappointment in its leadership. Backed by that segment of the lower middle class which supported the ideals of 1848 along with peasants and intellectuals. Justh broke with the leadership of Ferenc Kossuth and Count Albert Apponyi in 1909 and founded a new party. This party demanded universal suffrage and gradually recognized that both alliance with the radicals and land reform were inevitable. These developments constituted a great step forward. Justh's party, wrote Oszkár Jászi, had always been the party of the peasants, artisans and poor intellectuals, but it was thanks to Justh's efforts that it was led back to Lajos Kossuth's original 1848 programme.

From the very beginning the Coalition Government stood on shaky and precarious ground. In 1909 its internal unity disintegrated and, after a not very successful period in office, it fell in 1910. It was replaced in that year by the old Liberal group led by Count Károly Khuen-Héderváry and László Lukács, both supporters of István Tisza. Tisza reorganized the Liberals under the name of the "Party of Work". After his defeat in 1905, Tisza had retired for a few years and had reconsidered the political and social situation in the country. When antagonism towards him began to wane, Tisza returned to the political scene with a new approach. He now realized that the real enemy of the existing socio-political order was not the parliamentary opposition, but the growing of democratic and socialist popular movements. Accordingly, the most important task of the ruling class was to preserve its power and property intact. This was his primary objective and not the proper working of the parliamentary system.

In the 1910s Tisza made great efforts to rally the propertied classes and the forces of conservatism. He did not reject negotiations with Croatian and Roumanian national minority leaders and had no qualms about using force to break parliamentary obstruction. In May 1912, Tisza was elected President of the House, a development most unpopular with every shade of opposition thinking. On 23 May a huge mass demonstration swept the Hungarian capital. Demonstrators built barricades against the mounted police and gendarmes sent to deal with them. Trams were overturned and finally the army had to be called in to calm the situation. The Government ruthlessly supressed the wave of unrest which swept not only Budapest but the provinces too. Tisza used coercion to silence parliamentary opposition and forced through the long-disputed Army Bill, together with draft legislation preparing for war.

By this time, though, conflict involving the Habsburg Empire was not far off. In 1912 the members of the Balkan League (Greece, Bulgaria, Serbia and Montenegro) waged war on the Ottoman Empire to shake off the Turkish yoke once and for all. These states enjoyed quick and remarkable success, the Turkish army was defeated and Turkey driven out of Europe almost entirely. Austria–Hungary looked helplessly as hostilities engulfed the region to the south of her and was unable to intervene. The first Balkan War did not bring peace to the region. In a squabble over the spoils, the other states turned on Bulgaria and the fighting started again. Bulgaria was considered to be friendly to Austria–Hungary but received no assistance from her. The Second Balkan War ended in crushing defeat for the Bulgarians and a heavy blow to Austria–Hungary's prestige.

The Treaty of Bucharest (August 1913), which ended the Second Balkan War, stripped Bulgaria of the fruits of her previous victories and substantially added the size and prestige of Serbia. Moreover, it also strengthened Roumania, which had also joined in the hostilities, and accentuated the Monarchy's serious loss of face. Powerful and self-conscious states had emerged on the southern and eastern frontiers of Austria–Hungary, which with Turkey already defeated, could soon turn against the Empire itself. The small Balkan states could also expect backing from France and Russia, both major powers. In contrast, the Triple Alliance, to which Austria–Hungary belonged, began to lose cohesion. Italy drifted away somewhat and Germany was not prepared to give full-hearted support to Austro–Hungarian expansionism in the Balkans.

In this way the situation of Austria–Hungary became potentially very grave. The Balkans could explode at any time and nationalism among the peoples there threatened the very existence of the Habsburg Empire. The Serbians, Roumanians and Italians all wished to recover areas for national unity. At home the struggle was still on for suffrage and parliamentary control when World War cast a shadow over Hungary and the whole of Europe.

171

The Declaration of War

The inevitable was finally brought to pass by a revolver shot. On 28 June 1914, Gavrilo Princip, a Serbian student, assassinated the heir apparent to the Austro–Hungarian throne, Archduke Francis Ferdinand—together with his wife—in Sarajevo. The events of Francis Ferdinand's visit to the Bosnian capital, from the ceremonial procession there to the assassination itself, from the start of the sabre-rattling to the outbreak of war itself, are known to almost everyone. Yet many still continue to regard them as chance happenings. The truth, however, is that fate was neither blind nor anonymous in Sarajevo. It sprang from imperialism, the bonds of which the Great Powers had been loosening for years.

At first, news of the assassination caused sensation rather than indignation. In his summer residence at Ischl the Emperor-King, Francis Joseph, received the news with resignation and as the will of a just God. So did his Hungarian Prime Minister, Count István Tisza (1861–1918), at his Geszt estate. However, the war party, and especially the pugnacious Chief of Staff, Conrad von Hötzendorf, wanted to exploit the sympathy generated by the assassinations to settle scores with Serbia. Immediately after the Viennese Government received the go-ahead from Berlin: preparations for war commenced.

Although the events themselves are well-known, the same cannot be said of the causes, their relatedness and the secret motives behind the public actions. To begin with, the question immediately arises why, once the military and diplomatic leaders of Austria–Hungary had decided on war and obtained Germany's support, they failed to attack straight way. The answer lies in the opposition they encountered from the Hungarian Prime Minister, István Tisza, the same strong politician who afterwards so zealously committed himself and his country to the struggle. Tisza initially regarded the international balance of power as extremely unfavourable from the point of view of Austria–Hungary. He believed that Bulgaria, her only reliable ally to the south, had been utterly exhausted as a result of the Balkan Wars (1912–3). He also believed that Germany had shown definite signs of sympathy towards Roumania which, the Hungarian leadership feared, would eventually break into Transylvania. Tisza resisted for almost a fortnight. In spite of this, though Austrian and German politicians, together with the military, finally convinced him that the time was now ripe for the Central Powers to go to war. Any delay would serve the interests of the Entente—made up of the "enemies": France, Britain and Russia. Furthermore, they convinced him that Roumania would be neutral in any conflict.

But what actually was the Austrian case against Serbia? On what grounds did she send her ultimatum? Austria claimed that Serbia was responsible for agitation against the Empire and, in addition, for a host of terrorist acts

172

within its borders. Were these accusations true? Could the Serbian government have known about the plans for the assassination of Archduke Francis Ferdinand? The Serbian Prime Minister, Pašić, denied throughout the charge that it did. In 1924, however, one of his fellow ministers admitted —and his admission seems to be substantiated by a number of documents —that the Serbian Goverment had in fact known of the plan, disapproved of it, but was unable to prevent it. What is more, owing to a tense domestic situation, it did not dare to notify the Government in Vienna.

It does indeed appear as though the Serbian Government was to some extent responsible for having failed to warn Vienna. However, in July 1914 the Viennese Government was entirely unaware of this. In fact, a special commissioner of inquiry dispatched to Sarajevo reported that there was nothing to substantiate allegations of the Serbian Government's complicity. In short, the leading politicians of Austria–Hungary, among them Tisza, had drafted and dispatched the unacceptable ultimatum of 23 July in the belief that the Serbian Government was innocent.

It was not, however, on grounds of innocence that the Pašić Government rejected the important demands of the ultimatum on 25 July. The real reason was that Russia and France encouraged and prompted it to do so. When French President Poincaré visited St Petersburg on 20 July 1914, both France and Russia—counting on the support of their British friends —believed that the balance of power at that time would favour the Entente, should a war with the Central Powers break out. As a result, the assassination in Sarajevo soon assumed an importance extending well beyond narrow dynastic interests. The relationship between tiny Serbia and a decaying Austro–Hungarian Empire became a crucial issue between world-wide power interests. The assassination of Francis Ferdinand was only the spark which set off the powder-keg already in existence.

Neither the explosiveness of the international situation nor the mutual antagonism of the Great Powers can, however, overshadow the responsibility of individuals for events. The war was, after all, planned and started by individuals. What is certain is that this responsibility rests chiefly with the Empire's war party, including Francis Joseph himself—who, as he put it in his general order to the army had "considered everything and thought over everything" but in reality had given way to pressure from his soldiers and from the German General Staff. In this sense part of the blame must rest with István Tisza who, in spite of having realistically assessed the balance of power at the time and the likely consequences of aggression, did not vote against the declaration of war and did not resign when it was decided upon. The German military and political leadership, including Emperor Wilhelm himself, who pledged their support during this critical time, must also take much of the responsibility.

Naturally, seventy years afterwards, it is not really the assessment of responsibility which should be the task of historians. More important by far is the clear presentation of the causes and consequences of the war and the thorough understanding of a system in the nature of which expansionism and war were inherent.

The Austro–Hungarian Empire declared war on Serbia on 28 July. That same night her Danube flotilla began to bombard Belgrade. On 30 July Russia and Austria–Hungary simultaneously began mobilization against each other. On 1 August Germany ordered mobilization and declared war firstly on Russia and, two days later, on France. On 5 August Austria–Hungary declared war on Russia and on the same day Britain declared war on Germany. A week later a state of war was declared between the Anglo–French alliance and the Austro–Hungarian Empire.

By this time the report of the Sarajevo revolver had been entirely drowned in the clamour of marching armies, the sound of guns—and the explosion of empires.

Problems at the Front—and at Home

News of the declaration of war was received in Hungary with a sudden outburst of patriotic enthusiasm. Everywhere colourful and noisy ceremonies were staged to see the soldiers off to the war—which everyone believed would be short. However, the rapturous enthusiasm of the early days was soon eroded by the humiliating and catastrophic defeats of the first few months. The inadequately prepared and poorly-commanded armies of the Empire suffered defeat in every theatre of war. Her offensive ground to a halt in Serbia and on the Eastern front advance gave way to retreat as the Russian army pressed forward into the Carpathian Mountains. It was only with German military assistance that Austria–Hungary was able to halt Russia's winter offensive of 1914–15, to break through on the Russian front in May 1915, (and to press into Serbia to the south). However, Italy's entry into the war that same year on the side of the Entente reduced the value of these military successes. This was because Austria–Hungary now had to divert resources to yet another front, as the Italians attempted to advance into her mountainous southwestern areas.

In 1915 the Central Powers (by now Germany, Austria–Hungary, Bulgaria and Turkey) scored considerable success on the Eastern Front and in the Balkans.

However, they were unable to turn these to good account. The following year another enormous Russian offensive pushed the frontline back to within Austro–Hungarian territory. Thus Russian advance prompted Roumania to enter the war against the Central Powers. In August 1916 Roumanian troops invaded Transylvania—only to be repelled by an Austro–Hungarian army assisted by German troops. This force afterwards occupied most of Roumania.

In 1917 the growing plight of the Central Powers was alleviated by the

174

Russian revolutions and Russia's subsequent withdrawal from the war. This advantage was, however, soon offset by the entry into the conflict of the United States on the side of the Entente. Thereafter, despite Germany's tactical victories on the Western Front, and Austria–Hungary's in the war against Italy, the enemy's superiority, both material and military, gradually became overwhelming. By the end of 1917 the Empire which had sustained serious material losses and had suffered a heavy death toll since the very beginning of the war, became utterly exhausted. Discontent, desertion and mutiny also began to affect the army.

The civilian population behind the lines also suffered greatly from the war. The most important factories were turned over to war production and placed under military supervision, with attendant military discipline. In the first year of the war there was already a shortage of basic commodities and the black market flourished. In 1916 the production of cereals used for bread fell back to two thirds of the pre-war level and in 1918 it was down to half. The Government soon introduced the compulsory handing in of produce, livestock and horses, and resorted to requisition. While this hit the peasantry very hard, it did not, even with rationing, solve the problem of keeping the urban population supplied.

The living conditions of the workers had seriously deteriorated by 1915–16. Throughout the country people had to go without food and fuel. Moreover, the head of the family, the normal breadwinner, was usually absent through military service. Everywhere the dead were mourned and the captured and crippled lamented. Those on fixed incomes suffered the most. The volume of paper money in circulation increased fifteen-fold during the war. Sharply accelerating inflation was aggravated by the raising, on eight separate occasions, of war loans. War-widows, orphans and disabled servicemen received just enough aid to keep them from starving. According to contemporary estimates the real earnings of skilled workers dropped to half of their pre-war level, while those of white-collar workers and day-labourers fell to forty per cent of their 1913 value.

The growing discontent of the masses gave considerable encouragement to the anti-war activities of the Social Democrats and radical leftists. In turn these men and women imparted a growing consciousness to the anti-militarist sentiments of the workers. Mihály Károlyi's anti-war move in Parliament at the end of 1916 was received with sympathy by the workers. Despite military discipline, strikes erupted in many places. In 1917, for the first time during the war, May Day was celebrated. The yearning for peace, which was filling every stratum of the population at home spread irresistibly under the influence of the Russian revolutions of February and October 1917—and as a result of increasingly confident socialist agitation. This longing even began to reach the rank-and-file soldier at the front. This encouraged the belligerent Governments to put forward peace initiatives.

On 21 November 1916 Francis Joseph I, Emperor of Austria and King of Hungary, died. In keeping with his life, his burial was dispassionately cold and almost bureaucratic. Francis Joseph's death marked the approaching end of an empire and of an entire epoch. His successor, Charles IV of Hungary, reigned for just two years and was a weak and gullible character. Although Charles realized that only extensive reforms and the immediate conclusion of a peace treaty could save his empire in its desperate situation, mere good will was inadequate at such a decisive stage. Reforms remained at the level of promises, and Charles's feeble and half-hearted peace attempts were doomed to failure. His greatest act in the eyes of the masses was the sacking of the intensely hated István Tisza, who had stubbornly rejected any change in direction. Although they were more flexible, Tisza's successors continued his policy towards the war and, in the final analysis, no change of any substance were introduced in Austria–Hungary right up to the final collapse.

The war dragged on—despite powerful mass protests. During the winter of 1917–18 the soldiers at the front and their relatives back home were going hungry, suffering and dying. As before, strikes, mutinies and protest movements in the country itself were suppressed. The continuation of the war was the chief means of procuring peace at home—aided by the gendarmerie and police. In 1918, however, these traditional methods became increasingly ineffective. Letters confiscated by military censors bear witness to widespread destitution, bitterness and a powerful desire for peace. "This is no life", wrote a peasant woman from Mezőgyán to her prisoner of war husband in autumn 1917,"we, the poor cry ourselves to sleep, wake up crying, eat crying, thinking over the course of our life and why the ground does not open beneath our feet to swallow us up". As for the rich, "would the Good Lord send a war on those of them who have not had enough of this bloodshed, and make them homeless too".

The situation became even more explosive during the long, hot summer of 1918.

IV. OUR MODERN HISTORY

Revolutions—1918–1919

The Military Collapse and the Revolution of 1918

Each event of the last year of the war brought nearer the inevitable collapse of the Austro–Hungarian Empire. The military situation, internal decay and the policy of the Entente Powers all served to precipitate it.

On 8 January 1918 Woodrow Wilson, the President of the United States, delivered an address to Congress in which he outlined his famous Fourteen Points. Regarding "the peoples of Austria–Hungary", stated that they "should be accorded the freest opportunity of autonomous development". Vienna and Budapest would have liked to achieve survival for the Empire and a favourable peace on the basis of the Fourteen Points. For their part, the politicians of the non-Magyar peoples used them as pretexts for secession and territorial expansion for the emerging new states. These new states were, however, guaranteed by secret treaties and promises made during the war. These involved the meeting of Italian, Czechoslovak, Roumanian and Southern Slav demands.

In Soviet Russia, Lenin's Bolshevik Goverment concluded, on 3 March, a separate peace treaty with the Germans at Brest-Litovsk. Germany was therefore able to re-deploy substantial forces on the Western Front. Tens of thousands of captured Hungarian soldiers fought in the Russian Civil War on the side of the Bolsheviks and also helped them oppose the interventionist armies. In March Béla Kun formed the Hungarian section of the Russian Communist (Bolshevik) Party.

At home not a single day passed without strikes and demonstrations demanding an end to the war, universal suffrage, a secret ballot and internal democratization. In line with an initiative in Vienna, a three-day general strike was organized in January. On 1 February sailors staged a mutiny in the Adriatic port Kotor (Cattaro). This was suppressed on orders from Admiral Miklós Horthy.

On 20 May a major mutiny of troops broke out in Hungary which the authorities were only able to put down after a day of heavy fighting.

Desertion rates grew higher and higher. The Minister of the Interior dissolved the Galileo Circle, the left-wing youth and intellectual organization, and put its leaders—among them Ilona Duczynska—on trial. The Government of Sándor Wekerle attempted to resign, first in January and subsequently on several occasions in the course of the year. However, Charles IV and his advisers refused to concede political leadership to the opposition rallying around Count Mihály Károlyi.

On 8 April the Empire's national minority leaders declared in a joint resolution in Rome that those they claimed to represent no longer wished to remain within an Austro–Hungarian Empire. This contributed to the final decision of the Entente Powers to accept the French concept of a *cordon sanitaire*. What this actually meant was that crumbling Austria–Hungary would be replaced by independent bourgeois states. The purpose of these new states was to isolate revolutionary Russia by creating a "protective band" around it, as well as to close off Germany's path of possible future expansionism. In February 1916 *émigré* Czech and Slovak politicians formed the Czechoslovak National Council. From September 1918 onwards the other national minorities formed similar bodies of their own.

Meanwhile the Hungarian units of the Imperial and Royal Army suffered devastating defeat on the Italian front. The names Piave, Isonzo and Doberdo left their indelible mark on the memories of this generation. On 20 June, workers of the MÁV Engineering Works in Budapest demonstrated against the futile destruction and bloodshed of the war, and against the methods employed by the factory's military commanders. The law-enforcement detachments ordered to the scene opened fire on them. In response, a wave of strikes once again engulfed the country. In many places Workers' Councils, or Soviets, organizations hitherto unknown in the Hungarian working class movement, were formed.

Early in August the Entente armies broke through and pressed victoriously ahead on the Western and Balkan fronts. In September Bulgaria capitulated, followed in mid-October by Turkey. Under its commander, Franchet d'Esperey, the Balkan Army of the Allies pressed forward in the direction of Hungary.

Vienna now made a last desperate effort to retrieve the situation. On 16 October Charles IV proclaimed Austria to be a federal state. On 17 October István Tisza, having survived an assassination attempt the previous day, made a statement to the Hungarian Parliament. He declared simply, "We have lost war." Coming from him, this statement was like a bombshell.

On 25 October—much later than the national minorities—Mihály Károlyi formed the Hungarian National Council in Budapest. Oszkár Jászi then drafted its twelve-point programme for the establishment of Hungary's own independence, an immediate separate peace treaty, universal suffrage with secret ballot, land reform and recognition of the rights of the national minorities. It was taken for granted that the King would replace

178

Wekerle, who had once again tendered his resignation, with Károlyi, as by now quite a few politicians and organizations—among them the Budapest police force—had joined the National Council. However, Count János Hadik became the new Prime Minister. In protest, the people, on 28 October, marched from the Inner City to Buda Castle to demand Károlyi's appointment. A veritable battle broke out between demonstrators and law-enforcement detachments on the Chain Bridge.

On the very same day the Czechoslovak Republic was proclaimed in Prague. On 29 October Croatia joined the newly-emerging Yugoslavia and on the day after that the Provisional National Assembly in Vienna proclaimed Austria to be an idependent state. Although the Austro–Hungarian army was still fighting against the Italians, the Empire itself had almost entirely collapsed.

During the night of 30–31 October, 1918 Budapest's streets were crowded with people, soldiers and civilians, who initially cheered the National Council based in the Astoria Hotel. Later, however, the people occupied public buildings, prevented the movement to the provinces of army divisions loyal to Károlyi and captured Budapest's Military Governor. As in March 1848, they freed political prisoners. Asters and rosettes replaced the torn-off insignia on the soldiers' uniforms and also appeared in the buttonholes of civilians' suits. Although asters are generally considered to represent death, in Autumn 1918 they greeted a new spring.

"We did not want to take over power yet, we wanted to organize our forces", wrote Károlyi in his 1923 memoirs. "But in the meantime the entire revolution developed." At this point the Emperor-King Charles himself was forced to retreat: on 31 October he asked Károlyi to form a new government.

During the afternoon of the same day a few armed soldiers and workers forced their way into Count István Tisza's town house in Hermina Street where, after a brief verbal exchange, they shot dead the former Prime Minister. In the minds of the people Tisza had come to represent the entire dualist system and its pro-war policy. Popular wrath had long been fermenting against him, and in his death contemporaries saw the administration of justice by History.

Revolution triumphed and, for the first time since 1848, an independent Hungarian government had been formed. It seemed that the collapse of the dualist system was paving the way to the democratization of Hungary and the more harmonious co-existence of the various peoples of the Danube Basin. However, the legacy of the past obstructed this path and no one at the time estimated correctly the enormous effort required to clear it.

Hopes for a Bourgeois Democracy

The appointment of Mihály Károlyi as Prime Minister in Autumn 1918 was received with unprecedented enthusiasm and general approbation. Never before did a Hungarian statesman have to lead the nation under such tragically difficult conditions. Everyone expected Károlyi to secure for Hungary favourable treatment and fair peace terms. This general hope stemmed from the fact that in Hungary Károlyi had always been regarded as having not just sympathy for the Entente but also contacts with it.

The Great Powers, however, treated Hungary as a vanquished nation. They considered the new government as no more than the legal successor to the old. They appreciated neither its bourgeois democratic nature, nor its pro-Entente orientation. It was under Károlyi that the country's territorial disintegration took place, and under conditions which caused profound disturbance to the whole of Hungarian society. Its acceptance therefore became even more difficult.

On 3 November 1918, a week before the Germans, the Austro–Hungarian army and the Italians facing them signed an armistice in Padua. However, Franchet d'Esperey, overall commander of the Entente Forces in the Balkans, did not recognize the validity of this agreement for his own section of the front. With him the Károlyi Government signed, on 13 November, a military convention in Belgrade. This was the first occasion the victors acknowledged the existence of an independent Hungary and its new government. Unlike the armistice agreement of 3 November, the military convention established a demarcation line between Hungary and her enemies within the borders of the historic state.

This was not the only development which undermined confidence in the government. Adding insult to injury, Roumania and the new Czechoslovak and Yugoslav states ignored this agreement entirely. Even before the signature of the Belgrade Convention, firstly Czechoslovak and later Roumanian forces crossed the line—with full authorization from Paris. In spite of vigorous protests from the Károlyi Government along with limited resistance, they halted only in mid-January, 1919. The limits of their advance corresponded roughly to what eventually became the new Hungarian frontier in these areas. In the meantime, however, Roumanian and Yugoslav units had also clashed over possession of Bácska. French troops were forced to intervene and occupied Szeged in the process.

At home, consolidation was rather slow for the new government. The failure of the negotiations with the Entente was an important reason for this. The Károlyi Government regarded the revolution as now complete and subsequently as if wished only to introduce constitutional reforms. For their part, however, the industrial workers, the smallholders, the poor peasantry and the many prisoners returned from Soviet Russia regarded it as only a beginning. For them it was merely the prelude to another revolution—a revolution along Soviet lines. Although law and order were successfully maintained in Budapest, in the provinces public buildings were attacked, some of the officials and gendarmes driven out and even executed, shops looted and very often armed skirmishes occurred. Only the introduction of martial law could stem the tide of revolt.

This spontaneous discontent soon acquired both purpose and direction. On 24 November, 1918, the Communist Party of Hungary (CPH) was formed under the leadership of Béla Kun. The Communist Party had a political programme and an organizational framework and its popularity grew rapidly among the workers, demobilized soldiers and unemployed. The CPH aimed at the transformation of the bourgeois democracy into a dictatorship of the proletariat.

Within the Social Democratic Party (SDP), the principal party supporting the Coalition Government, a pro-communist left-wing group was becoming increasingly influential. Inside Károlyi's own Independence Party and even in the Government itself, opinions differed as not just with regard to policy, but the way in which it should be implemented. A group of Károlyi's supporters left the Independence Party because they thought the Government too weak in the face of the revolutionary left-wing. The right-wing groups supported by members of the former ruling circle, the middle class and especially the army officers wanted to do away with bourgeois democracy and bring back the former conservative system. Under the leadership of Count István Bethlen, a Transylvanian aristocrat, and Gyula Gömbös, an army officer, they began to organize against the Károlyi regime.

It was therefore under very difficult conditions that the Government implemented its programme. On 16 November, amid great ceremony, Hungary's independence was proclaimed and the constitutional form of Republic adopted. On 11 January 1919 Mihály Károlyi became Hungary's first President. Legislation was enacted to introduce universal suffrage with secret ballot and to guarantee freedom of the press, assembly and association. The democratization of the public administration was begun and, at the suggestion of Jenő Varga, in March 1919 it was decided to set up a separate ministry to begin nationalization. Oszkár Jászi, Oszkár Asbóth, Gyula Szekfű, Marcell Benedek and others were all appointed university and college professors. The *Nyugat* circle of writers and intellectuals established the Vörösmarty Academy with Endre Ady as its first president. Following his death on 27 January 1919 Zsigmond Móricz took over. Members of the National Council's Artistic Committee included József Rippl-Rónai, Ödön Márffy, Károly Lyka, Mihály Babits, György Lukács, Gyula Krúdy, Lajos Kassák, Ferenc Molnár, Béla Bartók, Zoltán Kodály, Ernő Dohnányi and Jenő Hubay among others.

However, neither higher wages, nor unemployment benefit could enable ordinary people to make ends meet. In addition to shortages of food and basic commodities, there was also a shortage of heating fuel. Industry was paralysed and unable to offer much employment. The families fleeing inland from areas under foreign occupation needed food and accomodation, and providing these was a serious burden. To make matters worse still, the influenza epidemic of that time was also taking its toll.

On February 16 the Government's Land Reform Act was passed. This was a piece of legislation justly described by Zsigmond Móricz as being historically significant. However, the distribution of land it was supposed to bring about only commenced on the Károlyi estate. The reaction of the land-hungry peasants was to take possession of the large estates unilaterally. On the whole they regarded their collective possession of the land as only the first step to its distribution among individuals. This was in spite of the fact that the Social Democrats and the Communists had both advocated collective farming.

The government was unable to prevent these developments, just as it was unable to prevent the expulsion from office of the newly appointed Lord-Lieutenant Government Commissioner *(főispán–kormánybiztos)*. The administration of a number of towns (for example, Székesfehérvár and Szekszárd) and a number of counties (for example, Hajdú-Békés and Barcs) came under the control of so-called Directories.

The Károlyi Government failed to come to agreement with the country's non-Magyar peoples. Oszkár Jászi had earlier developed the concept of a "Danubian United Nations" or an "Eastern Switzerland". This offered a confederation of democratic states and, within it, autonomy for the national minorities. The Hungarian nationalists rejected the idea, as did the leaders of the neighbouring peoples. Since these leaders were hostile and since Budapest had lost its authority over the minorities, negotiations for the implementation of this scheme were impossible.

At the beginning of 1919 the Károlyi Government struck at its left-wing and right-wing critics. Attempts were made to curtail the right-wing opposition and to liquidate the Communist Movement. On 21 February 1919, Béla Kun himself and fifty-four Communist leaders were imprisoned on the pretext of a street demostration and a shooting incident. Shortly afterwards, a mass of demonstrations was staged demanding their release. Károlyi, however, ensured for them such liberal conditions (for example a separate building and unrestricted visiting) that Béla Kun and his colleagues were able to control the movement from jail. They planned to topple the government on 23 March. This, however, was done by the Paris Peace Conference.

In connection with the French and British military intervention against Soviet Russia it was decided to create a neutral zone along the Hungarian–Roumanian border. A note to this effect was handed to Károlyi on 20 March 1919 by Lieutenant-Colonel Vix of France, the Allies' representative in Budapest. Under the terms of the Vix Note, as it became known, the Hungarian Government was to pull its troops back some fifty kilometres from their forward positions. As it did not want to comply with this demand and since it was in no position to offer armed resistance, the Károlyi Government resigned.

The Social Democratic and Communist leaders, having negotiated for some days, now quickly added the finishing touches to an agreement. The two parties were to merge and take over power. Károlyi would have been prepared to serve in a new government but his services were not requested.

The Republic of Councils, 1919

On 21 March 1919 the Revolutionary Governing Council took office and Hungary was proclaimed a Republic of Councils. Béla Kun became the People's Commissar (Minister) for Foreign Affairs and was in effect the leader of the new Government. Hungary now entered into an alliance with Soviet Russia. At the same time she called on the workers of the neighbouring countries, urging them to join the common struggle against the imperialist powers and the bourgeoisie.

The young communist movement, under Lenin's direction, had counted on a wave of revolution in Central Europe which would then have spread to the victorious Western countries. "We had based the revolution on the international revolution", said Béla Kun on 27 March 1919. For a short time it appeared that his expectation of his had been justified; on 13 April council power was—temporarily—established in Bavaria as well.

The Dictatorship of the proletariat in Hungary was accepted without resistance, even by those who did not agree with its domestic programme. The reason for this was its rejection of the humiliating Vix Note.

At both central and local level, public administration came under the control of Workers' Councils. Industrial, mining and transport companies employing more than twenty people were taken into public ownership. Also nationalized were the banks, other financial institutions and even retail and wholesale businesses. The Red Guard was responsible for maintaining law and order at home and plans drafted for a Red Army. Schools were nationalized in order to complete the process of separating Church and State. Wide-ranging schemes were launched in the field of public education. Hungarian intellectuals of European renown participated in the cultural work of the Republic of Councils. György Alexics, Lajos Fülep, Károly Mannheim, Irén Dienesné Götz, who had studied under Madame Curie, Béla Balázs, Lajos Kassák, Tibor Déry, Milán Füst, Géza Gárdonyi, Frigyes Karinthy, Dezső Kosztolányi, Anna Lesznai, Alexander Korda, Béni Ferenczy and many others all contributed. Initially Zsigmond Kunfi was responsible for cultural and scientific affairs but later György Lukács took over.

On 4 April 1919 every medium-sized and large estate passed into "the possession of the Proletarian State". No compensation was paid. The distribution of the land was, however, prohibited. As the government saw it, this was the only way of guaranteeing the production of sufficient food and of preventing the "expansion" of the rural petite bourgeoisie. The nationalized estates were organized for the most part along the lines of today's state farms. Eventually, where this was inevitable, small plots for building were allocated. This, however, did not alleviate the profound disappointment and discontent of those in agriculture. Once again the landless were not given land and the landed peasants feared that their lands too would soon be taken. One serious consequence of this was that later on the peasants refused to sell their produce for so-called "white money", the banknotes issued by the Council Republic. The counter-revolution was afterwards able to exploit this situation to its advantage.

The delegates at the Paris Peace Conference were shocked by these developments in Hungary. Heated arguments took place between the politicians and the military on the reasons for them. The Anglo–American position was that much of the blame lay with France's attempts to extend the influence of her client states. Finally, General Smuts was despatched to Budapest to assess the situation on the spot and to persuade the Hungarian Government to accept a slightly modified neutral zone. In the meantime, however, the French military leadership, with the active co-operation of Prague and Bucharest, was already organizing a military offensive against Hungary.

Although Smuts lent a sympathetic ear to Béla Kun's proposal for the calling together of an international conference on the economic future of the Danube Basin, he was not authorized to sign an agreement. For their part, Kun and his colleagues, hoping that their intransigence would bring about further negotiations, rejected the new suggestion for a neutral zone.

It is unlikely that any negotiations could have led to more favourable frontiers for Hungary and ensured the survival of the Republic of Councils. The existence of a proletarian dictatorship was entirely contrary to the wishes of the victors. These included the fullest possible satisfaction of the territorial claims put forward by Hungary's neighbours as well as the isolation of Soviet Russia. To put the matter briefly, in the long run the Allies could not allow the Republic of Councils to exist. Subsequent events confirmed that the victors were only manœuvring for position. The possibility of actually deciding events did not rest with the Hungarian Government.

On 16 April the Roumanians launched their offensive and this was followed on the 27th by a Czechoslovak incursion. Now only partially organized, the Red Army was driven back. On 1 May the Roumanian troops halted at Szolnok and the Czechoslovak forces at Miskolc but, in spite of this, the situation appeared catastrophic.

In the meantime Budapest and other areas not under occupation celebrated May Day. The Government and the Central Workers' Council remained constantly in session and Béla Kun pursued various diplomatic avenues. Finally, the crisis was resolved. The Government remained in office and started to organize the country's defences. Under the command of such outstanding leaders as Vilmos Böhm, Aurél Stromfeld, Jenő Landler and others, the Red Army was able to launch its counter-offensive as early as 20 May. The Red Army hoped that the successes on the northern front would enable it to link up with the Soviet troops.

Success attended the Red Army's endeavours. On 6 June it entered Kassa (now Košice, Czechoslovakia) and ten days later the Slovak Council Republic was proclaimed at Eperjes (now Prešov).

The prosecution of the war placed a great burden on the organized workers serving in the Red Army. It also put a great strain on the country as a whole. The various counter-revolutionary groups could easily exploit the growing economic and political difficulties which resulted. They provoked strikes and insurrections in almost every part of the country. On 24 June they even felt bold enough to make a bid for power in Budapest. However, central and local forces countered every counter-revolutionary move. The result was that the Government faced no serious challenge in July.

Meanwhile the representatives of conservative, upper-class Hungary rallied around Count István Bethlen in Vienna. In Szeged, now under French occupation, Major Gyula Gömbös organized the so-called National Army with Admiral Miklós Horthy as its supreme commander. The National Army contained officers commissioned in the days of the Empire and of a reactionary disposition. Exhibiting both chauvinism and anti-Semitic feeling, these men represented the extreme right-wing of the counter-revolutionary elements.

It was extremely embarrassing for France that the offensive mounted by her small allies had failed to overthrow the Republic of Councils. Shelving military measures for the time being, French Prime Minister Clemenceau launched a diplomatic offensive. His most successful effort was a note which reached Budapest from the Peace Conference on 13 June. The new frontiers in Central Europe had been decided and the note gave details of these. It also called upon the parties concerned to withdraw their forces behind them. After an extremely heated debate the Revolutionary Governing Council decided to comply with the order. The Red Army was immediately pulled back from its advanced positions. However, the neighbouring countries ignored the note completely, refusing to withdraw in turn. By conforming with the Paris instruction, Hungary made a tactical error. Early in July the Peace Conference began preparations for decisive military intervention. These progressed only slowly, though, and the Hungarian Government could have used the note as a basis for negotiation. This would have enabled it to play for time. The withdrawal of the army led to general demoralization and put the Governing Council in a hopeless position. During the course of July the trade-unions, the workers generally and other sections of the population were coming round to the view that Hungary should settle its differences with the Entente.

Since their advance of earlier in the year, Roumanian troops had occupied the region east of the Tisza river. The Peace Conference had acknowledged this area as Hungarian in its note of 13 June but no Roumanian withdrawal had taken place. After several unsuccessful protests, the Governing Council ordered the launching of its offensive at the River Tisza to drive the Roumanians out. This was a decision which undoubtedly hastened the fall of the Republic of Councils. Taking full advantage of its relative strength, the Roumanian army drove the advancing Hungarian troops back. This time the Roumanians did not stop at the line of the Tisza but pressed on towards Budapest.

On 1 August, 1919, the resignation of the Revolutionary Governing Council was announced at the final, dramatic session of the Budapest Central Workers' Council. The trade-union leader Gyula Peidl was appointed to form a new government. Between 3 and 4 August the Roumanian army entered Budapest. The dictatorship of the proletariat in Hungary was at an end.

Hopes for a rapid spread of the revolution had remained unfulfilled. It had been demonstrated that in the small country that Hungary had become, an isolated dictatorship of the proletariat could not survive a concerted foreign onslaught.

The attempts of 1918 and 1919 to resolve the social and political problems of Hungary within first a bourgeois democratic and then a socialist framework failed. However, memories of the two revolutions lived on in Hungary throughout the inter-war years, so did recollections of the territories lost at that time.

Hopes, Realities, Consequences

From this distance in time it is difficult to assess the attitudes of Hungarian writers, artists and intellectuals towards the Republic of Councils, following as it did the failure of the Károlyi Government and widespread disillusionment with the policy of the Great Powers. For the most part their view reflected an idealistic expectation and an almost Messianic sense of mission more typical of the age than a realistic assessment of what the possibilities actually were. Also rather lacking was the conscious acceptance of what proletarian dictatorship would really mean. In March 1919, however, few thought of the difficulties and conflicts likely to occur.

On 16 April 1919 Gyula Krúdy wrote: "There is no need to fear the future, a new Hungary, a flowering of human aspirations and ideals thrown up by revolutionary fervour. Let the old world be destroyed, crumble and disappear." According to Zsigmond Móricz "Communism, which naïve dreamers had feared because they saw in it the prison or the phalanstery, will bring about the magnificent era of the genuine flourishing of the individual... now begins a true, happy, really human life."

Freedom for creative work and participation in public life were not merely the privileges of Lajos Kassák and his circle, of the activists and of the socialist writers and artists. Zsigmond Kunfi and György Lukács's policy in the field of culture and science was liberal even by present-day standards.

The experience of the years 1918–9 left its mark not only on the works and careers of mature, established intellectuals, but also on the minds of Gyula Illyés and László Németh—grammar-school pupils at that time and future writers. Also influenced was Péter Veres, a member of the Workers' Council and another writer. This held true even for those who did not necessarily identify with what either of the two revolutions stood for.

The valiant efforts of the country as a whole to put up some form of resistance to the hostile world surrounding it impressed a wide circle. Oszkár Jászi, the most consistent supporter of bourgeois democracy, who neither at the time nor later regarded communism as a possible solution, never criticized the Republic of Councils openly—although he saw it leading to military intervention. This, he confidently expected, would be followed by counter-revolution and the loss of the bourgeois democratic achievements. It was fear of counter-revolutionary terror which caused him to leave Hungary on 1 May 1919. Mihály Károlyi remained in the country until the July crisis, and even tried to assist the Government. From exile, Károlyi was more than willing to co-operate with Béla Kun and the communists. Staff officer Aurél Stromfeld not only served in the bourgeois military, but also masterminded the great military success of the Red Army. Rudolf Andorka, Géza Lakatos, Ferenc Szombathelyi, Döme Sztójay and Henrik Werth, all prominent under Horthy, did not refuse to serve either.

Of the social democratic leaders only Ernő Garami emigrated. Jenő Hamburger, Jenő Landler and the other prominent left-wingers had already given support to the Communists before 21 March. Péter Ágoston, Vilmos Böhm and Zsigmond Kunfi also accepted the dictatorship of the proletariat.

The Republic of Councils' sense of mission also extended to the idea that Hungary should play a mediating role between East and West, and that it should attempt to spread the revolution. "Today, we Hungarian proletarians, are the vanguard of the liberation struggle originating from Russia", wrote the *Tata–Tóváros Courière* on 30 March 1919.

Were conditions, then ideal? By no means. The confident expectations of spring 1919 were not fulfilled, just as the high hopes in autumn 1918 turned to disillusionment. The Revolution did not spread further and was unable to establish direct contact with Soviet Russia. The country had to contend with foreign invasion in April, and living conditions deteriorated instead of getting better. It turned out that the dictatorship of the proletariat was exactly what its name implied and which did not shrink from the use of terror if necessary. Károlyi and his colleagues would have liked to preserve the bloodless character of the October Revolution. In November, however, they resorted to violence in an effort to maintain law and order. From the very beginning the Republic of Councils was determined to use force. When deemed appropriate, this also included the taking of hostages. It did not hesitate to send Tibor Szamuely, Ottó Korvin and the feared security detachment (the "Lenin Boys"), to suppress strikes and uprisings.

The Communists believed that the Soviet system could be established much more quickly in Hungary than in Russia. The fact that Hungary was economically and socially much more developed than Russia meant, so they thought, that traditional steps such as the distribution of land to the peasants could be missed out.

They also thought that nationality problems in Hungary and in the Danube Basin would disappear with the establishment of internationalist, and therefore allied, proletarian dictatorships.

Aiming to preserve Hungary's territorial integrity, Károlyi and his colleagues were unable to counter the occupying forces either through diplomacy or through military means. The Government, however, which in a note addressed to the neighbouring countries stated, "we acknowledge without reservation the territorial-national claims you have announced", sent the Red Army as far as Kassa (Košice) and Eperjes (Prešov) in the hope of spreading the revolution.

Political conflicts unresolved by the merger of the Social Democratic and Communist Parties also began to emerge more sharply. The situation was further complicated by the fact that the line of division did not necessarily lie between the two parties themselves. The communist József Révai pressed for the abolition of the trade-unions, Tibor Szamuely, Ottó Korvin and Mátyás Rákosi advocated firm application of dictatorship, while Ervin Sinkó, together with Jenő Landler, had doubts as to its expediency. Jenő Hamburger was just as much against the idea of distributing the land as were his fellow Communist People's Commissars.

It fell to Béla Kun to mediate between the various shades of social democracy and communism. He was sufficiently flexible to reach a compromise even in the most critical of situations and to prevent the split which would have endangered power itself.

The Revolutionary Governing Council was also compelled to acknowledge that by July its support in the country had fallen off considerably. The landless had not been given land, the peasantry had been hit by requisitioning and livelihoods of shopkeepers and artisans had been shaken. Moreover, the abolition of the land tax had produced an unfavourable effect, as had the prohibition of alcoholic drink beverages, which was in force throughout the country. The abolition of religious education in schools was also unpopular. The trade-union leaders strengthened the conviction among workers that "the dictatorship must be eased" and that Hungary "must

188

come to an agreement with the Entente". However, worker power which excluded the communists was unlikely to last. After the end of May, the enthusiasm of the majority of writers and artists supporting the régime began to wane and disillusionment spread in their ranks. Despite doubts and reservations, however, they did not turn against the Republic of Councils.

The impact of the events of 1918 and 1919 was as wide-ranging and perplexing as the history of the revolutions themselves. Several outstanding social democratic leaders such as Jenő Landler and Jenő Varga became communists. After the collapse of the Republic of Councils, Stromfeld joined the left-wing of the working-class movement. After August 1919, differences emerged between the Hungarian communists and social democrats over the causes of their joint failure. Controversy as to correct strategy and tactics became even more heated than before, indeed becoming incorporated into the fierce exchanges within the Communist International. The communists split into factions (the Kun and the Landler factions), with Kun and his entourage advocating an extreme brand of communism condemned by Lenin as an infantile disorder.

The international communist movement attached great significance to the fact that in Hungary the Republic of Councils had come into existence without the need for armed struggle. In Hungary, however, a sizeable segment of the bourgeoisie and the intelligentsia later turned away even from bourgeois democracy because of the experiences of 1918–9. These people drew the conclusion that dictatorship of the proletariat was "a corollary" of bourgeois democracy. During the thirties, ideas for the reformation of Hungarian society and the improvement of Hungary's status in Europe in some ways bore the mark of the defeat suffered by both bourgeois democracy and worker power. Men for radical changes searched "a third way" between East and West, Communism and bourgeois democracy. Even the counter-revolution, which was to emerge victorious, could not free itself from its legacy. Its existence was based not only on the negation of the dictatorship of the proletariat, but also of bourgeois democracy. Its authority was initially asserted by means of unrestricted terror then through legislation, the civil service, propaganda and such like. Not only were communists, left-wing and centrist social democrats forced into exile, but also prominent representatives of bourgeois democracy as well. This inevitably weakened within Hungary the political opposition to the Horthy regime.

In spite of this though, it was under the counter-revolutionary regime that this opposition succeeded in achieving what had been impossible in the days of the Empire: representation in Parliament and local government. The possibility for this was a concession the regime had to make in order to survive. The Communist movement was, however, outlawed and forced underground. In spite of these unfavourable conditions the part and movement not only survived the two-and-a-half decades of the Horthy regime but also kept alive the memory of the Republic of Councils.

Memories of what happened in 1918 and 1919 persisted in the years that followed. However, domestic and international development during the inter-war period proved to be significant to the evaluation of those events. When the advocates of radical change began to draw up the outlines of a new Hungary in the early forties, only very few of them regarded Károlyi's bourgeois democracy as a model to copy. On the other hand, supporters of socialism regarded the Republic of Councils as an inspiring historical precedent rather than the blueprint for the future.

Between Two World Wars

The Rise to Power of the
Horthy Regime

Although the counter-revolution proved to be victorious and enjoyed the support of the Great Powers, its consolidation was slower and more difficult than anyone had expected.

After Peidl's so-called "Trade-Union Government" had been forced to resign, István Friedrich formed a new administration in Budapest on 7 August 1919. Nevertheless, the counter-revolutionary government formed in Szeged under the Republic of Councils, was still operating and demanding its share of power. The counter-revolutionary High Command soon transferred its headquarters from Szeged to Siófok in Transdanubia. Shortly afterwards, its leader, Miklós Horthy, became the most important figure in the counter-revolutionary group. This rival government, its civilian functionaries and its special officer detachments launched in the area under its control, a massive and brutal campaign of reprisal. This was directed against those involved in both revolutions. Even before taking complete power, the counter-revolutionary regime was accompanied by general terror and absence of legality. The detachments headed by Prónay, Ostenburg-Moravek, Héjjas and others carried out ruthless executions and, in places, staged pogroms against the Jews. For the first time in Hungarian history, internment camps were set up in which men and women were held without trial for years. In the areas under their control, the Roumanian authorities staged similar campaigns of reprisal.

Owing to unfavourable international reaction, the "White Terror", as it became known, created difficulties for the counter-revolution. Count István Bethlen, his colleagues, and later Count Albert Apponyi, head of the Hungarian peace delegation in Paris, pressed for the restoration of legality.

It was only after intervention by the Great Powers that an official government acceptable to the Entente was formed in the Hungarian capital. Following the visit to Budapest by British diplomat George Clerk, Károly Huszár took office on 4 November 1919. An alliance of the so-called Christian-National parties gave the Government its majority in the National Assembly, although the social democrats and the bourgeois opposition were also represented. After dispatching much property under the guise of "reparations", the Roumanian troops first evacuated Budapest and eventually, in March 1920, the region east of the River Tisza. In accordance with the wishes of the Entente, the new Hungarian political system had to be

191

based on bourgeois parliamentarism and legality for the SDP and the bourgeois opposition. By these stipulations a more liberal system could have been built up than it happened but the Great Powers were not particularly interested in promoting this.

On 16 November 1919 Miklós Horthy and his army marched into Budapest. In January 1920, in accordance with Clerk's wishes, a general election was held on the basis of wide suffrage and secret ballot. The SDP was, however, browbeaten into inactivity. The social democrat journalist Béla Somogyi and his colleague Béla Bacsó were killed by the Ostenburg-Moravek detachment. The investigation led by the Minister of the Interior Ödön Beniczky revealed the responsibility of the High Command. Therefore Beniczky let the affair fizzle out. Under the leadership of István Nagyatádi Szabó, the Smallholders' Party became the largest political party in Parliament. In spite of unfavourable conditions, Vilmos Vázsonyi's National Democratic Party, representing the bourgeois opposition, also won seats in the new National Assembly.

The Great Powers and Hungary's neighbours insisted that the Hungarian throne remain unoccupied. Either the return of Charles IV or the election of another Hungarian king would, as they saw it, have constituted a move towards the restoration of the Austro–Hungarian Empire. This did not mean, though, that Hungary was to remain a republic.

The new National Assembly brought back the monarchy as an institution. There were two reasons for this. The monarchy not only ensured legal continuity but also justified any future claim to the lost royal territories. However, there was to be no king. The office of Regent was re-instituted—along the lines of that in the 15th century.

On 1 March 1920, with armed officers inside the Parliament building the deputies elected the fifty-two year-old Miklós Horthy to fill this position. Although the voting was overwhelmingly in his favour, neither Horthy's education nor his previous career made him suited for the office. His political views were characterized by staunch conservatism, anti-Soviet sentiment and a powerful desire to regain the lost territories. Initially, Horthy's chief support came from his army and the officers' detachments, but after a short while he was able to accept the political consolidation advocated by Count István Bethlen. Horthy was the figure who balanced the conflicting elements in the regime, as well as being its symbol.

By now the Peace Treaty was nearing completion and its acceptance was a prerequisite for the international acceptance of the Horthy regime. Ironically, the regime which was forced to sign the treaty was the same one which regarded the treaty's revision as the cornerstone of its policy.

Headed by Count Albert Apponyi, the Hungarian peace delegation in Paris requested modifications to the Treaty and the holding of plebiscites in the disputed areas. The Great Powers, however, refused to make any concessions. On 4 June 1920 the Peace Treaty was signed in the Trianon Palace at Versailles.

Under the Trianon Peace Treaty only thirty per cent of the territory and forty per cent of the former Kingdom of Hungary remained to the new state. One from three Magyars found themselves under the authority of alien state. About half of the three million Magyars in the lost areas lived in compact ethnic blocs immediately across the new frontiers. The Treaty limited Hungary's armed forces to a long-service force of 35,000 soldiers and regulated the use of ports, waterways and railways. The building of new railways was to be controlled and Hungary was obliged to pay reparations. The situation of the Magyars absorbed into the new states was aggravated by the facts that their rights as defined by the Peace Treaty, were not respected. Every section of society and every political party, including the workers' parties, joined in rejecting Trianon. Public opinion, however, was divided over the extent and form of revision to aim at. Unlike the revisionists who wanted to recover everything, the Social Democrats and bourgeois left-wing demanded only the return of predominantly Magyar areas. For their part, the Communists looked to the proletarian revolution to sweep away the Trianon Treaty.

On 19 July Count Pál Teleki became Prime Minister. Wishing to strengthen the position of the traditional ruling classes which included the big landowners and industrialists, he promoted political consolidation on the basis of conservatism. Teleki introduced firm measures to suppress the extremist army officers who were still pursuing suspected revolutionaries. To provide an outlet for anti-Semitism and partly to alleviate the problems of the middle class, Teleki introduced the so-called *numerus clausus*, a measure which restricted the ratio of Jews among university students. He started talks with the Social Democratic leaders with a view to pacifying the working-class movement. He introduced limited land reform in order to mollify discontent among the peasants. This succeeded in conferring on about another two million people the security and status coming from land ownership. Teleki's scheme did not affect the pattern of land distribution significantly. Only seven per cent of the land in Hungary was involved —far less than in the neighbouring countries, which introduced their own land reform programmes after the First World War. However, these states could afford to be more radical as their schemes were based on the distribution of large estates formerly in Austrian and Hungarian ownership. The greatest mistake of the Hungarian land reform was that it failed to increase significantly the number of viable small and medium-sized peasant farms and did not curtail the oppressive predominance of the *latifundia*. Under the land reform members of the "Vitéz Order" also received land. This had been founded by Horthy and was made up of officers and soldiers who had rendered valuable military services. Each *Vitéz* (Brave Man) received a "Vitéz Plot" and owed allegiance to Horthy himself.

Despite his achievements Teleki was unable to bridge the gulf between the pro-Habsburg legitimists and the "free electors" advocating the election of a national monarch. On 26 March, 1921 Charles IV staged an

193

unsuccessful bid for his throne. Nevertheless the issue of who was to be king remained unresolved. Other urgent tasks included setting up a political party of the ruling elite, the effective and lasting curtailment of the extreme right wing and the normalization of the situation of the trade unions and the Social Democratic Party. Other priorities were the creation of a post-Trianon national economy and the formulation of an independent Hungarian foreign policy. The size and complexity of these tasks both stemmed from the greatly changed political and economic situation which now prevailed in the country.

Political Consolidation under István Bethlen

Count István Bethlen served as Prime Minister of Hungary from 14 April 1921 until 19 August 1931. Although his political career began as early as 1901, Bethlen did not occupy Government posts up to the collapse of the Empire. Bethlen became the key figure of the counter-revolutionary era. Not only was he an excellent tactician, but also a statesman of vision and the most eminent politician to emerge during the Horthy years.

István Bethlen successfully tackled a host of problems of crucial importance to the consolidation and stabilization of the regime. On 20 October 1921, Charles IV again arrived in Hungary and attempted for a second time to win back his crown. Exploiting the commotion caused by this, and the threatening moves in the neighbouring countries, Bethlen passed a law dethroning the House of Habsburg. This was a decisive victory over Legitimism. By means of skilful diplomacy, among other things, he secured the return to Hungary of the area Pécs in the south-west occupied by Yugoslavia despite the Peace Treaty. Sopron and its surrounding in the far west were given back by Austria as a result of the referenda of December 1921.

Bethlen created a political alliance embracing not just the large land-owners, financiers and industrialists but also the gentry, army officer, civil servant elements of the middle class. Therefore, compared to the situation before 1918, the ruling group became broader and bigger. In 1923 Bethlen forced Gömbös and his fellow racialist supporters out of the Government Party. From this time until 1944, the extreme right-wing had—for the most part—an oppositional position.

In 1922 Bethlen brought together a number of political groups in the National Assembly to form a single Government bloc. The United Party, as this was known, absorbed and thereby eliminated the Smallholders' Party which had stood for more extensive political rights and a more radical land reform. While in the neighbouring countries peasant parties similar to the Smallholders' played an important role at this time, in Hungary the peasantry was to lack an independent political party of its own until 1930.

Bethlen also reached agreement with the Social Democratic Party. In return for concessions, the Social Democrats were given greater freedom of action and were allotted a place in the constitutional structure. Act III of 1921 banned the Communist Party. Its activity was subject to official persecution for the rest of the period.

Bethlen introduced an electoral system which restricted the size of the electorate. Budapest and twelve other towns enjoyed secret ballot but in the rest of the country open voting, with all its opportunities for intimidation and other abuse, was restored. Throughout the period the Government Party had an absolute majority in Parliament and showed obedience to the Prime Minister. The international trend at this time towards the strengthening of executive power at the expense of the legislature's monitoring role showed itself in Hungary too. This was well suited to Bethlen's purpose.

In company with the new states established at Trianon, Hungary also had to rely on foreign credit to stabilize her economy, to establish a separate national bank and to introduce distinctive currency. This was necessary to eliminate inflation and to effect an economic recovery. At the beginning of March 1924, Bethlen, with support primarily from Britain and Italy, procured a loan guaranteed by the League of Nations. In May the same year the National Bank of Hungary was established. On 1 January 1927 the old unit of currency, the Crown, was replaced by the new and stable Pengő. One gold crown was to be worth 1,16 pengős. Bethlen and his Finance Minister, Tibor Kállay, also pressed for the development of industry together with the active participation of leading—predominantly Jewish—financial and business circles.

During the second part of the decade Bethlen built on his achievements. He restored the previously abolished Upper House of Parliament in order to counterbalance the popularly elected House of Deputies should the latter exhibit signs of extremism. Bethlen went on to restrict the areas of competence already allocated to local government at the county and municipal levels. His measures here strongly limited the autonomy of Budapest, the stronghold of a powerful opposition. To fill the gaps, the power of central government was extended, as were the functions and responsibilities of the centrally controlled Civil Service.

At the same time the Government's social security legislation brought benefits to almost a million people. Between eighty and ninety per cent of the urban workforce profited by it. Obligatory retirement, disability and other insurance schemes were introduced, but these did not extend to the agricultural proletariat. In 1928, the Government modified the anti-Jewish numerus clausus legislation, restricting the admission of Jews to Hungarian universities and similar institutions.

Count Kúnó Klebelsberg, Minister for Education and Culture, implemented Bethlen's general policy in his own area of responsibility. With a view to proving the superiority of Hungarian culture, he devised a scholarship scheme for the training of Hungarian scholars abroad. He established Hungarian institutes abroad (for example, the Collegia Hungarica in Vienna and Berlin and the Accademia Reale d'Ungheria in Rome) which still function today. Also set up was the Biological Institute at Tihany, still also surviving. As well as developing the secondary-school network, the Bethlen Government had spent 48 million pengős from the state budget on the building of elementary schools by 1930. This was more than the total spent for this purpose by all the Hungarian Governments between 1869 and 1918. Their expenditure had amounted to the equivalent of 46 million pengős. By this five thousand elementary school classrooms and teacher's homes were built.

After becoming Prime Minister, Bethlen won the confidence of the Great Powers, and especially of Great Britain, by appearing to accept the provisions of the Peace Treaties. At the close of the decade, however, when consolidation was complete, Bethlen was openly declaring revision of Hungary's Trianon frontiers to be the aim of the country's foreign policy. This coincided with much criticism of Trianon in the West, and Lord Rothermere's *Daily Mail* even launched its "Justice for Hungary" campaign. In 1925 the Bethlen Government's opposition to Trianon involved it in a big scandal. It was discovered that several million French francs had been forged in Hungary, and that their purpose was to serve revisionist propaganda. Commitment to a revisionist policy drove Bethlen to conclude a treaty of friendship with Mussolini's Fascist Italy in 1927, and he would have liked to expand this into a Hungarian–Italian–German alliance.

The Wall Street Crash of October, 1929, however, caused a chain of events which was to bring down the Prime Minister. The collapse of the American stock market resulted in such a profound economic crisis that on 19 August 1931, Bethlen and his government resigned. At this time no one seriously thought that Bethlen's departure from office would be permanent.

It is impossible to sum up in a single word the system created by Bethlen, and which remained unchanged until the German occupation of Hungary in 1944. Bethlen's system rested on the balance between the three groups within the ruling élite, a balance which fluctuated during the years of the Horthy regime. These fluctuations showed themselves in the differences between the policies of the various governments. This balance made it possible for the Social Democrats and left-wing bourgeoisie to be represented in Parliament and at local government level right up to 1944—something impossible anywhere else under nazi domination. In spite of this, the functioning of the political apparatus in Hungary precluded the possibility of a shift to the left. Although it ensured more favourable conditions for a shift to the right throughout the period, Bethlen's system did make it impossible for the extreme right to take power unaided. Moreover, when, with German assistance, the extreme right did actually take power, the whole order collapsed.

Bethlen created a rigid and conservative political structure. His was a regime which not only made use of traditional constitutional forms and governmental pratices but also curtailed their normal workings from the very beginning. In addition he did not hold back from using new authoritarian and dictatorial methods.

The Great Powers and the member states of the Little Entente not only found Bethlen's political system acceptable but helped it in difficult situations. To the Great Powers the Bethlen regime constituted a guarantee against both revolution and the restoration of the Habsburg Monarchy. Moreover, seen from the neigbouring countries the Bethlen regime was preferable to democracy. For them, revisionist demands made by a democratically elected Hungarian Government would have been more difficult to resist.

This was why, the social democratic and bourgeois liberal opposition was unable to procure any support either from the Great Powers, or from the Little Entente for the liberalization of the system and for Bethlen's dismissal. Removal of the Prime Minister was attempted on several occasions during the loan negotiations and at the time of the forged francs affair.

At the time, the principal complaint of the left-wing opposition was that, although Bethlen had introduced a multi-party system, the government party was over-dominant, thereby preventing its proper working. Furthermore, it was not possible for the Government to be changed through the ballot-box—unlike in Britain, where this regularly happened. After 1933, however, owing to international and domestic changes, efforts centred on the preservation of the Bethlen structure and the prevention of its replacement by a nazi-type dictatorship.

The Great Depression and the Shift to the Right

As well as economic consequences, the Great Depression brought in its wake long-term political ramifications. In response to growing unemployment and falling production on both sides of the Atlantic, new governmental methods appeared. State intervention became more extensive. Under Roosevelt's "New Deal", America also adopted measures which curtailed some traditional liberties.

The Depression hit Hungary in 1930–1, slightly later, than some other countries. Accordingly, the problems it brought were resolved also later. There were two main reasons for this delay. Firstly, the initial results of the economic stabilization appeared only two to three years before the Depression. Secondly, agricultural exports, of decisive importance to the Hungarian economy, ground to a virtual standstill.

The peasantry became indebted, the production flagged and some

600,000 people became redundant in agriculture. Industrial output dropped by between forty and eighty per cent. Employment in industry was thirty per cent lower in 1932 than in 1928. The general decline in middle-class living standards was accompanied by a new phenomenon, the "over-production" of intellectuals and white-collar workers. This gave rise to a sizeable group of unemployed graduates, who were reduced to doing casual labour. It was not uncommon to find them clearing away snow from the streets and among the regular customers of the soup kitchen. It was only during the economic boom preceding the Second World War that Hungary's economy and society were able to recover from the tribulations and disruptions of the Great Depression.

Naturally, unemployment gave an impetus to the working-class movement and intensified Communist activity. On 1 September 1930 a huge demonstration was staged in Budapest and several hunger marches were organized in the provinces. The socialist working-class movement had almost no contact with the impoverished segment of the agricultural population, while the various right-wing organizations (e.g. the so-called "Scythe and Cross", *kaszáskeresztesek*) exerted considerable and increasing influence. Once again the various religious sects offering consolation for the sorrows of this world became extremely popular.

Developments in the thirties increasingly attracted attention to the state of the Hungarian village and the plight of the poor peasantry. The so-called Reform Generation, made up of young intellectuals and populist writers, turned to the hopelessly backward conditions in rural settlements—conditions unlikely to get better. The year 1930 witnessed the foundation of the Independent Smallholders' Party. This party was led by politicians of standing—Tibor Eckhardt, later Zoltán Tildy, and Endre Bajcsy-Zsilinszky.

The Depression, with its attendant unemployment and mass poverty, created conditions conducive to the rise of new, national socialist parties in Hungary. These found support among the middle classes, members of the officer corps and the bottom groups of the lower middle class. Also attracted to them were the unskilled, politically uneducated workers flocking to the towns from the countryside.

Indicative of the confusion reigning in the ruling circles was the appointment of Count Gyula Károlyi to succeed Bethlen as Prime Minister. Károlyi, the old Szeged leader and distant relation of Hungary's first President, Mihály Károlyi, formed a new Government on 24 August 1931. At first Károlyi would even have been willing to include members of the bourgeois liberal opposition in the government, but this did not happen. As regards the mass movements, Károlyi introduced martial law following the Biatorbágy viaduct explosion after which the Vienna express plunged into the valley below. Two communist leaders, Imre Sallai and Sándor Fürst were executed. In spite of these steps, Károlyi was unable to stem the tide of discontent and on 29 September 1932 Gyula Gömbös succeeded

198

him as Prime Minister. From Gömbös the ruling élite expected strong government and the restoration of law and order.

On 29 January 1933, Hitler came to power in Germany. From this time on, the international climate in Central Europe was radically changed, and the extreme right in Hungary now received foreign support. All this imparted an ominous quality to Gömbös's appointment as head of the government. Admittedly, as Prime Minister Gömbös was unable to pursue his former extremist race-protection policy. Although he did not enact anti-Jewish legislation, he did attempt to bring about a transformation of society similar to that in Mussolini's Italy. This was done by drafting a ninety-five point National Work Plan, by increasing the Prime Minister's role as controller of the machinery of state, by encouraging a spirit of militarism and by trying to organize a corporate system.

In economic affairs Gömbös achieved unquestionable results. (Restrictions to do with foreign exchange were part of his policy in this field.) When, however, he began to extend intervention to the realm of politics and society, Gömbös encountered powerful resistance. His attempt to abolish completely the self-government rigths of Budapest gave rise to an "Alliance for the Protection of the Constitution". This comprised not only the parties of the left-wing opposition, but also the majority of the Christian-National parties. Under collective pressure from some members of the Government, conservative political circles and the left-wing opposition, Gömbös had to abandon his plan to transform the hitherto club-like Government Party into a Fascist-type mass organization. Such an organization, with its suggestions of totalitarianism, would have subordinated to itself the State and public administration apparatus. Gömbös's reform policy was advantageous in some respect. He brought about a slight rise in the social hierarchy for certain groups in the middle strata, introduced social welfare measures and initiated major construction projects. Under his Prime Ministership, the slum area of Tabán—near Budapest's Royal Palace—was demolished. The National Competition Swimming Pool was also built. On the whole, however, the Gömbös period was less than satisfactory. It triggered off changes in the membership and political orientation of the officer corps and public administration apparatus which led to a strengthening pro-German sentiment. This was to have serious consequences during the Second World War. It was also under the Gömbös Government that the "Levente", a para-military youth organization, turned into a serious movement, and that the activities of the various fraternal societies and rifle associations began to be extended. Gömbös dealt firmly with the working-class movement and the year 1933 witnessed the arrest, among others, of János Kádár.

In 1934 the Government found itself at the centre of a serious international scandal. Italy had organised a plot to assasinate French Foreign Minister Barthou and King Alexander of Yugoslavia. The Croatian

"Ustachi" responsible for their murder had, with Gömbös's connivance, been partly trained in Hungary.

Gömbös was the first statesman to visit Hitler after the latter's accession to power. Throughout his period in office Gömbös strove to strengthen Hungarian–German links. At the same time, however, he strove to ensure a role for Budapest as mediator between Berlin and Rome and to exploit the benefit of this to serve his policy of territorial revision. Since the proposed German annexation of Austria aroused concern in Hungary and was at this stage opposed by Mussolini himself, the Hungarian Government played and active part in forging an Italian–Austrian–Hungarian alliance.

Gömbös's attempt to create a totalitarian state failed. His death in 1936 made it easier for the ruling conservative circles, afraid of an excessive shift to the right, to set a new course for Government policy. On 10 October 1936, Horthy appointed Kálmán Darányi as Prime Minister.

After the Bethlen years, a characteristic fluctuation can be observed in the policy of successive Hungarian Governments. Whenever involvement with Germany and leniency towards the Arrow-Cross and other extreme right-wing parties reached dangerous proportions, a change of Government took place and a certain amount of backtracking occurred. In actual fact, however, it was impossible to prevent the general drift of government policy towards alliance with Germany abroad and a shift to the right at home.

The Course and Difficulties of Foreign Policy

The possibilities for and goals of an independent Hungarian foreign policy were influenced by many factors. One major determinant was that the small states emerging from the ruins of Austria–Hungary did not individually, or even collectively, possess the strength and international standing which had once characterized the Habsburg Empire. In the economic and political sphere they came under the influence of their larger and more powerful neighbours. Consequently, their fate became inextricably linked to the balance of power between the Great Powers.

After the revolutions of 1918–9 and the subsequent signature of the Peace Treaty, Hungarian foreign policy was determined by the desire to bring about its revision. However, because Hungary was too weak to effect this by herself, suitable foreign allies would be needed. At the same time the function of foreign policy was to ensure the survival of the counter-revolutionary system at home. Hungary could appear on the international diplomatic scene not merely by her signature of the Trianon Treaty. Also needed was the dethronement of the House of Habsburg and admission to the League of Nations. France and the neighbouring states were opposed to the latter but in spite of the difficulties they raised, Hungary became a member in September 1922.

From 1920 on, however, Czechoslovakia, Roumania and Yugoslavia concluded mutual agreements, giving rise to the "Little Entente". This alliance was dedicated to the preservation of the *status quo,* the isolation of Hungary and the consequent frustration of Hungarian revisionist hopes. Initially inspired by Rome, the alliance eventually came under France's patronage and became an instrument of French security policy. This circumstance, together with the fact that Britain had given its full backing to the counter-revolutionary regime as early as 1919 had a curious effect on British–Hungarian relations. In her own way, Britain supported Horthy's Hungary and helped that country in its various difficulties. The bourgeois radical politician Rusztem Vámbéry pointed aptly to one of the reasons for this. In his view, Hungary was for Britain "a naval base restraining French influence in Central Europe".

Although closer Franco–Hungarian co-operation was made impossible by Trianon and the existence of the Little Entente, links between the two countries were not completely broken in the thirties. The bourgeois left especially advocated the strengthening of ties to offset Hungary's pro-Italian and pro-German orientation. French loans played an important part in the reconstruction of the Hungarian economy after the Depression.

Relations with most of the neighbouring countries remained tense and in the twenties, when Social Democracy had considerable influence over Austrian policy, they were not very close with Vienna either. On the other hand, Hungary made several attempts to improve relations with Yugoslavia. The main purpose of these efforts was Hungary's wish to break up the Little Entente. Historical traditions, lack of disputes, and similarities between the two regimes all contributed to the maintenance of good relations between Hungary and Poland.

The British Prime Minister Lloyd George, head of the British delegation at the Paris Peace Conference, had pointed out to other representatives the likely consequences of their decisions in 1919. For him, the Peace Settlement would lay the foundations of an eventual alliance of dissatisfied states desiring revision and that this would include, among others, Germany and Hungary. The foreign policy of the Horthy regime was headed precisely in this direction, although not to the exclusion of all others and not from the very beginning.

The Hungarian Government did not aim at closer links with pre-Nazi Germany and when Bethlen eventually tried to improve relations he achieved fairly little. The road to Berlin actually passed through Rome. From the economic point of view there were good reasons for this and, in the meantime, the illusion of Hungary's mediating role between Italy and Germany had to be forgotten.

It was only towards the end of the twenties—after the completion of political consolidation and the stabilization of the economy—that the Horthy regime had its first opportunity to launch an independent foreign policy initiative. There was only one path open to the Hungarian Government: in 1927 Bethlen concluded a treaty of friendship with Mussolini's Italy and this constituted the first major diplomatic move of the Horthy years.

Hitler's appointment as Chancellor was quickly to alter the international balance of power and with it the course of Hungarian foreign policy. The rapid build-up of the Reich's military strength after 1933 was accompanied by a powerful drive to overthrow the Treaty of Versailles, Germany's "Trianon" and signed reluctantly in 1919. Germany too now aimed at territorial expansion. On the one hand this strenghtened the pro-German faction in Hungary. On the other, though, it increased concern amongst the moderate groups in the ruling circles as to whether Hungary would be able to preserve some independence in her domestic and foreign policy. While official policy aimed at the realization of Hungarian revisionist goals by joining hands with the Germans, the socialist and bourgeois opposition were strongly opposed to this.

At first Britain and France rejected the German aspirations for territorial aggrandizement and, as long as Italy constituted a significant counter-balance to Berlin, the Hungarian regime strove to base its policy on Italian support. From 1938 onwards, however, this changed. Germany's position internationally, together with her influence in the Danube Basin, became stronger. Hungarian foreign policy now rallied behind Germany lest the opportunity of revision be missed. The appeasement policy of Britain and France also played a part in this, as it became clear that Germany would not encounter resistance from the Western democracies—in the immediate future at least. Hungarian foreign policy decisions were also motivated by the fact that Hungarian agricultural products did not find an adequate export market in Italy whereas in Germany they did.

In March 1938, with Italy's acquiescence, Hitler annexed Austria. The *Anschluss* gave Germany a common frontier with Hungary—causing justified concern to the latter. This was followed in the same year by the Munich Agreement which sanctioned German annexation of Czech territory vitally important to the security of the Czechoslovak state. Britain and France had discarded the entire post-1918 Peace Settlement as well as their own previous policy. The Horthy regime owed the success of the majority of its revisionist claims to the Munich Agreement, albeit only indirectly. The impact of this success, which was considerably exaggerated by a massive supporting propaganda campaign, was undoubtedly increased by the fact that the frontier adjustments, which for the most part followed the ethnic principle, were achieved through peaceful means. The government was able to add its revisionist successes even after the outbreak of the Second World War. In spite of this though, Hungary did not become Germany's comrade-in-arms.

Often, Hungarian foreign policy moves were initiated by Rome or Berlin. A case in point is the establishment of Soviet–Hungarian diplomatic relations, the way for which had been prepared by Bethlen during the first half of the twenties, but which had been overrated at the time by Horthy. Later on, it was on advice from Mussolini that, in 1934, the Gömbös Government established diplomatic links with the Soviet Union. These were endorsed, at Hitler's suggestion after the signing of the Nazi–Soviet Non-Aggression Pact of August 1939. Because it fitted in with German war preparations, Berlin approved of the conclusion of the Treaty of Eternal Friendship between Yugoslavia and Hungary in 1940.

Count Pál Teleki, who took over as Prime Minister in February 1939, strove to maintain Hungary's "non-belligerence" when the Second World War broke out. In the same year, however, his Government signed the Anti-Comintern Pact, directed against the Soviet Union and originally concluded by Germany and Japan in 1936. On 20 November 1940 Hungary signed the Tripartite Pact—the formal alliance of Germany, Italy and Japan made some two months earlier. In sum, Hungary's bonds to the Axis Powers were becoming stronger.

The efforts to keep Hungary out of the war failed, indeed as they were bound to fail. Premier Pál Teleki's suicide on 3 April 1941 could not divert the government from the revisionist path which it had chosen and which chained Hungary to German policy. The Hungarian army participated in the German attack against Yugoslavia (11 April 1941) and the top military leadership, especially Chief of the General Staff Henrik Werth, pressed for voluntary participation in Hitler's war against the Soviet Union. It was in vain that Soviet diplomacy tried, through József Kristóffy, Hungary's Ambassador to Moscow, to dissuade the Hungarian Government from taking this fateful step and even offered support for Hungary's claim to Transylvania. In spite of all this though, on 27 June 1941 Hungarian troops crossed the Soviet border, just five days after the initial German assault.

Entry into the war against the Soviet Union followed inevitably from the course of Hungarian foreign policy had set for itself, and led the country to disaster. Hungary became subordinate to the German war machine and the loss of the entire Second Hungarian Army on River Don (January–February 1943) was a futile sacrifice of human life. Based on revisionism and the bolstering of the counter-revolutionary system, Hungarian foreign policy was by its nature unsuited to the normalization of relations with the neighbouring countries. The alliance with Italy inevitably led to commitments to the Germans, to war against the Soviet Union and, consequently, to the hostility of Britain and the United States. All this was in spite of the fact—realized by Teleki himself—that Hungary would not be able to keep the territories recovered when the war was over.

J. F. Montgomery, United States' Ambassador to Budapest, described Hungary's relations with Germany as those of a "reluctant ally". This, however, was only part of the truth. From the very nature of Hungarian foreign policy it followed that it was not only reluctantly that successive Hungarian governments adjusted to German wishes. Hungary's revisionist claims had not been completely satisfied by the two Vienna Awards and hopes of further territorial gains gave her an interest in keeping Hitler happy. Indeed, Germany's overall satisfaction with the various Hungarian governments was the reason why Hitler did not, up to 19 March 1944, consider it necessary to occupy the country.

Competition between Hungary and Roumania for Hitler's favours was an important element in Hungarian–German relations. Budapest strove to procure further territory from the Roumanians while Bucharest wanted to recover the areas already lost to Hungary. This played into Germany's hands and Hitler did not hesitate to play them off against each other. On the personal level though, the Führer's preference was much more for Roumania's Marshal Antonescu than with Horthy.

On some issues, however, Hungary showed reluctance to fall in with the Germans. In 1939 the Teleki Government opened the borders to about 100,000 Polish refugees, among them Polish troops bearing arms. These Poles were given work in Hungary and had their own schools, qualifications form which were afterwards officially recognized by post-war Poland. Hungary also gave sanctuary to French prisoners of war escaping across the border from Germany. Despite strongly-worded and repeated demands, the Hungarian Government refused either to confine the Jews to ghettoes, or to deport them. After the annihilation of the Hungarian Second Army on the Don, it also refused to send major new Hungarian forces to the front. Finally, it was this reluctance and the attempt to salvage the regime for the post-war period which gave rise to a peace initiative in 1943. Under the Kállay Government, secret negotiations were started with the representatives of the Allies.

The Left-Wing Opposition to the Horthy Regime

From the earliest days of the counter-revolutionary regime there existed an increasingly powerful left-wing opposition to those in power. This opposition criticized government policy from a democratic standpoint and sought a democratic course for change. This left-wing opposition lacked social, ideological and organizational homogeneity. Hitler's accession to power, however, brought some moves towards unity and later, in the search for a way out of the Second World War, these received greater impetus.

The most significant and most radical element of the left-wing opposition to the Horthy regime was, understandably, the working-class movement. This was divided. After the overthrow of the Republic of Councils the alliance between the Communist and the Social Democratic parties was ended and they once again became separate entities. Under Horthy though, only the SDP could operate legally. The top Communist leaders (Béla Kun and Jenő Landler etc.) were forced into exile, along with centrist and left-wing Social Democrats prominent during the revolutions. The Communist Party was hard hit by its illegal status and brutal persecution by the public administration and police. Severe losses were caused by repeated arrests, imprisonments and even executions. Put to death during this period were such prominent Communist leaders as Imre Sallai, Sándor Fürst and Zoltán Schönherz. In spite of all these difficulties though, the Communist Party was able, time and again, to reorganize its ranks, although its numerical strength remained modest. The setting aside of internal differences, the easing of dogmatism within the international working-class movement, the need to fight Nazism together with the People's Front policy emerging from this all enabled the Communists to work out a programme more in harmony with the domestic situation. Although this programme continued to regard the overthrow of the Horthy regime as its main aim, it no longer included the establishment of the dictatorship of the proletariat as a short-term goal and attributed appropriate importance to the distribution of the land.

From the mid-thirties on, the Communist Party played an important role in the more broadly-based popular movements against fascism (for example, the March Front). In 1943–4 it became a significant force in the Resistance Movement aiming to throw off German control. At the end of the period the governing circles themselves were forced to negotiate with the communists and to treat them, albeit reluctantly, as a serious political force. In addition to the party leaders in exile (Béla Kun, Mátyás Rákosi, Jenő Landler, György Lukács, Ernő Gerő, József Révai and others) a leadership also emerged inside Hungary, running all the risks underground operation implied. Such leaders included Ferenc Donáth, Lajos Fehér, János Kádár, Gyula Kállai, Gábor Péter, László Rajk and István Szirmai.

The Social Democratic Party represented the left-wing of the legal opposition to the Horthy regime. The top positions in the party were filled by politicians of lower calibre than those forced into exile, and who were prepared to compromise and make concessions. The strength of the Social Democratic Party derived throughout the period from its close relationship with the trade-unions, whose membership fluctuated between 100,000 and 150,000 in the inter-war years. No other political party or organization could boast mass backing to this degree. The socialist trade-union and, to some extent, the Social Democratic Party were the chief areas of the Communist Party's illegal activity. Although aiming at radical change in the political system, the Social Democratic Party did not desire revolution and dissociated itself from the Communists. The Communists, for their part, up to the mid-thirties generally regarded the social democrats as "social fascists".

Its legality did not protect the SDP from harrassment by officialdom and the police. Neither did it safeguard the organizers of strikers from arrest. The Social Democrats continued their cultural work amongst the workers and ran a vigorous sports movement. Despite innumerable libel suits and other forms of persecution, the party paper *Népszava* came out until March 1944. During the Second World War cultural programmes organized on trade-union premises effectively counted as political meetings.

From the thirties onwards, the younger generation within the Social Democratic Party became increasingly influential. These men, such as Árpád Szakasits—who became Secretary-General in 1939—György Marosán represented the more consistent or left-wing section of the party and took their place alongside Károly Peyer and the moderate leadership.

For a long time ideological, tactical and personal differences between the two workers' parties militated against their co-operation. However, the nazi occupation of Hungary in 1944 brought the former antagonists closer together and led to the conclusion of a formal alliance between them. After the Liberation of Hungary from German occupation, this alliance became the foundation on which central political authority was based.

Despite the numerical weakness of the left-wing opposition to the Horthy regime, the proponents of bourgeois liberal democracy constituted an important counterbalance. Their attitudes reflected the political outlook of the entire Hungarian bourgeoisie and its interpretation of the experiences of the two revolutions. Their opportunities, however, were limited by the fact that their most prominent and able leaders had been forced into exile. Another important handicap was that right-wing and extreme right-wing propaganda blamed not only the working-class movement for the revolutions and for Trianon but bourgeois liberalism and democracy as well. Because the bourgeois opposition contained many Jews in its ranks, antisemitic feeling in the country was a further disability.

The aim of the National Democratic Party, headed by Vilmos Vázsonyi, and, after his death, by his son János Vázsonyi, did not aim at the abolition of private ownership, but instead the transformation of the capitalist order in Hungary along the lines of that achieved in Western Europe. The same held true for the Kossuth Party, led by Vince Nagy, Rusztem Vámbéry and Rezső Rupert, and for Károly Rassay's party. This was known by several names and was the most important of the three from the thirties and from 1935 on as the Bourgeois Liberty Party, it established closer ties first with Bethlen and then with Miklós Kállay.

Credit must go to these parties mainly for their consistent struggle for the promotion of greater equality, for their resistance to any dictatorial moves, and to any withdrawal of rights. Their political position was voiced on the pages of the *Esti Curir* (Evening Courier), the *Újság* (Newspaper), the *Világ* (World) and the *Magyar Hírlap* (Hungarian Daily).

During the thirties the left-wing became more powerful and associated itself with new political trends—representing primarily concern for the interests of the agrarian population and a solution to nationality problems.

In addition to the Independent Smallholders' Party, formed in 1930, the National Peasant Party was set up in 1939. The latter had many members who sympathized with the working-class movement and the Communist party. Leading members of these two parties were in the forefront of public life during the Second World War, and in some cases even afterwards. Examples of these prominent members were Endre Bajcsy-Zsilinszky, Tibor Eckhardt, Ferenc Nagy, Zoltán Tildy, István Dobi, Imre Kovács, Béla Varga.

A substantial contribution to the shaping of public opinion and to the strengthening of opposition to the regime was made by sociologists and populist writers concerned with rural life. These included Ferenc Erdei, Géza Féja, Gyula Illyés, János Kodolányi, László Németh, Zoltán Szabó, Péter Veres and others. Their influence was so profound that it is still discernible today. The sensitivity of contemporary writers to social problems and the illusory nature of Gömbös's reforms prompted Lajos Zilahy in April 1936 to launch the "New Intellectual Front". Soon, however, the majority of populist writers backing the Gömbös reforms realized that the prime minister's goals were completely different from their own.

On 15 March 1937 the new Left-Wing—for a while with powerful Communist support—organized the "March Front", and, as in 1848, formulated its political, social and national demands into twelve points. The Social Democratic Party and the bourgeois liberal parties placed far greater emphasis on the attainment of a just political democracy than the sociologists, the populist writers and their followers.

In the Christmas 1941 issue of *Népszava* the writings of anti-fascist citizens, social democrats and communists including Marcell Benedek, Gyula Szekfű, Árpád Szakasits, Gyula Kállai etc. appeared side by side. This bore witness to the growing unity within the opposition. It was this more general collaboration which in 1942 gave rise to the Historical Memorial Committee.

During the Second World War, and more especially in its latter half, the role of the left-wing opposition became increasingly important. It first protested against Hungary's entry into the war and later pushed hard for a break with Germany. In 1943 the Independent Smallholders' Party allied itself with the SDP and the communists formed the legal "Peace Party". In 1944 an alliance between the social democrats and the communists was also established. The left-wing opposition organized resistance against the German occupation forces and, after Horthy was deposed, against the rule of the puppet Hungarian nazis, the Arrow-Cross. In May 1944 it formed the "Hungarian Front" and later the Hungarian National Liberation Committee. In these organizations Endre Bajcsy-Zsilinszky, Vilmos Tarcsay, János Kiss, György Pálffy, László Sólyom, Lajos Fehér, György Markos and others risked their lives to organize resistance. The Nobel Prize Winner Albert Szent-Györgyi and the middle-class groups rallying around him also joined the Resistance Movement. In 1944–5 the armed Hungarian

Resistance units helped expel the Germans and their Arrow-Cross allies from the country.

The struggles and sacrifices of the Resistance Movement, which fought for the establishment of a new Hungary, bears witness to the fact that in Hungary there were still men and women with a genuine desire for democratization.

Yet the anti-fascist left-wing opposition was unable to achieve a breakthrough, to mobilize and rally behind itself the overwhelming majority of society. The opposition was still divided as late as 1944. In the campaign for political democracy the conditions in the countryside were not given the attention they deserved. The opposition programme of the populist movement laid its emphasis on national independence, inevitably associated it with right-wing nationalism, with its connotations of Magyar supremacy in the Danube Basin. At the root of the differences within the left-wing opposition lay the future of post-war Hungary. The entire left-wing opposition wanted a change of regime, but only a minority wished to go beyond this to the abolition of private property and the putting into effect of socialist transformation. As elsewhere in Europe, genuine, armed resistance emerged in Hungary only when that country was occupied by the Germans. In Hungary there was in fact very little time to establish this armed resistance and the Soviet army crossed into Hungary as early as September 1944. Partly divided and not properly organized, the left was unable to produce a force that would have been capable of seriously challenging the Horthy regime, its pro-German military leadership, and the German army itself. The left was just not strong enough, to prevent the Arrow-Cross takeover of power on 16 October 1944.

Economy and Society between the Two World Wars

Hungary's territorial losses after 1918 were to have serious economic consequences. A sizeable proportion of her existing natural resources was lost and her industrial structure became even more distorted than it had been under the Empire. The Hungarian economy became much more dependent on the world economy and, because of this, foreign trade acquired crucial importance. Under Habsburg rule, Central Europe had been an integrated economic unit, the various areas of which were mutually interdependent. Trianon did not contain provisions for the establishment of economic ties between the new Hungary and her neighbouring states and, later, political factors militated against such links. Hungary's export capacity was overwhelmingly agricultural and Germany was the most promising market for her farm products. Germany gradually became the greatest buyer of Hungarian agricultural produce, accounted for half of Hungary's foreign trade in 1938. After Trianon, protectionism and isolationism were general in Central Europe. The various states were all attempting to strengthen and consolidate their new economies. Hungary herself was no exception and the conditions of the time demanded substantial government support for industry. Because of this, the role and influence of big capital became greater within the ruling groups than they had previously been. The National Association of Manufacturers, the Association of Banks and Savings-Banks and the National Hungarian Agricultural Union all played a decisive part in the shaping of economic policy. By the end of the 1920s, industrial production reached its 1913 level, having in one period actually exceeded it by twelve per cent. The average of growth rates for Europe as a whole was, however, more than double this figure.

Light industry developed the most dynamically. The number of workers in the textile industry increased five-fold and the tinned-food industry became competitive even in the world market. New branches of industry were created and old ones were modernized. As early as the twenties, production of crude oil and bauxite began in the western half of the country. The aluminium industry was started up with German assistance and output of electricity trebled. Hungary's new diesel railway engines and rail-cars were marketable even in the United States. The chemical industry (for example the Pét Nitrogen Works) was one of the most modern, and rapidly developing in the country, as was the pharmaceutical industry (for example Chinoin and the Gedeon Richter Works). There were outstanding achievements in the electrical industry. Good examples include Ottó Bláthy's voltmeter, the United Incandescent Lamp factory's crypton bulbs, and Orion radio sets. Owing to the general standards of Hungarian industry and technology though, Oszkár Asbóth's helicopter and György Jendrassik's turbine engine could not be manufactured in Hungary.

During the inter-war period Hungary became a slightly more industrialized country but the output of Hungarian industry reached only forty-three per cent of the European average. What is more, small workshop production accounted for a quarter of all industrial production in the country.

In agriculture, arable land accounted for sixty per cent of the total. Although yields per hectare also improved, lack of capital and credit made serious development impossible.

In 1938 there were only seven thousand tractors in the whole country and —in the aftermath of the Depression—the number of livestock in 1938 was still below its 1925 level. The development of agriculture elsewhere in Central and Eastern Europe was greater than in Hungary. Owing to a number of reasons (for example, the economic crisis after the First World War, the Great Depression, and low demand resulting from the bulk of the population's poor living standard), the domestic market did not expand at the necessary rate.

As regards the density of her railway network, Hungary was the seventh in Europe. During the inter-war period electric locomotives were put into service on the main line from Budapest to the Austrian border. Civil aviation was introduced and Budapest's Ferihegy Airport counted as one of the largest in Europe.

On the whole, the pace of economic development between the wars was slower than during the period between 1867 and 1918. Nevertheless, between 1920 and 1941, the industry's share in the national income rose from thirty to thirty-six per cent. In Austria during the same period, this figure exceeded fifty per cent but in the Balkan countries reached only twenty to twenty-five per cent. On the whole, Hungary's agricultural character was slightly lessened. Even in 1937–8, however, per capita national income was only 120 US dollars. This was only half the European average and between a third and a quarter of that for the Western European countries. All of this put Hungary in the ranks of the moderately developed countries.

The Treaty of Trianon also brought about a change in the country's social structure, a change that was strengthened by the developments of the following twenty-five years. The proportion of those employed in industry, commerce and transport grew, while the proportion in agriculture declined. Nevertheless, those working the land still accounted for almost half of the population. The white-collar workers grew in number, partly as a result of large-scale middle-class immigration from the lost territories, and partly because of the proliferation of the bureaucracy. About one-third of white-collar workers were employed in public administration.

Hungary's social structure at this time resembled a pyramid at the apex of which were two groups. The first was made up of over five hundred aristocratic and big landowning families (for example, the Zichy, Pallavicini, Festetics, Esterházy families) and by about fifty finance-capitalist families (for example the Chorin, Kornfeld, Perényi, Vida, Weiss families).

The character of the middle class was determined by its inclusion of slightly more than twelve thousand gentry, senior civil-servant and senior military-officer families. Their financial position was weaker than that of the big landowners but this was offset by their predominance in the state apparatus and in county administration. They occupied key positions in the army and most politicians of the period came from among their ranks. Civil servants and officers of gentry background, together with those of more plebeian origin rigidly preserved the forms and trappings of the upper-class way of life. A sizeable proportion advocated racism, sympathized with the extreme right and pressed for a pro-German policy.

The number of middle-ranking urban capitalist families in the upper middle class was roughly the same as the number of gentry and senior civil servant families. These capitalist families were much better off financially than they were in terms of social prestige and political influence. Although they basically supported the system, the fact that many of them were Jews led to their rejection of extreme right-wing sentiments. At the same time the liberal opposition parties could count on a certain amount from them.

In the heterogeneous mass of the urban petite bourgeoisie between 300,000 and 350,000 artisans, shopkeepers and traders made up the self-employed groups. Over sixty per cent worked without even one assistant and in reality their independence was therefore no more than an illusion. The living standard of the *petite bourgeoisie* was not as good as many thought. Junior white-collar workers and junior officers for the most part lived rather modestly, but at least they had a regular salary and a state pension on retirement.

The rapid rise in the numbers of qualified professionals and freelance intellectuals was a new phenomenon during the inter-war period. Developments in technology, in education and in health policy triggered off an ever-growing demand for teachers, engineers and doctors of medicine. The sharpening of social tensions within the intelligentsia's ranks was another characteristic feature of the era. At the beginning of the 1930s, the dramatic rise in the number of unemployed professionals became a serious problem. Lack of job prospects made some professionals receptive to right-wing radicalism and it ran high within their ranks. Owing to the characteristic features of Hungarian bourgeois development and the policy of the Horthy regime, the majority of Jewish intellectuals were in freelance occupations. Indeed, there were virtually no other opportunities open to them. The "Changing of the Guard" was demanded not only by the Christian intelligentsia, but the entire Christian middle class as well. This—aimed at removing Jews from important positions—became one of the demands of the political movements and parties of the extreme right.

Even at the top of society, dual stratification existed and this was present to a greater extent within the middle classes. Two groups existed – the "historic" or "traditional" elements and, distinct from them, those circles associated with capitalist development. Throughout the Horthy period, the simultaneous coexistence and segregation of these groups became increasingly conspicuous. The fairly high proportion of Jews in the latter group was an important reason for this segregation. Similarly, a prosperous artisan, capitalist or shopkeeper could not compete with a landowner or civil servant in terms of social prestige, even if the landowner or civil servant was worse off financially. Birth and social standing were esteemed more highly than wealth derived from industrial or commercial activity. Before 1918, a grammar-school certificate and especially an officer's commission were the two most important requirements for entry into upper-class Hungarian society. After 1918, however, grammar-school qualifications became more common and the social origins of those attaining them became wider. Accordingly, the prestige of the grammar-school certificate declined and became insufficient in itself for admission. Also, the circle of those finding their way into the officer corps also slightly expanded. As a result, the narrowness of upper-class Hungarian society was—very slowly and slightly—reduced.

At the bottom of the pyramid were the urban proletariat and the peasantry. The urban proletariat numbered over a million and was largely made up of miners and industrial workers. Within the peasantry the most affluent segment section numbered some 50,000, and was made up of those with substantial farms. 300,000 were smallholders with land adequate to provide a living. Another 200,000 were dwarfholders—occupying land normally insufficient to sustain themselves. In addition there were some 780,000 farm hands and labourers—with no land and the worst off group within the peasantry.

Some remnants of feudalism continued to persist in Hungary even between the World Wars. The social prestige of the aristocracy surpassed that of every other stratum. The process of embourgeoisment progressed slowly —very slowly in the peasantry. Birth, titles, and rank were far more important than individual achievement and success. Caste-like discrimination existed in forms of greeting, address and in social life generally. After the revolutions the state, educational institutions and the Churches all fought to strengthen the principle of authority.

All societies depend for their existence on stability but Hungarian society in the inter-war period approached rigidity. Opportunity to rise on the social ladder was lacking and social mobility remained restricted. The sons of the more prosperous peasants could enter the public administration and could study at an agricultural college or even the university. The sons of small peasants could advance socially as teachers or priests. For the poorer strata, jobs in the postal service, on the railways, in the gendarmerie and in the police offered not just opportunities for advancement but also state retirement pensions. The impoverished agricultural labourers flocked to the towns and the capital to find semi-skilled industrial work perhaps, or to do unskilled jobs. In the latter category were caretakers, servants and, say, messengers. Within the intelligentsia, however, there emerged a highly important, though not very large, group which had risen from the ranks of the peasantry.

The dual structure of Hungarian society thus lived on. Even though, on the whole, this structure was slightly affected by the process of embourgeoisment, in terms of politics and outlook generally the conflict between the "historic" and "traditional" elements on the one hand and the new bourgeois groups on the other was greatly accentuated.

Changes in Life-Style

The living conditions of the various social classes was invariably determined by the kind of work they were engaged in, the sort of income they derived from it, and indeed by whether there was any available work at all. Unemployment hit not only the industrial work force, but the middle-class intellectual and white-collar strata as well. Full employment was achieved only during the economic boom created by the Second World War. The problem of unemployment in the middle class was "solved" by the need for white-collar workers to administer the returned territories, conscription legislation removing Jews from certain positions of employment.

In industry the working day was between eight and twelve hours. Mechanization and the introduction of electricity had improved working conditions, especially in big industry. In agriculture, however, threshing was almost the only mechanized process, and work largely filled the hours of daylight. White-collar staff in ministries and offices worked between nine and twelve in the morning and perhaps stood by for duty during the afternoon hours as well.

In 1941 almost forty per cent of Hungary's population lived in towns, seventy-one per cent lived in settlements with electricity.

Urbanization, however, remained rather patchy. Whilst the population of Budapest rose to over a million, that of other major Hungarian towns remained around the hundred thousand mark. Forty-six thousand new homes were built in Budapest between 1930 and 1941, among them a host of "small urban flats", as they were known. A number of big industrial concerns, among them the State Railways and Ganz-Mávag, built accommodation for their workers. Consisting of a single room and lacking even such basic amenities as a bathroom, these were hardly luxurious. A three-roomed flat was considered as a good middle-class home during this period. Some of these were located in Budapest in buildings which already bore the marks of the *Bauhaus* architectural style. The miserable, slum-like housing estates of the post-1918 years which, incidentally, had all been called after Habsburg archduchesses (Augusta, Zita, Maria-Valeria) still existed in Budapest at this time.

The 200–400 pengős of monthly salary of the non-senior civil servant was considered adequate for a comfortable life during the thirties. This was shown by the light-hearted song of the time "With 200 for a salary, it's easy to be happy!" During the thirties a minimum wage was fixed for industrial workers and the forty-eight-hour working week was introduced which, however, remained in force only until the Second World War. In spite of official measures though, the average monthly wage of factory workers was only about one hundred pengős and not every worker was able to earn even this much. The agricultural work force earned less still and received most of its payment in kind. The small peasant had an average yearly income of about one hundred pengős per *hold* (0.57 hectares, or 1.42 English acres).

In 1930 social security provisions covered a million people and new hospitals were built in the county towns and in Budapest. Compared with the size of the country's population, the number of doctors in Hungary was high even by European standards. Quality of health care, especially in the villages, showed improvement.

As a result of increased attention to public education and to school building, illiteracy dropped to between a half and a third of its 1914 level

213

and the number of university students doubled. All of this was undoubtedly connected with the unquestionable, albeit uneven, general improvement in living conditions. The quality of everyday life was far more favourable in the towns than in the villages. There was running water in only twenty-five towns and in these, with the exception of Budapest, it was mainly limited to the inner districts. Tram services operated in Budapest, Miskolc, Debrecen and Pécs. There was an expanding bus service in Budapest and the first traffic lights there were installed in 1928. Although the number of taxis rose rapidly—especially in Budapest—the hansom-cab and the fiacre could still be seen on the streets. Private cars were considered a luxury and in 1930 their numbers barely exceeded thirteen thousand in the whole country. On the other hand the number of people who owned bicycles and motor-cycles, indispensable in rural areas, rose quickly. The motor-cycle and side-car was tremendously popular at this time and was the equivalent of today's small family car.

Changes in dress and fashion altered the outward appearance of people. Men were less affected than women but important changes for them included the eclipse of the starched shirt-collar. The traditional suit remained but there emerged also a vogue for sporty clothes. Women's fashions had, of necessity, to take account of the fact that thousands of women now worked in factories, shops and offices. Although the traditional garb persisted in the village, women in the towns no longer wore long skirts and girdles. Dress lines became simpler and one reason for this was that initially even clothing-material was scarce. The ready-to-wear clothing industry, although still very small, also contributed to the standardization of women's clothes. Long hair went out with the long skirt. It was replaced at first by the very boyish "Eton" style and later by a style utilizing the newly-invented "perm". A "lady" would never be seen in the street without hat and gloves, although she would wear ankle-length trousers for sport —something previously unimaginable.

In the towns, goods were increasingly sold in specialized shops. By the second half of the thirties the Meinl delicatessen chain—which had thirty-three branches in Budapest—traded in twenty-two towns and villages. There were Del-Ka shoe shops in Budapest and in fourteen provincial towns. In 1926 the first truly big and modern department store, the "Corvin" was opened in Budapest. Inside, escalators carried shoppers from the ground floor to the upper stories. Budapest's shops stood comparison to those of Berlin, Munich and Vienna. Nevertheless, in the provinces the general store remained the chief source of supply and in Budapest the small shop retained great importance. It was in the thirties that specialized shops began to appear in rural areas.

New types of entertainment and recreation came in, while the old ones increased their appeal among the general public. Christmas 1922 witnessed the opening of the Operetta Theatre in Budapest and Hungarian Radio began to broadcast on 1 December 1925. At this time there were only 21 radio sets per 10,000 people, a number which had risen to 462 by 1938. From 1931 on the Hunnia Film Studio produced talkie motion pictures and cinemas were opened in the towns and larger villages. The gramophone became very popular—but was beyond an ordinary family's financial means. Sport and hiking, on the other hand, became a pastime of the masses between the two World Wars. Tennis, fencing and sailing (the so-called "white sports"), remained the preserves of the rich, while swimming, hiking and soccer were accessible to everybody. Competitive sports also offered to the poor a chance of rising on the social ladder. In addition, the flourishing sports clubs reflected and promoted social and, to some extent, political segregation. The groups of enthusiastic fans rallying around the more famous football teams differed from each other in character. The football teams fielded by the various university sports clubs had an exclusive Christian middle-class character while that of the Ferencváros Sports Club (FTC) attracted the support of petit bourgeois, semi-proletarian following, elements partly sympathetic to extreme right-wing views. The football team of the Hungarian Sports Club (MTK) had a middle-class and Jewish following until it was banned. Between the two World Wars the Social Democratic Party created its own sports network which drew participation of factory and office workers, as well as that of intellectuals. Sport and hiking also provided useful cover for the working-class movement, and especially for illegal meetings. The Tourist Association of Nature Lovers contained many social democrats, communists and freemasons. Walks and excursions through deserted countryside would often turn into political assemblies.

It was during the inter-war period that Budapest became a "City of Spas". The Palatinus Baths on Margaret Island, the Széchenyi Baths in the City Park and the Gellért Baths at Hotel Gellért were all built in the capital before the Second World War. The Gellért Baths, with their wave-producing machine, were especially famous.

Going away on holiday was a new custom which spread chiefly amongst middle-class circles. Holidays spent within Hungary were just as popular as those taken abroad. In the twenties a great amount of land around Lake Balaton was divided into lots and a whole host of spas was built. These rapidly became enormously fashionable. This development of Lake Balaton boosted the development of local trade and provided employment opportunities. However, Siófok, Balatonföldvár, Balatonlelle, Balatonfüred and Tihany became holiday resorts for different social strata. During the early twenties the annual number of holiday makers was 50,000. By the end of the thirties, however, this number had risen to 200,000.

The café was an integral part of town life and cafés were often the centres of literary life and political discussion. In addition to the gentry-clubs there were artisans' circles and associations and the workers' cultural centres, the village reading circles together with boys' and girls' clubs made for a lively social and community life.

It was also during this period that newspapers began to be read on a mass scale. Up to 1938, hundreds of daily newspapers, illustrated magazines and journals were published. These included *8 Órai Újság* (8 O'clock News); *Friss Újság* (Latest News); *Esti Kurír* (Evening Courier); *Tolnai Világlapja* (World News of Tolnai) etc. The pictures and news items in *Színházi Élet* (Theatre Life) were popular amongst all social classes while the *Magyar Úri Asszonyok Lapja* (Hungarian Ladies' Journal) was read by middle-class women.

From the beginning of the thirties onwards there appeared indisputable signs of an improvement in living standards together with evidence of modernization. The value of these developments was limited, however, and further progress in these fields became impossible with Hungary's entry into the Second World War. This brought wide-ranging economic consequences, including rapid inflation and growing food and commodities shortages. In spite of the standardizing effects of fashion, the impact of cinema and radio and many other influences, society remained stratified with the lines of division between individual strata sharply defined.

Waves of Emigration

Between the two World Wars, several waves of emigration from Hungary took place. These resulted in the loss of Hungarian science and intellectual life generally of some of the country's finest minds. Those who publicly advocated democracy and socialism were also forced to leave.

The suppression of the two revolutions, the white terror which followed and the consolidation of a conservative and right-wing political regime caused many Hungarians to leave the country. Another reason was the fact that many contemporaries felt that Hungary was in a hopeless situation, and this seemed to make their own situation appear hopeless too. The economic disruption caused by Trianon, gallopping inflation, and continuing mass unemployment which characterized the early twenties did indeed make future prospects appear bleak. Accordingly, not only those who had taken part in the revolutions and those committed to bourgeois democracy or socialism decided to leave. Young professional people and intellectuals also felt that foreign countries would be more agreeable for them, as did numbers of skilled workers, smallholders and even landless peasants. This last group of emigrants left out of economic considerations: they just could not make ends meet at home.

Mines in Belgium and France (e.g. those of the Pas-de-Calais and Lens etc.) and the big industrial plants in the suburbs of Paris (for example in Billancourt and Boulogne sur Seine) provided jobs for several thousand Hungarian miners and industrial workers. At the beginning of the twenties difficulties of adjustment, the need to protect interests as well as democratic

216

conviction led the émigrés to establish in Paris the Hungarian section of the "League of Human Rights". For years this organization was directed by Mihály Károlyi and his wife, Katinka Andrássy. Ernő Bóta was one of those forced to emigrate when the counter-revolution asserted itself in autumn 1919 and he played an important part in the setting up of this body.

In contrast with the period of Dualism, in the years after 1919 emigration from Hungary occurred primarily for political reasons. Those leaving included not just leading political figures, but large numbers of lesser-known communists, social democrats, as well as bourgeois democrats. Before 1918 most emigrants from Hungary headed for America. Between 1918 and 1938 the overwhelming majority of those leaving for political reasons remained in Europe, however. During the twenties, some thirty thousand people emigrating out of economic necessity were taken in by the United States.

In spite of this, not everyone leaving the country at this time travelled westwards. To communists and those who had served as officials under the Republic of Councils the Soviet Union offered sanctuary and thereby relief from persecution. It was there that the economist Jenő Varga achieved international recognition. Béla Kun, György Lukács, Máté Zalka and others filled various posts in the international communist movement within the framework of the Third International. Hungarian Communist exiles in the Soviet Union, among them Mátyás Rákosi, Imre Nagy, József Révai, Zoltán Vas and many others, played an important role in promoting anti-fascist consciousness among Hungarian servicemen captured by the Soviets on the Eastern Front. These men subsequently rose to prominence after the Liberation of Hungary in 1945.

Political conditions in Hungary and bleak prospects for creative work drove many Hungarian social and natural scientists to other lands after 1919. Sociologists Karl Mannheim and Karl Polányi, aesthetician and art theorist Arnold Hauser, and Pál Dienes in mathematics all sought opportunities abroad. Also emigrating were John von Neumann, an expert in number theory and computer science, together with nuclear physicists Edward Teller, Leó Szilárd, Eugene Wigner and Theodore von Kármán. All made outstanding contributions in their fields. The history of British and even world cinema could not be written without mention of the Korda brothers, especially Alexander. Béla Balázs made an important contribution to the aesthetics of motion pictures. Outstanding Hungarian artists as Marcell Breuer and László Moholy-Nagy joined the Bauhaus group in Germany. Béni Ferenczy, Sándor Bortnyik, Károly Kernstok, József Nemes Lampérth, Béla Uitz and other prominent Hungarian artists too were forced to go into exile for various periods. The same fate befell Ferenc Molnár, the immensely popular playwright.

For those who emigrated, Vienna became the initial destination. It was there that many began their studies. From Vienna the majority went on to universities in Germany to complete their education. During the Weimar

217

period in Germany, cultural activity flourished and Hungarian artists took full advantage of the congenial atmosphere there. Some, however, went further afield, to France and to Italy. Hitler's rise to power in 1933, however, caused Hungarian exiles to move on from Germany. With the spread of Nazi control to other countries (for example Austria and Czechoslovakia), Hungarian émigrés left those states as well. A number moved on to Great Britain and the United States. Some were actually invited on the basis of their professional accomplishments.

In 1938 Austria was annexed to the Reich. Following this the Hungarian government enacted anti-Jewish legislation more stringent than any previously seen in the country. This triggered off another wave of emigration. This time Britain, the United States and South America were the destinations, with the latter two more popular on account of the greater security they seemed to afford. In 1940 Béla Bartók and his family emigrated to New York. Bartók's exacting artistic and moral principles made it impossible for him to remain even as an onlooker and thereby concone a system which had fostered the decline and destruction of human values. In protest he chose to leave the country.

Circumstances forced György Solti, among others, to pursue his career abroad. Those exiled artists whose work was in the Hungarian language led a hand-to-mouth existence during their time in foreign countries. A good example was the actor Gyula Kabos, a popular star of the Hungarian screen.

From Oberlin, Ohio, Oszkár Jászi made tremendous efforts on behalf of his fellow countrymen. Using his reputation and his extensive connections in the United States, he did much to procure entry permits to that country for Hungarian political exiles. This was in spite of the fact that strict immigration quotas were then in force.

During the inter-war period, many people emigrated from the countries of Central and Eastern Europe to more affluent states. These offered a better livelihood and, later, refuge from nazism. Hungary, however, was the only country with a sizeable group of political exiles from 1919 onwards. From the very beginning Mihály Károlyi was their acknowledged leader. First in France and then in Britain, Károlyi rallied around him these democratic refugees. Károlyi set up the "Hungarian Council in England", the aim of which was to work for the establishment of a democratic Hungary. Károlyi was ready to form a government-in-exile during the Second World War and attempted to organize the creation of Hungarian military units to fight alongside the Allies. The intention was that these would be recruited from Hungarian troops captured on the Eastern Front. However, for political and military reasons the Allies vetoed both courses of action. Accordingly, Hungarians opposed to their country's pro-nazi orientation were not given the opportunity afforded to Czechoslovak and Polish emigrés finding themselves in Britain and the Soviet Union.

Although Hungarian political refugees were divided on many issues, on one they were agreed—namely their duty to make the anti-democratic character of the Horthy regime known to the world. During the Second World War they made a collective effort to bring Hungary out of the war, to create a new, democratic Hungary and to promote harmonious relations amongst the peoples of the Danube Basin. Many actually took up arms against the nazis. Hungarians fought not only in the Soviet Red Army and amongst the Soviet partisans, but also in the American army, in De Gaulle's "Free French" and in the French Resistance.

The overwhelming majority of Hungarian exiles, regardless of age, social status and political beliefs, preserved their cultural indentity while abroad and retained their ties with Hungary even when they opposed her political system.

Culture and Art

In spite of highly unfavourable conditions and the drain on intellectual and artistic talent caused by the waves of emigration, Hungarian cultural life was extremely rich and colourful during the interwar period. Different generations worked alongside each other and diverse artistic trends coexisted peacefully. The varying social bonds and experiences of the leading cultural figures influenced art and the views artists had as to their role in society. Within individual fields of art a wide range of genres were cultivated. Contact with intellectual trends in the rest of Europe was not broken and these were enriched by Hungarian contributions. At the same time the official line on culture and science was determined by conservatism and academism. Consequently, most creative intellectual work was forced outside the official framework. In spite of this though, such work was able to reach the public.

Within the boundaries of the new state, Budapest's role in cultural life increased considerably. However, minor intellectual centres also grew up in Debrecen, Szeged and Pécs.

The aspirations of progressive bourgeois elements in the early years of the twentieth century, as well as the experiences of the two revolutions and the subsequent period, left their imprint on the work of Hungarian writers and artists. In many countries there was growing interest in society and in Hungary this acquired special significance in literature and the arts. Questions of vital importance to Hungary, the future of the Hungarians and interpretations of Hungarian and European identity occupied every creative intellectual. The special intellectual and ideological role of literature was not confined to Hungary, although conditions in that country gave to it added importance between the two World Wars. This explains the enormous impact of Gyula Szekfű's *Három nemzedék* (Three Generations), a historical analysis. Szekfű's subsequent inquiry as to where Hungary had gone wrong, and say, the work of Dezső Szabó, were similarly influential. Szabó's *Az elsodort falu* (A Village Swept Away) was particularly noteworthy. The special role of literature explains the long-lived influence of the populist writers though their ideas were by no means homogeneous. László Németh and others spoke of a middle course for Hungary between East and West, between the Soviet system and that implemented in capitalist countries. This conception of Hungary's role and a so called third way between East and West has triggered off heated debate ever since.

The period between the two World Wars was without doubt a significant period in the history of Hungarian literature. The great generation associated with the literary journal *Nyugat* was at the height of its creative talent. This generation included Mihály Babits and Zsigmond Móricz who were not only authors themselves but also edited the journal. Other writers were Dezső Kosztolányi, Gyula Krúdy, Frigyes Karinthy and Lajos Nagy to name just some. A new generation emerged at the end of the twenties: Attila József, László Németh, Gyula Illyés, Lőrinc Szabó, Tibor Déry, Péter Veres and many others. The youngest generation appeared on the scene in the thirties: Miklós Radnóti, Zoltán Jékely, Zoltán Zelk, István Vas, Sándor Weöres and others. During the 1920s "avant-garde" in literature was declining everywhere. When Lajos Kassák returned to Hungary from exile in 1926 this type of writing was already out of fashion.

As a result of the growing interest in society and politics, literature became partly sociological in character. Lajos Nagy wrote powerfully about the town, sociologists expert in rural life and the populist writers revealed, in a moving way, the infinite destitution of the village. *Puszták népe* (People of the Puszta) by Gyula Illyés, *Falusi krónika* (Village Chronicle) by Péter Veres, *Viharsarok* (Stormy Corner) by Géza Féja, *Futóhomok* (Running Sand) by Ferenc Erdei, *Cifra nyomorúság* (Odd Misery) by Zoltán Szabó, *Néma forradalom* (Silent Revolution) by Imre Kovács and many other works spoke of what was happening in the countryside.

A large majority of the younger writers considered even *Nyugat* to be conservative and launched their own publications. These included *Szép Szó* (Beautiful Word) started by Attila József, Pál Ignotus, Ferenc Fejtő, Zoltán Gáspár; *Válasz* (Answer), established by Pál Gulyás, Imre Németh, György Sárközi, Lajos Fülep and László Németh; and *Tanú* (Witness), set up by László Németh. As a successor to *Nyugat, Magyar Csillag* (Hungarian Star) was launched by Gyula Illyés and Aladár Schöpflin.

In the inter-war period, the traditionally high standards of Hungarian musical life were upheld by Béla Bartók and Zoltán Kodály. Further important contributions were made by Leó Weiner, Lajos Bárdos, Ernő Dohnányi, János Ferencsik, Ede Zathureczky, Mihály Székely, Endre Rösler, Mária Basilides and many others.

Official cultural policy towards the fine arts supported conservative nationalist academism and neo-Baroque eclecticism. In spite of this, achievements in these fields were very diverse during these years. In painting József Rippl-Rónai, Béla Czóbel, and Adolf Fényes followed the early post-Impressionist school. The Szentendre Group comprised Jenő Barcsay, Lajos Vajda and Dezső Korniss. The most prominent figures of the Alföld School were Gyula Rudnay, József Koszta, István Nagy and János Tornyai. István Szőnyi, Aurél Bernáth, Róbert Berény and Ödön Márffy harked back to the traditions of the Nagybánya School, while József Egry followed in the footsteps of the Eight. Vilmos Aba-Novák and Pál Molnár-C. belonged to the so-called Roman School. In sculpture Béni Ferenczy, Ferenc Medgyessy (who had an affinity for folk themes), and others produced outstanding work. Noémi Ferenczy created an entirely new trend in the art of tapestry weaving. Gyula Derkovits was the outstanding representative of socialist expressionism and of the neo-realism which evolved from this. In the mid-thirties the Socialist Fine Arts Group was formed. Around this rallied painters and sculptors representing various artistic trends. These ranged from István Dési Huber to Endre Szöllősi and to Tibor Vilt. The avant-garde architects Farkas Molnár, József Fischer and Lajos Kozma exerted profound influence over the younger members of their profession.

Artists who were socially and politically committed often clashed with the regime. Libel actions were brought against the populist writers and sociologists, the exhibition of the Socialist Fine Arts Group was banned in 1942.

The theatre enjoyed a boom in these years. In addition to Hungarian plays, classics of the foreign stage and modern drama were put on in Hungarian theatres. Margit Ladomerszky, Mária Lázár, Margit Makay, Mária Mezei, Anna Tőkés, Irén Varsányi, Andor Ajtay, Gyula Csortos, Gyula Hegedűs, Zoltán Makláry, Imre Ráday and Artúr Somlay all performed during this period and have become classic figures in the history of Hungarian theatre.

Owing to the one-sidedness of state support and lack of patrons, the majority of artists lived among difficult financial conditions and often on the poverty line. Writers and poets were generally unable to make a decent living out of their work. Although after the mid-thirties there was greater popular interest in books, paintings, concerts, and the theatre, interest in the arts was confined to a minority. The intelligentsia and the educated middle classes provided the market for artistic work but the tastes and demands of this section of the public coincided only marginally with the aspirations of the outstanding artists of the day. A case in point is Béla Bartók's *The Miraculous Mandarin* which won international renown outside Hungary. The general reading public preferred to read Zsolt Harsányi, Ferenc Herczeg, Sándor Márai and Lajos Zilahy rather than sociological studies of the village.

It was not in every field and not even uniformly that élite and mass culture interacted. The different strata in society had different means of access to culture. Works, authors, institutions and initiatives which at-

221

tempted bridge the gap between art and the public acquired special importance. In the thirties Hungarian writers and poets—including the populist writers and the poet Attila József—often spoke on Hungarian Radio. Géza Supka, the editor and publisher of the journal *Literatura* and also an archaeologist and well-known bourgeois radical writer, organized the first Hungarian Book Day in 1929. The János Vajda Society organized performances in which, among others, Mária Basilides, Vilma Medgyasszay, Erzsi Palotai, Tamás Major, Hilda Gobbi all participated. Many of these figures regularly performed to trade-union audiences. The socialist labour movement also played a role in the bringing of art to ordinary people. Indicative of this is the fact that Attila József held seminars.

The years between the two World Wars witnessed outstanding achievements in cultural and intellectual life. The greatest problem was, as the artists themselves were painfully aware, that the number of people receptive to art remained smaller than they would have liked.

On the Threshold of War

The period 1938–40 in Hungarian history was a time of strangely mixed developments and feelings. Lavish ceremonies took place in the midst of ominous international events and revisionist jubilation existed alongside grave anxiety for the future.

The year 1938 was the 900th anniversary of the death of King Stephen, the founder of the Hungarian State and who was afterwards canonized. 1938 was accordingly declared the year of Saint Stephen and the Roman Catholic Church's Thirty-Fourth Eucharistic Congress was held in Budapest during May. Afterwards various ceremonies were arranged. There was a special gala meeting of the Parliament in Székesfehérvár, Stephen's capital. On St Stephen's Day (20 August) the "Sacred Dexter" procession took place in Budapest and involved the leading figures in the State. The "Sacred Dexter" was the embalmed right hand of St Stephen. This was borne through the streets during the St Stephen's Day procession. This was followed by a colourful fireworks display in the evening. All of these celebrations were given a special and partly political significance.

While Hungary commemorated St Stephen, however, the prospects for the preservation of peace in Europe looked far from good. Encouraged by the appeasement policy of Great Britain and France, Hitler annexed Austria to the *Reich* in March 1938. The *Anschluss* gave the Reich a common border with Hungary and the existence of such a powerful neighbour did not reassure Budapest. While the Arrow-Cross Party declared that "1938 is ours!" the majority of the population feared that the German army might not stop at the frontier. In a radio address Miklós Horthy tried to calm public opinion, and stated that all disturbances would be firmly dealt with.

222

Also in March 1938, Prime Minister Kálmán Darányi gave a subtile indication of what was likely to come. In a speech delivered in Győr, he announced that the Government was launching a five-year-development programme involving the expenditure of 1,000 million pengős on the army and industry. At the time few realized the true significance of this programme. Indeed, for a while, positive developments resulted from it: unemployment disappeared and living conditions improved perceptibly.

In September 1938, Britain, France, Italy and Germany concluded the Munich Agreement which soon afterwards led to the partition of Czechoslovakia. By the terms of the Munich Agreement the mountainous Sudetenland areas of Czechoslovakia were annexed to the Reich. The incorporation of these regions, which contained three million ethnic Germans and the Czech army's main fortifications, was a grave blow to Czechoslovakia and made the rest of that country indefensible. Hitler was not satisfied with these limited gains, however. In March 1939 German troops occupied the rest of the Czech Lands and set up a Fascist puppet state in Slovakia. Munich paved the way for Nazi expansionism in Eastern Europe, and, in the same time, brought the outbreak of a new war.

The Peace Settlement imposed on Europe after the First World War now collapsed completely. Britain and France, moreover, had actively contributed to its demise. These events had a profound effect on the whole of Hungarian society. Memories of the disintegration of Historic Hungary were still vivid and the Horthy regime's propaganda was also effective. The fact that the Western Powers capitulated to Nazi demands caused shock and confusion among bourgeois and socialist opposition circles alike.

Hungarian foreign policy, based as it was on the desire to overthrow Trianon, was ready to support the Axis Powers. The map of Europe was being re-drawn and Hungary stood to gain if the architects of the new order were well-disposed towards her. In domestic policy too the Government was prepared to make concessions to Berlin to foster good relations and thereby advance the cause of territorial revision. Between 1938 and 1941 some of the lost territories were indeed recovered—and without the need for military action. After the Munich Agreement, the First Vienna Award (2 November 1938) returned the southern border areas of Slovakia. These areas had an ethnic Magyar majority and contained the towns of Komárom, Érsekújvár (Nové Zámky), Losonc (Lučenec), Kassa (Košice), Ungvár and Munkács. The First Vienna Award represented a major success for the Government and added 11,927 sq.km to Hungary's size. Another territorial gain was soon to follow. With the final disintegration of Czechoslovakia in March 1939, Hungarian troops occupied Ruthenia—the easternmost province of that state. Hungary thereby acquired control over the upper reaches of River Tisza and a common border with Poland.

Under pressure from Germany and the Arrow-Cross Party, the curtailment of Jewish citizens' rights now began. In May 1938 sixty Christian Hungarian writers, artists, scholars and public figures protested against

223

this. Their appeal "To the Conscience of the Nation!" was signed by Béla Bartók, Imre Csécsy, József Darvas, Noémi Ferenczy, Zsigmond Móricz, Aladár Schöpflin, Géza Supka, Árpád Szakasits and Lajos Zilahy.

Laws (Act XV of 1938 and others) were enacted to restrict the number of Jews in employment as well as to limit their voting and marrying rights. Jews were excluded from the armed services and instead could be conscripted into forced labour units. Jewish members of autonomous bodies were stripped of their seats. Since from 1939 onwards race and not religion determined identity, the proportion of the population affected by anti-Jewish legislation exceeded 6.2 per cent. This was higher than the percentage classified in 1941 as Jewish by religion. Although the Hungarian race laws were not as severe as the Nazi Nuremberg Laws (1934), they nevertheless seriously undermined Hungarian constitutionalism.

The Hungarian Government ensured special privileges for the ethnic Germans living in Hungary. Later on it enabled the German Government to organize these people into the "Volksbund" and to the SS.

On 1 September 1939 the German army invaded Poland and the Second World War broke out. Absence of pressure from Berlin to join in the attack made it easier for the Hungarian Government to keep Hungary non-belligerent. Count Pál Teleki, now Prime Minister for a second time, refused even to give non-military assistance to the Reich. German troops were not allowed to cross through Hungarian territory and thereby enter Poland from the south. The Hungarian railways were not used for the transportation of German military supplies. At the same time Teleki opened the border to Polish refugees. For the time being Hungary preserved her neutrality.

The fact that Hungary now recovered even more territory seemed to vindicate the policy of Teleki and the governing circles. After the Soviet Union reoccupied Roumanian-held Bessarabia and since Teleki was prepared to use military means to recover Transylvania, Germany and Italy made the Second Vienna Award (30 August 1940). By the terms of this Northern Transylvania (a total of 43,591 sq.km) was returned to Hungary. This area included the towns of Nagyvárad (Oradea) and Kolozsvár (Cluj-Napoca), together with the Szekler Land to the east. The population of these regions was 51.4 per cent Magyar, which meant a total of 1,123,216 people. This number was swelled by 60,000 Magyars who moved up from Southern Transylvania. In the same time 200,000 Roumanians left the areas annexed to Hungary and settled in the remaining parts of their country. The Magyar population of northern Transylvania greeted these changes with joy, but this was tempered by the fact that atrocities were committed when the Hungarians moved in. The Hungarian authorities persecuted the left-wing socialist movement and applied the race laws in the newly recovered area. As had previously been the case when Hungary annexed the Slovak border region, positions of authority in Northern Transylvania were filled by people from within the Trianon borders. In spite of all this though, the Magyar population of Transylvania considered the change favourable from the national standpoint.

The Second Vienna Award poisoned still further the already bad relations between Hungary and Roumania. It also helped Hitler to subordinate both countries to the service of the German war machine by playing them off against each other.

The general shift to the right, revisionist successes and the unrestrained propaganda of the Arrow-Cross Party produced dire consequences at the 1939 election. The left-wing opposition had secured use of the secret ballot for the entire country by forcing a change in the electoral law. However, in the political climate existing at the time it was the Government Party, the Arrow-Cross Party and the national socialists who could best exploit this. The extreme right gained far more seats than the social democrats or the Independent Smallholders' Party ever had before. Now the Arrow Cross constituted the most powerful opposition group in Parliament.

This undoubted shift to the right and the German alliance notwithstanding, conditions in Hungary differed vastly from those parts of Europe under Nazi occupation. The admission to Hungary of Polish and French refugees is indicative of this. Also, in spite of anti-Jewish legislation, the lives of Hungarian Jews were not directly threatened before the German occupation of the country (19 March 1944). Indeed, many people fled to Hungary from neighbouring countries where the deportation of the Jews had already begun. At first the reality of the war and the suffering attendant on it seemed remote. For the time being only the advantages of the German alliance—and, above all, the success of revisionist policy, were apparent. In the spring of 1941, however, the situation changed.

Under considerable pressure from Hitler, Horthy and the General Staff decided to participate in the projected German attack on Yugoslavia—despite the Treaty of Eternal Friendship which Hungary had concluded with that country on 12 December 1940. Prime Minister Pál Teleki, however, regarded this as a fatal step, and one which he was not prepared to endorse. In the small hours of 3 April 1941 Teleki committed suicide, thereby acknowledging the failure of his own policy together with the responsibility of revisionism for Hungary's entry into the war. "We have become treacherous", he wrote to Horthy in his last letter. "We have sided with scoundrels. ... We shall be robbers of corpses. The most worthless nation..."

Teleki intended his death to be a memento and anti-Nazi circles regard it as such. News of it caused a considerable international sensation, and was appreciated by a number of leading statesmen including Winston Churchill. Teleki's suicide was, however, unable to alter the course of Hungarian politics.

Hungary Enters the Second World War

Teleki was succeeded by Prime Minister László Bárdossy. On instructions from his Government, the Hungarian army crossed the Yugoslav border on 11 April 1941 and occupied the Bácska, the triangle of territory between the Danube and the Drava rivers. Also occupied were the Muraköz and the Muravidék. By these actions Hungary acquired a further 11,417 sq.km of territory and more than a million new inhabitants, among them 370,000 Magyars. About 150 thousands of non-Magyars had left the newly annexed territories. There could no longer be talk of peaceful territorial expansion. It was clear even to the governing circles that a great price would have to be paid for their joint adventure with Germany.

Great Britain now broke off diplomatic relations with Hungary. To the departing Hungarian Ambassador, György Barcza, Eden, the British First Secretary explained, that Britain would remember of this act of Hungary at the future peace conference. Britain and the Allied Powers would not forget that Hungary violated her agreement with Yugoslavia.

In 1941 Hitler was already preparing "Operation Barbarossa"—his planned offensive against the Soviet Union. Several gestures were made by the Soviet Union to dissuade Hungary from entering the war on the German side. The Soviets returned the Hungarian flags captured in the 1849 War of Independence and in return for Hungary's neutrality they expressed a willingness to entertain Hungarian claims to Transylvania.

On 22 June 1941 the German attack on the Soviet Union began. The Slovak and Roumanian Governments immediately offered to join the assault voluntarily. For its part though, the Hungarian Government was still waiting for a suitable pretext before doing the same. The opportunity came when, as the official statement put it, Soviet aircraft carried out a bombing raid on Kassa (Košice), Munkács (Mukachevo) and Rahó (Rachov). The anti-Soviet stand inherent in the Horthy regime and the vain hope of keeping the territories already returned led to Hungary's entry in war on the Soviet Union just four days after the German offensive opened. This crucial step was not debated in parliament but the decision was merely announced to the members. On 27 June the Hungarian army—joining the German army—crossed the frontier.

Despite its initial successes on the Eastern Front, the German army demanded active support from its allies. Italian and Roumanian armies also took up position along River Don and in 1942 the Hungarian Government committed itself to despatch the Second Hungarian Army to the front. In the General Staff of this army József Grassy occupied a high-ranking position. Grassy had been responsible for the massacres committed early in January 1942 at Újvidék (Novi Sad), Zsablya and vicinity in which five thousand people died. The Second Hungarian Army—totalling some 200,000 soldiers and Jewish members of labour battalions—arrived at the front during the summer. It was then placed under German military command.

After undertaking the attack on Yugoslavia and the declaration of war on the Soviet Union, László Bárdossy had fulfilled his ignominious role. On 9 March 1942 Miklós Kállay replaced him as Prime Minister of Hungary. Initially Kállay continued the policy of his predecessor but soon, however, his principle task was to effect some very delicate manœuvring. Kállay aimed, at a suitable time and in a suitable way, to break with Germany, to reach agreement with the Western Allies and to ensure the survival of Horthy Hungary for the post-war period.

During the war state intervention in the economy assumed unprecedented proportions. Industrial and agricultural production was made over for military purposes. Most factories were declared "war factories", the purchasing of agricultural produces was made a state monopoly and a new system of compulsory delivery was introduced. Nevertheless, shortages of food and commodities grew constantly and this state of affairs remained unaltered even with the introduction of rationing. The black market flourished.

The Hungarian economy was subordinated to German interests and demands. In 1942, 90 per cent of Hungary's bauxite production and over 50 per cent of her oil production went to Germany. Certain sectors of war industry produced more for the German than for the Hungarian army. The situation was similar with agricultural products. In addition to the entire food surplus of the Bácska, most of Hungary's maize, wheat, oil-seed etc. also went to Germany. What is more, Germany failed even to pay for what she received. The *Reich*'s debt to Hungary rose from 326 million pengős in 1941 to 550 million pengős in 1942. In short, Germany's war was in part financed by Hungary.

After Hungary's entry into the war, special measures were introduced at home. These banned political rallies, inaugurated censorship of the press, and rigourously punished the practice of listening to enemy radio stations. Communist activity was dealt with under summary penal procedure, a number of prominent Communist leaders were given long prison terms, the Communist Zoltán Schönherz was executed in 1942 and members of the Presidium of the Historical Memorial Committee were arrested.

In spite of all this, from 1941 onwards people opposing the regime rallied around various organizations, denounced the war, called for an end to the German alliance and for Hungary's withdrawal from the hostilities. These men and women received encouragement when the tide of the war began to change in autumn 1942. The Allied Powers now halted the hitherto unchecked advance of the German armies and launched a counter-offensive. In November 1942 the British defeated Rommel's army at El Alamein and Anglo–American units landed in North Africa. At the same time the Red Army surrounded and annihilated the German Sixth Army at Stalingrad. The Soviet victory at Stalingrad was the turning point in the war.

227

In January 1943 Soviet troops launched a successful offensive along River Don. In the course of the fighting the Hungarian Second Army stationed in the Voronezh region was destroyed. In combat readiness and fighting ability the Hungarian troops lagged far behind the Red Army. Owing to hostile behaviour on the part the Germans, the defeated Hungarian units, retreating in a disorganized way, suffered heavy losses. The number of dead exceeded 150,000. The Hungarian Government tried to remain silent about the catastrophe at Voronezh, and to play down the extent of the losses. Only those who listened to Moscow-based Radio Kossuth or to the BBC learned the truth.

After the annihilation of the Hungarian Second Army, the Kállay Government refused to send another to the Eastern Front—in spite of German pressure to do so. With the end of the war in sight, Kállay wanted to build up combat-ready forces in Hungary. His Government put out diplomatic feelers in the West in an attempt to pave the way for an armistice and to take Hungary out of the war.

The Attempt to Arrange a Cease-Fire and to Take Hungary out of the War

In 1943, the plans of the ruling circles and the ideas of the politically aware public were influenced by the experiences of the First World War. Many therefore expected that the Western Allies would once again land in the Balkans and that they would quickly reach the Hungarian frontier. This would enable Hungary to go over to their side. They did not want to see Hungary for a second time on the side of the losers. They also did not want the country to be militarily exhausted by the time a cease-fire was signed. Effective armed forces at home would prevent a repetition of 1918–9. With the exception of the Communists, the anti-Nazi and anti-German opposition did not wish for revolution.

The Horthy–Kállay–Bethlen clique, the majority of the bourgeois political parties, and even such well-known opposition figures as Károly Rassay wished to take Hungary out of the war and get at the same time preserve, as far as possible, the existing political structure. Therefore, although every anti-nazi group, including the communists, supported and approved of Kállay's negotiations and the proposed break with Germany, the majority wanted more than just this. The Social Democratic Party, the Communist Party, the majority of the Smallholders', the National Peasant Party, the Bourgeois Radicals and the Democrats all called for fundamental reforms. These included distribution of the land, the curtailment of big capital and the thorough-going democratization of political life.

From January 1943 onward, several representatives of the Kállay

228

Government conducted negotiations with the Western Allies in Istanbul, Stockholm and Switzerland. In Budapest a special bureau was opened with Horthy's younger son, Miklós Horthy Jr., as its head. For the period of transition, Horthy and Kállay assigned important roles to well-known opposition figures including, for example, Károly Peyer (Social Democratic Party), Zoltán Tildy (Independent Smallholders' Party) and Károly Rassay (Bourgeois Liberty Party). It was hoped that if Hungary succeeded in pulling out of the war she would be able to retain the territories annexed since the beginning of 1938. Horthy, Kállay, Bethlen and others would have liked to see this change of sides and withdrawal from the war accomplished independently of the Soviet Union. Only one person, Nobel Prize winner Albert Szent-Györgyi, conducted talks on behalf of that section of the Hungarian opposition which wished to see a change of regime. He met British representatives and London treated him with the respect due to the head of a possible Provisional Government. However, it was not the Hungarian opposition but the Government itself which possessed the means to undermine the German war effort to bring about an end to the German alliance and to reduce or refuse valuable deliveries of *materiél* and food to the *Reich*.

Initially Hungarian hopes had been raised by the Allies landing in Sicily and the arrest of Mussolini on the instructions of the Italian monarch, King Victor Emanuel III. However, the advance of the Anglo–American forces in Italy ground to a halt and German troops occupied Rome. Mussolini was freed from captivity by the Germans and formed a separate Government in the north of the country.

On 9 September 1943 representative of the Kállay Government received from the British conditions for a cease-fire. This would come into force when British and American troops reached the Hungarian frontier. Until then resolute signs of a break with Berlin were requested. This request echoed those of the anti-German opposition in Hungary which was trying to force the Government to act. Believing that the end of the war was at hand, convinced that the *Reich*'s defeat was certain and fearing the consequences of a German occupation of Hungary, the Kállay Government tried to play for time. Hungary was to stick it out until the decisive issue of events on the battlefield.

The Nazi intelligence service discovered Hungary's negotiations with the West and had up-to-date information about everything which had taken place. Accordingly, Hitler repeatedly demanded Kállay's dismissal, and the deportation of the Jews. The Arrow-Cross Party stood in the wings, ready to take over power. Fearing that an imminent Anglo–American military move in Hungary would enable the Kállay Government to go over to the Allies, Hitler issued orders for the implementation of "Operation Marguerite". A stormy meeting between Horthy and Hitler at Klessheim (near Salzburg in Austria) on 18 March 1944 ended in the Regent agreeing to the German occupation of Hungary.

On 19 March 1944 the German army moved into Hungary. The Third *Reich*'s Ambassador in Budapest, Edmund Veesenmayer, now became the *Reich*'s Imperial Commissioner and possessed full power.

Although Hungarian political circles had been afraid that a German occupation might take place, nevertheless they were both surprised and unprepared when it actually did happen. The supporters of a break with Germany were not united. None òf their groups could boast armed fighters and, in any case, this sort of resistance could not have been compared to that of a regular army. The Hungarian army remained passive. No one assumed the responsibility for issuing orders to resist. Under the official orders the occupiers had to be received as friends.

No sooner had the occupation taken place than the arrest—on the basis of pre-compiled lists—began of opponents of the Nazis. Politicians representing the labour movement and the bourgeois opposition were taken into custody, together with leaders of the opposition to Germany within the governing circles. In the course of March and April, some 3,000 people were arrested. Most of them were deported to German concentration camps.

The Kállay Government resigned and the Prime Minister himself was taken into custody by the Germans. Key posts in the Government and other bodies were filled by pro-German politicians. Every political party and organization that was not of the extreme right was dissolved. Every non-Nazi newspaper was banned. In May, Jews living in the countryside began to be confined to ghettos and in the course of the summer they were deported to the death camps. Half of all Hungarian Jews at this time died in Auschwitz and other concentration camps.

All of this took place while Horthy remained Regent and while the machinery of the Hungarian state continued to function. The arrests and deportations were not carried out by the Germans but by the Hungarian authorities who obeyed them and collaborated with them.

After the German occupation of Hungary—and in accordance with an earlier announcement—the Anglo–American aircraft started to bomb the country. Budapest experienced its first major air-raid on 3 April 1944. The horrors of the war had finally reached the homeland.

As everywhere in Europe, the Resistance Movement only emerged in Hungary after that country had been occupied by the Germans. In the Resistance the Communists played an important role; unlike the Social Democrats and anti-German bourgeois forces they could draw on quarter of a century's experience in underground organization. The anti-Nazi forces set up various groups which carried out military operations and undertook acts of sabotage. Bearing such names as "Szir", "Marót", "Laci" and "Szent-György", they issued pamphlets during armed opposition and prepared forged papers for the persecuted. The impact of the Resistance was, however, greatly reduced by the fact that the majority of its potential leaders and organizers had already been arrested in March. On 27 July,

Endre Ságvári, a prominent member of the communist movement, was shot dead in an armed clash with Hungarian policemen. In spite of this the Hungarian Front's Executive Committee was formed with Árpád Szakasits as President. Its membership was broadly based and included communists, smallholders and legitimist politicians alike. György Pálffy presided over the Communist Party's Military Committee.

On 23 August 1944, after the Soviet army crossed the Roumanian frontier, the Bucharest Government denounced its own German alliance and withdrew from the war. The Roumanian army capitulated. These developments, as well as the fact that in September 1944 Soviet troops arrived on Hungarian soil in Békés and Csongrád counties, had a decisive impact on Horthy and his clique. Having finally accepted the fact that they could not count on the appearance of British or American troops, they now discarded their strong anti-Soviet stand. On 28 September a delegation was dispatched to Moscow to negotiate an armistice.

On 11 October 1944 the Hungarian delegates signed the preliminary armistice agreement. Withdrawal from the war and a break with the Germans now became a distinct possibility. On 15 October, Radio Budapest broadcast Horthy's announcement the cease-fire. For one fleeting moment a wave of joy swept through the country.

However, the implementation of the armistice agreement and neutralization of the probable German opposition to it were inadequately prepared, both politically and militarily. Horthy had even informed Hitler about the armistice plan. In point of fact only the Germans made preparations for action. Hungary's ruling circles dismally failed this test of history. The price of their irresponsibility and dilettante approach was paid by the nation.

Encountering no serious resistance, the German army occupied the strategic points and institutions of Budapest, including Buda Castle. Threatening to abduct his son, the Germans blackmailed Horthy into appointing Ferenc Szálasi "Leader of the Nation", thereby creating the semblance of legal continuity. Szálasi, an ex-Major and the leader of the Arrow-Cross Party, became the symbol of Nazi power in Hungary. With Horthy and his family transported to Germany, power therefore passed into the hands of the Arrow-Cross movement, which was prepared to serve Hitler's Germany to the last.

On the Way to Socialism

The Liberation of Hungary

In the autumn of 1944, Soviet troops crossed the Hungarian border. In ferocious battles, the troops of the Second and Third Ukrainian Front pushed the German and Hungarian forces westwards. In October 1944, the town of Debrecen was the scene of a devastating tank battle, as was the Székesfehérvár area in March the next year. The German army launched the last major counter-offensive of the Second World War to the north of Lake Balaton. At Christmas 1944 the Soviet army blockaded Budapest. Prepared to spare the city the horrors of a siege, the Soviet army sent two officers under the flag of truce. They were to propose the surrender of the city by the Germans but without success. The two-month "Battle of Budapest", which devastated the Hungarian capital, therefore began. The country was now divided into two parts—the part liberated by the Soviet army and that in the hands of the Arrow-Cross.

In the constantly diminishing area of their rule, the Arrow-Cross instituted a reign of brutal terror. This primarily affected Budapest. The accession to power of the Arrow-Cross was accompanied by another wave of arrests and the Jews of Budapest were confined to the ghetto. Thousands of people were executed or died as a result of atrocious treatment. The inmates of the forced labour camps were moved westward, and mostly on foot. The majority was eventually murdered.

In October 1944 the communists and the social democrats agreed to establish a united front. This was a decisive development which not only strengthened resistance to the Germans but also laid the foundations for Hungary's post-war life. The agreement was valid not only for the struggle against the Nazis and their fellow-travellers, but also for the building of a democratic Hungary. In November the Liberation Committee of the Hungarian National Uprising was formed with Endre Bajcsy-Zsilinszky as President. Lieutenant-General János Kiss was responsible for its military operations. The Hungarian Front sent representatives to Moscow. The "Szir", "Marót" and other communist-led partisan groups, as well as the partisans working in the auxiliary law-enforcement units carried out successful operations. They blew up the statue of Gyula Gömbös in Buda and the Arrow-Cross Party's centre in the Újpest district of the capital. They also set off bombs at Szálasi's headquarters, the "House of Loyalty". In many places the partisans prevented the transportation of industrial and medical equipment to Germany. Hospitals, church organizations and mo-

232

nastic orders offered refuge to the persecuted. The population of Csepel refused to carry out evacuation orders.

The Gestapo and the Arrow-Cross, however, dealt ruthlessly with Hungarian patriots. They captured and executed Lieutenant-General János Kiss, Colonel Jenő Nagy and Captain Vilmos Tarcsay. When fleeing they took with them some of their prisoners. At Christmas 1944 Endre Bajcsy-Zsilinszky was executed, along with István Pataki, Barnabás Pesti and other communists.

In their flight from the oncoming Soviet army, the Germans and the Arrow-Cross took with them much of value to the country. Machinery, medical equipment, art treasures, food stuffs and many other things were moved by rail. The Hungarian Crown, the royal insignia and such national relics as King Stephen I's "Sacred Dexter" were taken out of Hungary. Most of the leading figures in the state and in the public administration fled the country. So did many misguided ordinary people who feared the fighting.

Hostilities in Hungary lasted 194 days and the last German military units were expelled from the country on 4 April 1945. After fierce street fighting, the Pest side of the capital was liberated on 18 January 1945. Buda had to wait until 13 February. To the liberation of Budapest the Buda Volunteer Regiment, under Oszkár Variházy's command, made its own modest contribution. In addition, the Soviet army was supported by a number of Hungarian partisan groups.

In those parts of Hungary which had been liberated, the organization of democratic forces began. As far as was possible, life was returned to normal. On 2 December 1944 the Hungarian Independence Front was born in Szeged. Communists returning from Moscow, the Social Democratic Party, the Independent Smallholders' Party, the National Peasant Party and the Bourgeois Democratic Party all joined in the establishment of this. By 20 December 230 members of a Provisional National Assembly had been elected in forty-five localities.

On 21 December 1944 the Provisional National Assembly convened in the oratory of the Calvinist College in Debrecen. The following day the Provisional Government was elected with Béla Dálnoki Miklós, the general who went over to the Soviet army, as President. Seen constitutionally, the democratic transformation of Hungary began with the formation of the Provisional Government. This was recognized by the Soviet Union and her allies as the *de facto* representative authority of the nation.

One of the earliest and most important actions of the Provisional National Government was to declare war on Germany on 28 December 1944. It also started to organize a new democratic army, and sent two Hungarian divisions to fight alongside the Soviet army.

The New Power

After the liberation of the whole of Hungary and the election of November 1945 Hungary was governed by a Coalition Government based on the four major parties of the Independence Front. However, from the very beginning the Hungarian Communist Party, now led by Mátyás Rákosi, played a decisive role.

Although the pre-Liberation programmes of the four coalition parties had much in common, on fundamental issues they profoundly differed. As to the form Hungary's government should take, convictions ranged from parliamentary democracy to dictatorship of the proletariat. This divergence of opinion within the coalition inevitably resulted in efforts to alter the balance of power within it, as well as in disagreements over policy and methods. These political struggles were influenced not only by domestic considerations. Developments external to the country played an important part in what was happening. The "Grand Alliance" of Britain, the United States and the Soviet Union was breaking up and giving way to East–West confrontation. The start of the "Cold War", along with Stalinist policy and its assertion in Eastern Europe had considerable influence on events.

In March 1945 the Government issued its Land Reform Decree. This was a step of historical significance in doing away with the shackles of the past. For the first time in Hungary's history, land was distributed to the peasants across the whole country. Land distribution began ceremoniously on 29 March 1945 at Pusztaszer, in Csongrád county. Thirty-five per cent of the country's land, 5.6 million cadastral yokes were distributed. Sixty per cent of this land went to 642,000 peasant families, while state and model farms were established over the rest. Ninety per cent of those receiving land were farm servants, dwarf-holders or peasants with no land originally. The land reform carried out in Hungary was one of the most radical of the post-1945 period. In itself the reform pointed beyond the final elimination of feudalism.

The Coalition Government settled the country's constitutional form, an issue unresolved ever since 1918. Act I of 1946 abolished the monarchy for good and proclaimed Hungary a Republic.

The new Government had to sign the Peace Treaty which formally put an end to the Second World War and in doing so accepted, to a certain extent, the consequences of the Horthy regime's policy. The Peace Treaty signed in Paris on 10 February 1947 restored Hungary's 1937 frontiers, restricted the strength of her army and ordered her to pay 300 million US dollars in reparations. At the same time an unprecedented population movement took place in the Danube Basin, and this deeply shocked Hungarian public opinion. Citing the legally and morally unjust principle of "collective responsibility", the authorities in Czechoslovakia resettled part of the Hungarian minority there in the Sudetenland. Simultaneously a greater number, over 100,000 people, was sent into Hungary. Meanwhile at home the same principle was applied. Members of the German-speaking population—not only those who had belonged to the "Volksbund"—had to move to Germany.

The liberation paved the way for popular creative spirit and talent and, throughout the country, committees were spontaneously formed. Formed from local democratic and socialist elements and free from any central control, these committees assumed political power. The total collapse of the public administration apparatus meant that the new committees could perform functions previously reserved to national and local government. With the re-establishment of central power, however, and with the growth of central control, these promising democratic forums were eliminated. In 1950 the council system was introduced and their services were no longer required. In the elections of 1945 the Independent Smallholders' Party got absoulute majority (57 per cent) of the votes. Its victory was counter-balanced by the close-knit alliance and power of the minority left-wing parties (Communist Party: 17 per cent, Social Democratic Party: 17 per cent, National Peasant Party: 7 per cent).

Hungary was being transformed, but not into a bourgeois democracy. In the face of much opposition, the Hungarian Communist Party attempted to drive quickly from power and public life those opposing the new democratic regime. Soon, however, it switched to the revolutionary interpretation of people's democracy, removing every bourgeois and non-socialist grouping from the political scene. In an atmosphere of growing suspicion and mistrust the Communist Party merged with the social democrats in June 1948. The resulting organization, known as the Hungarian Working People's Party, came into existence at a time of increasing central power in the country. In Hungary, as in the neighbouring states, workers' parties merged under communist leadership became the sole possessors of political power. The year 1948, which can be seen as a turning point, marked the replacement of coalition government by dictatorship of the proletariat, which graduly turned into autarchic rule.

The Stalinist conception of the building of socialism, and belief that this could be done in only one way, led, on an international level, to the break with Tito's Yugoslavia. Within Hungary it resulted in the predominance of coercion and violations of the law which sharply contrasted with the socialist interpretation of democracy. Those imprisoned included not just bourgeois and social democratic leaders, eminent democratic politicians (for instance, Prime Minister Ferenc Nagy) were forced into exile or were imprisoned, also well-known communists. In 1949 prominent figures in the Hungarian Communist Party were executed, as were numerous other party members. Included among these were László Rajk, György Pálffy, László Sólyom and András Szalai. In 1951 János Kádár and Gyula Kállai were sent to prison, as were others.

It was only after the death of Stalin on 5 March 1953 that a change of policy began. The line taken by the Government had caused growing

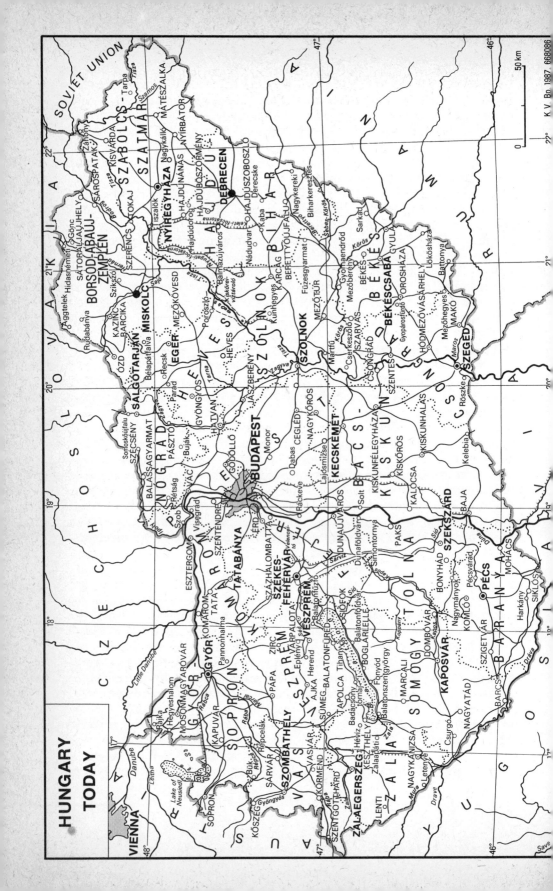

discontent and had undermined confidence in socialism but even now little altered. The dogmatism of the Rákosi leadership allowed no scope for important changes. This was even the case after the Twentieth Congress of the Soviet Communist Party in February 1956, when Khrushchev denounced Stalin's crimes. Therefore the tensions which had been building up over the years finally found expression on 23 October 1956. Hungarian society and its socialist system went through a profound and tragic crisis and only emerged from it at the cost of considerable sacrifice and losses.

After 3 November 1956 a new start was made. The Government, headed by János Kádár, renounced the rigid dogmatism, policy and methods of the Rákosi leadership. First he put down the strikes and other forms of opposition and then, introducing a new style of rule, it called for the active participation of the community in public affairs. Relying on broadly-based social support, it was able to open up a new chapter in Hungarian history. A consensus was established between leadership and people which had not existed before. The new policy of "those who are not against us are with us" extended to everyone with the exception of those who openly opposed the system. This not only led to improvement of the political atmosphere, but also renewal in economic, intellectual and cultural life.

Under the 1972 amendment to the Constitution, the Hungarian People's Republic is a socialist state. The National Assembly as its supreme representative and executive body elects the members of the Presidential Council from among its ranks and may remove them. It also elects the Council of Ministers—which acts as the Government—and the Council of Ministers is accountable to it. The subordinate organs of state power are the Councils, existing at county, town and village level. Deputies to the National Assembly and Council members are elected on the basis of universal suffrage with secret ballot. In the case of council elections, the law prescribes that there must be two candidates in every consituency, of whom one is elected. Under new regulations introduced in 1983, more than two candidates can stand for each seat. Deputies to the National Assembly are elected from the party list drawn up by the Patriotic People's Front. To guarantee legality, constitutionality and consistency in the application of the law, there exists a Supreme Court accountable to the National Assembly. The Constitutional Law Tribunal was set up in 1983. The extensive work of the Central People's Control Commission is assisted by the co-operation of citizens generally. The Hungarian Socialist Workers' Party is the only political party in the country and lays down the guiding principles for policy. Alongside its leading bodies (for example the Political Committee and the Central Committee) there function its branch organizations in towns, villages and factories. The task of the Patriotic People's Front, which ensures the broadest framework for the population's role in public life, is to rally and represent every stratum of society. Recent initiatives on the part of the Patriotic People's Front to raise the standard of political awareness and to expand its own sphere of activity have been a response to growing popular demand. Citizens wanted to have a greater say in the affairs of their residential areas—and, nation-wide problems. Local self-help activity has been considerably encouraged. Most recently it is widely required that the executive bodies should be subordinated to the legislative body and the self-government of local elected bodies should be restored.

The Economy

The reconstruction of the economy, along with its transformation, commenced in 1945—a time when conditions were extremely difficult.

War damage was estimated at 22,000 million pengős, the equivalent of 5,000 million dollars, or five times the country's 1938 national income. Approximately forty per cent of Hungary's national assets were destroyed in the war. Seventy-four per cent of the buildings in Budapest were damaged in the course of the hostilities and the retreating Germans blew up all of the Danube bridges. The Trianon areas of Hungary together lost over half a million soldiers and civilians in the course of the war. This number includes the dead, the wounded, prisoners of war, those who disappeared and the Jews who were exterminated.

Reconstruction together with the re-starting of production and supply began with tremendous zeal. From the very beginning this renewed econo-mic activity was coupled with restrictions on capitalist enterprise—for instance banks and industry. Indicative of the speed of reconstruction is the fact that the annual growth rate of the economy was seventy-six per cent in the year 1946–7. Between 1947 and 1948 it was still thirty per cent.

By 1 August 1946 inflation was halted and the Pengő replaced by a new, stable currency, the forint. The coal mines were nationalized and the major banks placed under supervision. A Three-Year Plan was launched on 1 August 1947. This further extended state intervention in the economy and introduced new methods of business operation. In 1948 the factories and banks were nationalized. Also privately-owned workshops and retail outlets were almost completely eradicated.

This burgeoning economic policy did not, however, take properly into account the conditions and possibilities existing in the country. It aspired to autarchy and was very much influenced by military considerations in the wake of the Cold War. It dictated a pace of development beyond the capabilities of both the economy and the society. In economic development, priority was given to industry in general and to heavy industry in particular. The new economic policy assessed economic opportunities more realisti-cally, reduced the enforced pace of investment and asserted the principle of production reached its 1938 level, while the output of light industry and the food industry lagged considerably behind this. Things were even worse in agriculture where various factors had conspired to depress the level of production still further. On the land output was between ten and twenty per cent lower than in 1937–8. Even in 1949 production of commodities reached only three-quarters of the pre-war amount.

The launching of the first Five-Year Plan on 1 January 1950 marked the beginning of a new system in the management of the national economy. The new system which was based on compulsory "plan targets", centralized production and management. It did not permit independent initiative and distorted incentives. Economic management under this system made necessary the complete restructuring of agriculture and the abolition of small-scale peasant farming. From December 1948 onwards compulsory collectivization began in agriculture.

During the inter-war period, Hungary's economy had something of a dual character. Agriculture was certainly important but industry had its part to play as well. The new economic strategy, however, aimed to transform the country into an industrial state in which farming would be of secondary importance. Accordingly, forty-eight per cent of investment went into industry, while agriculture only received thirteen per cent. On the land, motivation among the peasants fell off, causing a fall in output. Production targets for food were not met and this resulted in a serious disruption of supplies. The agricultural co-operatives and peasant farms were burdened with the need to make compulsory deliveries to the state and these were stringently enforced. The consequence was that fierce animosity was aroused in the rural population and, at the same time, the people generally were not supplied with food at the required level. By the mid-fifties, wages had dropped by over twenty per cent in real terms instead of a planned fifty-per-cent rise in living standards.

Tensions which accumulated in the economic spheres constituted a decisive cause of the political crisis of 1956.

After the consolidation of the political system, economic policy was reviewed and the method of planning modernized. However, the drawing up of a comprehensive and radical reform extending to the entire system of economic management commenced only in 1965. This gave rise to the "New Economic Mechanism", which was put into effect in January 1968. The new economic policy assessed economic opportunities more realistically, reduced the enforced pace of investment and asserted the principle of granted incentives. More resources were made available for the production of consumer goods and steps taken to raise the population's standard of living. The development of industry was made less of a priority, and agriculture along with the infrastructure generally were to receive more attention than before. In addition, it allocated considerable investment capital for the modernization of farming and abandoned the idea that Hungary should aim at economic autarchy.

As methods of management were corrected so co-operatives along with industrial and agricultural firms attained greater independence. Under the new system of regulation, they made greater efforts than previously to

239

adjust to market conditions and consumer demand. Economic links with other countries became more important and were established not only with states in the socialist bloc but with others too. In addition to production under licence there occured new developments in the Hungarian economy. These included co-operation with foreign firms both in production and in trades as well as the utilization of foreign labour and capital to develop the services sector. The results of the latter can be seen in the improvement of the hotel network. Radical changes have taken place in the overall character of Hungarian industry—changes which have reflected international trends. For example, the telecommunications and chemical industry sectors have both grown. Natural gas and crude oil became important as sources of energy. To offset shortages in this sphere Hungary has built her first nuclear power-station. In foreign trade, the export of industrial commodities, instruments and entire factory units has increased. The same is true of raw material and agricultural exports. In addition to the state and co-operative sectors, which dominate the economy, various forms of private enterprise have been given considerable scope. Private enterprise fills the gaps left by the State and co-operative sectors and operates in the fields of supply, repairs, catering and other services.

Between 1958 and 1961 the collectivization of agriculture took place. This time the main consideration was for the needs of production. Rapid development was not attempted and less force was used. Over seventy-seven per cent of Hungary's agricultural land was collectivized, with state farms established on sixteen per cent. Yields increased substantially, as did the pace of mechanization. By 1965 the amount of arable land per tractor had reached, and indeed surpassed, the figure for Greece and Spain. By the same year, harvesting had been completely mechanized, as had the major operations in soil cultivation. Between 1931 and 1940 an average of five kilos of artificial fertilizers was used annually per cadastral yoke. By the early seventies this figure had more than trebled. Substantial growth of the livestock population from the sixties onwards resulted in a better ratio between animal husbandry and the raising of crops. Household plots, as well as specialized agricultural co-operatives whose members are only part-time, are important in the supply of food for the population. The general growth of worker-motivation and the much greater independence of the co-operatives have decisively and favourably affected not only economic performance and commodity supply, but these the shaping of the public mood.

During the period that has elapsed since 1968, reforming ideas and their actual implementation have, to some extent, been influenced by both internal and external factors. These have included the adverse developments in the international economy which have mainly resulted from an increase in prices for raw materials and for energy. In spite of this, however, the reforms have brought about a favourable change in the structure of the economy and in its management. The necessary transformation is not yet complete. In spite of outstanding achievements in many areas—for example in machinery manufacture, technology, automation, overhead costs and consumption of materials—much remains to be done, first of all the streamlining of the pattern of production. Both agriculture and industry have not yet been able to measure up to world standards.

Changes in Society and Living Conditions

The whole face of Hungarian society changed after the Second World War. None of the social classes or strata from the inter-war years survived in its old form or position. The two classes at the opposite extremes of pre-1945 Hungarian society ceased to exist completely. Having lost the bases of their livelihood, the big landowners, and big capitalists who had formerly held power ceased to exist in their old capacities. Many left the country; the rest, especially their children, adjusted to the new conditions. The huge class made up of farm-servants and other landless peasants also disappeared, as the land distribution raised them to the rank of smallholders. In 1949, 90 per cent of earners in agriculture were private farmers.

The gentry middle class, who had played such an important political role in pre-war Hungary, also lost its powerful position. Leading posts in the Government, the public administration and the economy were filled from the ranks of the workers and peasants. It became a general tendency to promote manual workers from the shop floor to, say, company director or similar top white-collar position. By the early sixties, 40 per cent of earners in managerial and intellectual occupations came from a working-class background and 26 per cent from peasant families.

In education, too, the former proletariat enjoyed greatly improved opportunities. Before 1945 about four per cent of secondary school pupils and four per cent of university students came from working-class backgrounds. These figures increased to 44 and 33 per cent, respectively, during the period 1945–60. The numerical strength of the working class grew rapidly over a short period, and the number of workers in state industry and in the building industry doubled in the years 1950–70. This large growth inevitably changed the internal composition of the working class as well. Now integrated into it were the various *déclassé* elements and, most importantly, agricultural workers who were no longer needed on the land. In the sixties, half of the workers in Hungary came from peasant backgrounds. The policy of locating industry in particular areas substantially contributed to the emergence of a group of workers more than 300,000 strong who commute considerable distances to their place of employment. With greater decentralization of industry and with the increasing prosperity of agricultural co-operatives, the numbers of such workers have recently dropped considerably.

241

Private farming in the traditional sense of the term has disappeared almost entirely. The private farmer has either joined the producers' co-operative or left agriculture altogether. The proportion of private farmers among agricultural earners dropped to five per cent since the completion of collectivization. However, the former smallholder who joined a co-operative has seen considerable changes. Former differences in social status within the village have gradually disappeared as the work itself has altered. The growth of mechanization has produced new types of job and has shaped a new set of values with regard to employment on the land. Lowest in prestige are the various types of crop raising which still require manual work and which almost exclusively employ women. Most agricultural activity has become skilled work requiring special qualifications. The fact that the co-operative farms also carry on supplementary activities, mostly of an industrial character, has meant that members no longer do agricultural work only.

As a result of nationalization in the fifties, the employment position of self-employed tradesmen and shopkeepers, who numbered about 350,000 between the two World Wars, underwent transformation. These people became members of industrial co-operatives, factory workers and white-collar workers in the public sector. Only a few were able to preserve their self-employed status and only then in a few branches of the service sector. Since the launching of the new economic policy, self-employed tradesmen and shop-keepers have been setting up businesses in growing numbers. These mainly operate in the fields of services, catering and the clothing and food retail trade.

Nevertheless, the number of those who are self-employed has dropped to a negligible proportion among earners generally. Only two to three per cent of earners work for themselves.

Since the First World War, women have been entering paid employment in growing numbers. This process has speeded up so much over the past forty years that, in 1981, women accounted for almost 45 per cent of all earners. A number of occupations (for example, teaching, the judiciary and certain medical occupations) have become almost entirely dominated by women. The fact that women have entered paid employment in such a big way has affected not only the economy and public life, but also the traditional pattern of family life.

Clearly indicative of the structural changes which have occurred in Hungarian society are the developments which have taken place in the pattern of employment. In 1981 over 40 per cent of earners worked in industry. Slightly over 20 per cent worked in agriculture, and not exclusively in "peasant" occupations. Almost 10 per cent worked in commerce. This represented a great and many-sided change. In 1941 almost half of Hungary's active earners still worked in agriculture, with industry and construction work providing a livelihood for just over 23 per cent. Nowadays it is the services sector, and not industry, which shows a rise in the numbers it employs. All this has led to a transformation of the Hungarian way of life, a transformation also influenced by modernization generally, government measures, trends in fashion as well as new customs.

Accompanying this transformation has been the disappearance of unemployment. Even though it is difficult to find jobs in certain fields, the jobs market in Hungary is, generally speaking, characterized by a shortage of labour. After a certain number of years spent in paid employment, men may retire at the age of sixty and women at fifty-five. Almost the whole of Hungarian society is covered by social-welfare and health-care provisions, although standards tend to vary. Whilst in the thirties social-security provisions covered 31 per cent of the population, today free medical care is the constitutional right of every Hungarian citizen.

The introduction of the 48-hour working week was followed in the eighties by the switch to a five-day working week. Mechanization, together with health and safety regulations, have made work considerably easier. At the same time difficult manual work has been reduced considerably.

Under a special scheme greatly affecting the whole of society, a working mother is entitled to three years leave of absence for each of her children. During this period she receives a regular monthly allowance from the State. This scheme, unique even by international standards, has recently been extended to fathers. They may now stay at home with children more than twelve months old.

There has been growing movement of population into the towns and, in the countryside itself, a simultaneous drift from outlying areas into the villages. Urbanization, formerly centred on Budapest, has become more general throughout the country. Between 1931 and 1980 the proportion of those living in the capital has risen far more slowly than the urban population generally. Nevertheless, about one fifth of Hungary's population lives in Budapest, and more than half in towns and urban settlements. In 1949, 17 per cent of the people lived in homesteads, isolated from larger communities.

By the mid-seventies this figure had dropped to about seven per cent. The benefits and comforts made possible by modern technology have become accessible to all. In 1980 there was electricity in almost every home in the country and 65 per cent of homes had running water. Almost half the country settlements also had running water. Traditional cooking stoves burning wood or coal have been replaced by electric and gas cookers. The use of washing machines has become widespread and the same holds true for electric refrigerators, radios, and television sets. In 1960, there were only 104,000 television sets in the country but, twenty years later, this figure had risen to almost three million.

The improvement in living conditions has also affected nutrition. It seems that Hungarians still wish to eat more and eating habits are still very much bound up with tradition. Between 1934 and 1938, average annual per capita consumption of meat was slightly less than thirty-four kilogrammes.

In 1980 the annual figure was seventy-three kilos. Over the same period consumption of sugar increased from an annual per capita figure of ten and a half kilos to a figure of thirty-five kilos. Carbohydrates and fats yield the overwhelming majority of the 3,054 calories consumed on average each day. As a result of medical advice and trends in fashion, healthier eating habits have struck root. However, progress towards a more healthy diet has been slow.

Taking holidays and the pursuit of recreational activities was part of the middle-class way of life between the two World Wars. Today all sections of society can afford a holiday, thanks largely to the network of subsidized trade-union, company and co-operative holiday centres. The spread of motoring has made people more mobile and has helped the expansion of both domestic and foreign tourism. In 1930 there were slightly over thirteen thousand automobiles on Hungary's roads, a number which had risen to 1,2 million by 1983. Sport (mainly soccer), which in the fifties served as an outlet for enthusiasm and as an opportunity for social advancement, has become the main way for people to refresh their spirits. Even the so-called "white" sports (fencing, tennis and sailing), which were formerly the privilege of the upper classes, are now pursued on a mass scale.

It is a fact that the standard of living of millions has reached a level unimaginable during the inter-war period. However, the changes that enabled this to occur also created difficulties. Dramatic changes in social position and way of life brought problems even for those who rose in society and were successful. Consolidated conditions and relative affluence also engendered other problems and contradictions. In addition to the opportunities for social mobility, there appeared a danger that the new structure of society would rigidify and that inequality and lowly status would be recreated in different forms. The difference between the well-to-do ruling elite and the less well-off strata started to increase once again. The consequences of technological advance, so familiar to the industrially more developed societies, are not invariably beneficial. The overcrowdedness of cities and the pollution of the environment have become markedly discernible in Hungary.

Cultural and Intellectual Life

The Second World War, as well as bringing great material destruction, caused serious losses to literary and intellectual life as well. As members of forced labour battalions died among others the painter Imre Ámos and *literati*: György Bálint, Gábor Halász, Miklós Radnóti and Antal Szerb. Those who survived the Holocaust drew upon their appalling experiences even decades afterwards. In the spring of 1945, however, the prominent figures of Hungarian intellectual life enthusiastically joined forces to create an entirely new culture, one accessible to the whole people.

To make education accessible to all and to raise the standards of culture the Government issued a decree in August 1945. This made the introduction of the eight-grade elementary school system compulsory. In 1948 the schools were nationalized, including those run by the Churches. With education taken out of the Church's hands, religious instruction at school became optional. Various agreements were concluded to normalize relations between the State and the Churches. The first of these was the agreement with the Calvinist Church and the last with the Roman Catholics. Sects wich had been tolerated became officially acknowledged denominations. The Churches received certain financial assistance from the State and were allowed to run nine of their own theological colleges as well as thirteen secondary schools. In 1951 the State Office for Church Affairs was set up. It was, however, only from the sixties onwards that relations between the State and the Churches could substantially improve. The peace movement among the priests played a considerable role in this.

With the reform of the educational system, education became free at every level. The old four-class secondary school (which followed four years of primary school education) was replaced by various types of vocational secondary schools. Although the grammar school, which had been designed to provide an all-round general education, continued in existence, it lost much of its appeal. New textbooks and curricula were prepared for every educational institution and level. In 1945 all the university faculties opened their doors to women. The network of people's colleges, which was established in the forties, together with the new university admission system, made it possible mainly for young peasants and workers to pursue further education studies. Later, by means of evening and correspondence courses, those who already started work could also acquire a degree. In 1949 the autonomy of the universities was restricted, and the old teaching staff replaced. At the same time the network of people's colleges was dismantled —out of political considerations.

The general educational level of the people improved substantially. The number of secondary school pupils rose from 52,000 in 1939 to 334,000 in 1980, whilst in institutions of further education almost ten times as many students pursued their studies as had done so in 1938.

The former duality and division of culture disappeared. Initially, the new cultural policy acknowledged those artists and values officially shunned during the inter-war period. Culture became a public affair, the concern of the people generally. As early as summer 1945, a time when conditions were very difficult, the traditional book day was held. In 1948 the Kossuth Prize was founded. This was followed in 1950 by the creation of the titles "Outstanding Artist" and "Meritorious Artist", given in recognition of outstanding artistic work. The whole of Hungarian cultural and scientific life was affected by the new possibilities of approach and the methods and

245

themes preferred by Marxism, which by now was intensively studied. Already the Marxist philosophy greatly influenced the representation and evaluation of the phenomenal world.

The cultural life of the second half of the Forties was extremely rich and colourful. Side by side in the literary life of the day were writers of considerable diversity. These included advocates of socialism, communist authors, the populists, members of the *Nyugat* generation and those belonging to the "urban" trend of bourgeois democracy. Among all these writers were Lajos Kassák, Lajos Nagy, Gyula Illyés, László Németh, Pál Szabó, Péter Veres, Lőrinc Szabó, Milán Füst, Tibor Déry, István Vas, László Cs. Szabó, Sándor Márai and Lajos Zilahy. In fine art the Szentendre School, the European School, the one-time Group of Socialist Artists and others all represented different styles and forms of expression. In 1947 Hungary became a member of UNESCO and this broadened her cultural and scientific links internationally.

From the late-forties on the distortions apparent in Hungarian political life also affected every area of culture and science. Here, too, central control became stronger. Political and ideological struggle, lack of artistic confidence, the mistaken interpretation of socialist realism, and easy understanding all had their effect. The result was the spread of stereotyped work, empty formalism and monotony. The representation of genuine social and individual conflicts became impossible. This was not, however, a state of affairs exclusively confined to Hungary, but merely a part of a general that took place in Eastern Europe at this time. In the fifties, Hungarian cultural policy was directed by József Révai.

In 1949 the publication of a whole host of journals ceased. Various artistic groups disbanded. Centralized organizations were established for writers, painters, sculptors, architects, etc. Artistic debate acquired political significance and could have serious consequences on the livelihood of people concerned. Writers and artists were denied opportunities to publish and exhibit their works. Considering their situation hopeless many left the country. Examples of those who did are Cs. Szabó, Márai, and Zilahy.

After 1956, the normalization of the relationship between the political leadership and artistic circles did not occur immediately. It took longer than the achievement of the other preconditions for consolidation. However, the renewal freed every branch of literature and the arts from the oppressive burden of dogmatism and stereotyped expectations. The renewal gave rise to pluralism in both genre and mode of expression, and thereby brought about the linking of Hungarian intellectual life to the mainstream of world culture. This openness was manifested in the expansion of liberty to create, in the publication of books and in the policy of theatres and exhibitions alike.

In this new atmosphere the life work of Gyula Illyés and the work of his and Lőrinc Szabó's generation reached its zenith. At the same time the work of István Örkény, Zoltán Zelk and Sándor Weöres struck root.

246

Writers whose careers took off after the liberation in 1945 include László Nagy, János Pilinszky, Sándor Csoóri and Ferenc Juhász. Behind them a new generation is already clamouring for similar renown, for example, Péter Esterházy, Péter Dobai and György Spiró.

Hungarian novelists and playwrights have turned with passionate interest to those national issues of the past which are topical today also (cf. the historical plays of Illyés and Németh). Some works search for the responsibility of the Hungarian people for what happened between the two World Wars, for example *Cold Days* (Hideg napok) by Tibor Cseres. Others uncover the dramatic experiences of the fifties, for instance *Studfarmer* (Ménesgazda) by István Gáll, and the writings of Erzsébet Galgóczi. The volumes of the "Discovering Hungary" series reflect an interest in both literary sociography and the present.

Excellent new Hungarian plays have been performed in the theatres. Long-forgotten or deliberately ignored authors and works (for example, Milán Füst and *Moses* by Imre Madách) were rediscovered. István Örkény's *Cat's Play* (Macskajáték) and *The Tóth Family* (Tóték) were highly successful both inside and outside Hungary, winning recognition even in the United States. Outstanding actors and actresses of the post-war period include Margit Dayka, Mária Sulyok, Margit Lukács, Klári Tolnay, Elma Bulla, Ferenc Bessenyei, Ferenc Kállai, György Kálmán, Lajos Őze, Sándor Pécsi and Lajos Básti.

Painters Endre Bálint, Ignác Kokas, Béla Kondor, Dezső Korniss, Ferenc Martyn and Jenő Barcsay together with sculptors Miklós Borsos, József Somogyi, Erzsébet Schaár, Imre Varga and Tibor Vilt are substantial contributions to Hungarian art. The recognition and acceptance of artists as good as Tivadar Csontváry Kosztka brought enrichment to the fine arts in Hungary. The Hungarian National Gallery, established in 1957, along with the galleries and museums of a number of provincial towns, bring art to a far broader section of the population.

One of the great achievements of musical life is that the works of Béla Bartók have now won in Hungary not just acceptance but also appreciation. Hungarian concert audiences are likely to contain very many people whose musical education at school was based on the Kodály Method. This method of teaching music has been introduced in many countries, from Canada to Australia. The Kodály Seminar in Kecskemét is regularly attended by foreign teachers of music. In addition to the composition of many new pieces of music (for example by Pál Kadosa, András Mihály, Zsolt Durkó and György Kurtág), Hungarian opera (with Sándor Szokolay and Emil Petrovics) has recently experienced a revival. A number of Hungarian opera singers (for example, Éva Marton and Sylvia Sass) have become famous abroad, as have some instrumentalists (for example Zoltán Kocsis and Dezső Ránki). Every year concerts are organized at the former Esterházy palace at Fertőd, where Haydn himself worked. These are intended to give young musicians the opportunity of an impressive international debut. Musical life in Hungary has been further enriched by the reconstruction not long ago of the Vigadó concert-hall in Budapest. Another achievement has been the restoring in all its old splendour, of the Budapest Opera House for the centenary year of its foundation.

As well as operetta, which has always had its followers, new genres such as the musical and the rock opera have become widely liked. The popularity of the first Hungarian rock opera, which dealt with Stephen, the first King of Hungary, surpassed all expectations.

The cinema, the art form of the twentieth century, acquired a special role in Hungary after 1945. There emerged directors who were capable of presenting Hungarian problems of the past and of the present and yet at the same time making them relevant to everyone. While primarily serving the cause of national self-knowledge, they brought happenings and conflicts of general interest onto the screen. The new wave of films commenced with Géza Radványi's *Somewhere in Europe* (Valahol Európában) and was followed by the works of Zoltán Fábri, Miklós Jancsó, András Kovács, Márta Mészáros, István Szabó and others. Over the years Hungarian films have scored great international successes. Miklós Jancsó was the first Hungarian film director to win international acclaim. The greatest success of all has been achieved by István Szabó, whose *Mephisto* was awarded an Oscar award for the best foreign picture.

During the past few decades cartoons and animated films have emerged as an independent branch of cinematographic art. A special contribution has been made to this by the works of Ottó Foky, Gyula Macskássy and József Nepp. Ferenc Rófusz's *The Fly* (A légy) won an Oscar for short animated productions.

After the war, architecture in Hungary was confronted by an enormous task. In addition to all the rebuilding which had to be done, architecture was burdened by fixed ideas on design. Another problem was the strangeness of such things as pre-fabricated building sections and the technology which went with them. Together these factors paralyzed the imagination of Hungarian architects and, in the face of large-scale home building and limited financial resources, the aesthetic side of architecture became overshadowed. A monotonous uniformity was produced in Hungarian towns and villages. Recently, however, there have been favourable changes—aesthetic criteria have again become important in architecture and urban development generally. The new hotels in Budapest and Keszthely together with the musical centre in Kecskemét bear witness to the new approach.

Regular and fruitful contacts have been established with Hungarian writers and artists who, for many years, have lived outside Hungary. Among these are György Cziffra, Amerigo Tot, Victor Vasarely, László Cs. Szabó and Győző Határ. Hungarian intellectual life also keeps contact with the cultural development of Hungarians living just beyond the country's borders, as well as in other parts of the world.

In the twentieth century Hungary has joined the ranks of those small nations whose very existence had become threatened—partly because of their own division, weakness and backwardness. The history of the past few decades, the achievements and the pitfalls, just as much as the repeated experiments, bear witness to the fact that Hungary has waged an unceasing struggle not only for survival as a nation, but also against isolation and backwardness. Efforts have not always produced the expected results. What is certain, however, is that Hungary, a small nation, seeks her place in world economy, she wants to strengthen her activity in the community of the nations and in universal cultural life.

INDEX OF NAMES

251

FERENCZY, ISTVÁN (1792–1856),
Sculptor: **109**

FERENCZY, KÁROLY (1862–1917),
Painter: **168**

FERENCZY, NOÉMI (1890–1957),
Painter: **221, 224**

FESTETICS, GYÖRGY, Count (1755–
1819), Aristocrat, economist: **100**

FISCHER, JÓZSEF (1873–1942),
Architect: **221**

FOKY, OTTÓ (1927), Director of
puppet films: **248**

FORGÁCH, FERENC OF GIMES (c.
1530–1577), Historiographer: **55**

FRANCHET D'ESPEREY, LOUIS-FELIX
(1856–1942), French general: **178,
180**

ST FRANCIS OF ASSISI (1182–1226),
Italian poet, confessor, founder of
the Franciscan Order: **25, 27**

FRANCIS FERDINAND OF HABSBURG
(1863–1914), Crown prince: **172–173**

FRANCIS II OF HABSBURG (1768–1835),
Holy Roman Emperor 1792–1806,
Emperor of Austria 1804–1835, as
Francis I King of Hungary and
Bohemia 1792–1835: **97, 103**

FRANCIS JOSEPH I OF HABSBURG
(1830–1916), Emperor of Austria
1848–1916, King of Hungary
1867–1916: **119, 121, 123–125,
130–132, 134–136, 147–149, 155,
159–163, 169, 172–173, 176**

FRANGEPÁN, FERENC KRISTÓF, Count
(1620–1671), Aristocrat: **69**

FRANKEL, LEÓ (1844–1896), Worker's
leader, Commissioner of Labour of
Paris Commune 1871: **141**

FRÁTER, LÓRÁND (1872–1930),
Song-writer: **167**

FREDERICK I OF HOHENSTAUF,
BARBAROSSA (c. 1120–1190), Holy
Roman Emperor 1152–1190: **24**

FREDERICK II OF HOHENZOLLERN, the
Great (1712–1786), King of Prussia
1740–1786: **83**

FREDERICK III OF HABSBURG
(1415–1493), Holy Roman Emperor
1442–1493, as Frederick IV King of
Germany 1440–1493: **35–36**

FREDERICK V OF PFALZ (1596–1632),
King of Bohemia 1619–1620: **58**

FRIEDRICH, ISTVÁN (1883–1958), Prime
Minister 1919: **191**

FÜLEP, LAJOS (1885–1970),
Philosopher and historian of art:
183, 220

FÜRST, SÁNDOR (1903–1932),
Communist leader: **198, 205**

FÜST, MILÁN (1888–1967), Writer and
novelist: **183, 245, 247**

GAJ, LJUDEVIT (1809–1872),
Croatian writer and publicist: **111**

GALEOTTO, MARZIO (c. 1427–1497),
Italian humanist historiographer: **46**

GALGÓCZI, ERZSÉBET (1930), Novelist:
247

GALILEI, GALILEO (1564–1642), Italian
mathematician and philosopher:
164, 178

GÁLL, ISTVÁN (1931), Novelist: **247**

GARAI, LÁSZLÓ (?–1459), Palatine of
Hungary 1447–1458: **34**

GARAMI, ERNŐ (1867–1935), Social
democrat leader: **163, 187**

GÁRDONYI, GÉZA (1863–1922),
Novelist: **166, 183**

GARIBALDI, GIUSEPPE (1807–1882),
Italian statesman: **125, 127**

GÁSPÁR, ZOLTÁN (1901–1945),
Publicist: **220**

GAULLE, CHARLES DE (1890–1970),
French general, Prime Minister
1944–1946, 1958, President
1958–1969: **219**

GELLÉRT, GERARD, SAINT (980–1046),
Bishop and ecclesiastic writer of
Italian origin: **20–22**

ST GEORGE (?–c. 303), Martyr, patron
of England: **44**

GERŐ, ERNŐ (1898–1980), Communist
leader, First secretary of Hungarian
Working People's Party 1956: **205**

GÉZA OF ÁRPÁD HOUSE (940–997),
Taksony's son, Prince of Hungary
972–997: **19**

GÉZA I OF ÁRPÁD HOUSE (?–1077),
Béla I's son, King of Hungary
1074–1077: **22**

KÁDÁR, JÁNOS (1912), Prime Minister 1956–1958, 1961–1965, First secretary (1956–), General secretary (1986–) of Hungarian Socialist Worker's Party: **199, 205, 235–236**

KADOSA, PÁL (1903–1983), Composer: 247

KÁLDI, GYÖRGY (1573–1634), Jesuit translator of Bible: 59

KÁLLAI, FERENC (1925), Actor: 247

KÁLLAI, GYULA (1910), Politician and journalist, Foreign Minister 1949–1951, Minister for Culture 1957–1958, Prime Minister 1965–1967: **205, 207, 235**

KÁLLAY, MIKLÓS (1887–1967), Prime Minister 1942–1944: **204, 206, 227–230**

KÁLLAY, TIBOR (1881–1964), Finance Minister 1921–1924: **195**

KÁLMÁN, GYÖRGY (1925), Actor: 247

KÁLMÁN, IMRE (1882–1953), Composer: **167**

KÁN, LÁSZLÓ (?–c. 1318), Voivode of Transylvania 1297–1315: **29**

KARA MUSTAPHA (1634–1683), Turkish Grand Vizier 1676–1683: 71

KARADŽIĆ, VUK STEFANOVIĆ (1787–1864), Serbian linguist and poet: **111**

KARINTHY, FRIGYES (1887–1938), Writer and translator: **167, 183, 220**

KÁRMÁN, TÓDOR/THEODORE VON (1881–1963), Engineer and inventor: 217

KÁROLYI, GYÖRGY, Count (1802–1877), Officer, politician: **105**

KÁROLYI, GYULA, Count (1871–1947), Foreign Minister 1930–1931, Prime Minister 1931–1932: **198**

KÁROLYI, MIHÁLY, Count (1875–1955), Prime Minister 1918–1919, President 1919, Ambassador to Paris 1947–1949: **165, 175, 178, 180–183, 186–188, 190, 198, 217–218**

KÁROLYI, SÁNDOR, Count (1668–1743), Kuruc, later labanc general: **80**

KASSÁK, LAJOS (1887–1967), Poet, writer and painter: **181, 183, 187, 220, 245**

KATONA, ISTVÁN (1732–1811), Historiographer: **86**

KATONA, JÓZSEF (1791–1830), Dramatist: **107**

KAUNITZ, WENZEL ANTON/KAUNITZ-RIETBERG, Prince (1711–1794), Austrian Chancellor 1753–1794: **84**

KAZINCZY, FERENC (1759–1831), Poet and writer: **95, 107**

KEMÉNY, JÁNOS (1607–1662), Prince of Transylvania 1661–1662: **59**

KEMÉNY, ZSIGMOND, Baron (1814–1875), Writer and politician: **105**

KEMPIS, THOMAS/THOMAS OF KEMPEN (c. 1380–1471), Chronicler: **47**

KERNSTOK, KÁROLY (1873–1940), Painter: **168, 217**

KÉZAI, SIMON (13th cent.), Chronicler: 45

KHRUSHCHEV, NIKITA SERGIEVITS (1894–1971), First Secretary of Communist Party USSR 1953–1964, Prime Minister 1958–1964: **235**

KHUEN-HÉDERVÁRY, KÁROLY, Count (1849–1918), Prime Minister 1903, 1910–1912: **170**

KINIZSI, PÁL (?–1494), Military commander, Lord Chief Justice 1494: **35**

KISS, ERNŐ (1799–1849), Honvédgeneral: **122**

KISS, JÁNOS (1883–1944) Lieutenant-General: **207, 232–233**

KISS, JÓZSEF (1843–1921), Poet and editor: **166**

KISS, LAJOS (1881–1965), Ethnographer, archeologist and historian: **156**

KLAPKA, GYÖRGY (1820–1892), Honvédgeneral and politician: **127–128**

KLEBELSBERG, KUNÓ, Count (1875–1932), Minister for Education and Culture 1922–1931: **195**

260

NEPP, JÓZSEF (1934), Director of animated cartoons: **248**

NEUMANN, JÓHN/JÁNOS (1903–1957), Mathematician of Hungarian origin: **168, 217**

NICHOLAS I OF ROMANOV, NIKOLAI PAVLOVITS (1796–1855), Tsar of Russia: **121**

NÓGRÁDI, SÁNDOR (1894–1971), Antifascist colonel and diplomat: **233**

ÖRKÉNY, ISTVÁN (1912–1979), Novelist and dramatist: **246–247**

OSTENBURG-MORAVEK, GYULA (20th cent.), Officer of a detachment: **191–192**

OSVÁT, ERNŐ (1877–1929), Editor and publicist: **166**

OTTO I, THE GREAT, OF SAXE (912–973), King of Germany 936–973, Holy Roman Emperor 962–973: **17, 19**

OTTO OF FREISING (**c.** 1111–1158), German chronicler and bishop of Freising 1137–1158: **37**

OTTO III OF WITTELSBACH (1261–1312), Prince of Bavaria, as Otto I King of Hungary 1305–1307: **30**

OTTOKAR II OF PŘEMYSL (1230–1278), King of Bohemia 1253–1278: **29, 35**

ŐZ, PÁL (**c.** 1766–1795), Lawyer and jacobinist: **95**

ŐZE, LAJOS (1935–1984), Actor: **247**

PÁLFI/PÁLFFY, ALBERT (1820–1897), Editor and writer: **121**

PÁLFFY, GYÖRGY (1909–1949), Antifascist general: **207, 231, 235**

PÁLFFY, JÁNOS, Count (1663–1751), General, Palatine of Hungary 1741–1751, Lord Chief Justice 1731–1751: **80**

PÁLFFY, PÁL, COUNT (**c.** 1580–1654), Palatine of Hungary 1649–1654: **61**

PALOTAI, ERZSI (1907), Actress: **222**

PÁPAI-PÁRIZ, FERENC (1649–1716), Doctor, scientist, dictionary-maker: **74**

PAŠIĆ, NIKOLA (1845–1926), Serbian Prime Minister 1906–1926: **173**

PASKIEVICH, IVAN FEDOROVICH, Prince (1782–1856), Russian Field-Marshal: **121**

PATAKI, ISTVÁN (1914–1944), Communist leader: **233**

PÁZMÁNY, PÉTER (1570–1637), Jesuit ecclesiastic writer, Archbishop of Esztergom 1616–1637: **57–58, 60, 65, 73**

PÉCHI, SIMON (**c.** 1575–1642), Humanist scholar, Chancellor of Transylvania 1613–1621: **57**

PÉCSI, SÁNDOR (1922–1972), Actor: **247**

PEIDL, GYULA (1873–1943), Minister of Labour 1919, Prime Minister 1919: **186**

PERO **see** SZEGEDINAC, PERO

PESTI, BARNABÁS/GETZLER, JÓZSEF (1920–1944), Chemik, communist leader: **233**

PETER I OF ROMANOV, THE GREAT (1672–1725), Tsar of Russia 1682–1721, Emperor of Russia 1721–1725: **78, 80**

PÉTER, GÁBOR (1906), Communist leader: **205**

PETER ORSEOLO OF ÁRPÁD HOUSE (1011–1058), Doge's of Venice son, King of Hungary 1038–1041, 1044–1046: **20–21**

PETŐFI, SÁNDOR (1823–1849), Poet and revolucionary: **106, 108, 115, 118, 144–145**

PETROVICS, EMIL (1930), Composer: **247**

PEUERBACH/PURBACH, GEORG OF (1423–1461), German mathematician and astronomer: **46**

PEYER, KÁROLY (1881–1956), Social democrat leader, Minister of Labour 1919–1920: **206, 229**

PILINSZKY, JÁNOS (1921–1981), Poet: **247**

269

INDEX OF PLACES

The name of the locality is followed by the name of the county or province (C. stands for county), the old Hungarian, Latin and German name, where that applies, and the country where it is situated today. No country is indicated for localities situated in Hungary.

273

277

Printed in Hungary, 1988
Zrínyi Printing House, Budapest
87.1081/66–12